Enormous Prayers

For Father Steve Deaver —

With my best wishes.

[signature]

Enormous Prayers

A *Journey into the Priesthood*

Thomas Kunkel

Westview Press
A Member of Perseus Books, L.L.C.

Published in 1998 in the United States of America by Westview Press, 5500 Central Avenue, Boulder, Colorado 80301-2877, and in the United Kingdom by Westview Press, 12 Hid's Copse Road, Cumnor Hill, Oxford OX2 9JJ

Library of Congress Cataloging-in-Publication Data
Kunkel, Thomas, 1950–
  Enormous prayers : a journey into the priesthood / Thomas Kunkel.
    p.   cm.
  ISBN 0-8133-3464-0 (hc)
  1. Catholic Church—United States—Clergy—Biography.   2. Catholic
Church—United States—History—1965–   3. United States—Church
history—20th century.   I. Title.
BX4670.K86   1998
282'.092'273—dc21
[B]   97-43527
                                                                                          CIP

The paper used in this publication meets the requirements of the American National Standard for Permanence of Paper for Printed Library Materials Z39.48-1984.

10   9   8   7   6   5   4   3   2

For my mother and father,
who have always been people of faith

Acknowledgments

My debt extends to hundreds of people, none more than the many priests I met and interviewed in the course of my travels. Some of their stories are told here; most are not. Yet every conversation was insightful, and more than a few were inspirational. In particular I would like to thank a group of men in my Indiana hometown who took me into their confidence at the earliest stages of this project and who encouraged me throughout. I believe they represent the very core and commitment of the American Catholic clergy. In every sense, they have kept the faith.

Of the many print sources I consulted, two I found especially instructive were Richard P. McBrien's *Catholicism* (revised edition) and Kevin Orlin Johnson's *Expressions of the Catholic Faith*. When I completed a first draft, two friends, Monsignor Kenneth Knapp and Father James Sauer, were kind enough to read it and make suggestions and corrections.

I must also thank the men of the National Federation of Priests' Councils, and the organization's executive director, Brother Bernard Stratman, for their generosity and support of my project.

My agent and friend Peter Matson adroitly steered the book through some early turbulence, for which he earned my gratitude yet again. He eventually delivered it into the hands of editor Laura Parsons, whose enthusiasm and encouragement were—are—most appreciated. Also at Westview, Alice Colwell edited the book with taste and precision. I must also thank my colleague Linda Davis and her husband, Chuck Yanikoski, for providing so many leads as well as moral support.

Finally let me thank my wife, Debra, whose help and support quite literally made this book possible. Writers often say that; this time it happens to be truer than the reader can ever know.

Thomas Kunkel

 A Communion

SAN DIEGO

Snaking my way through the crowded conference room, I have an unsettling thought: what is the penalty for impersonating a priest? Back in beginning catechism, I thought we had covered the waterfront where perdition was concerned, everything from little white lies to coveting thy neighbor's wife (a tough concept for a nun to put across to a second-grader, I can tell you, or at least it was in 1962). But I don't recall her addressing the surely grave sin of clerical impersonation.

I hadn't *meant* to be misleading, mind you. It's just that I was one of the few civilians in a room brimming with men who had come to San Diego for the annual convention of the National Federation of Priests' Councils (NFPC). And since most of the delegates were only now arriving, having made their way to California's own paradise from all over the country, they were still casually dressed in blue jeans, in slacks and blazers, some even in cowboy boots—scarcely a collar in sight. A well-tanned San Diegan rollerblading by might have peeked in and taken us for another graying assemblage of insurance agents or snack-food distributors. On top of that, we all sported those minimalist name tags; no "Father Smith" or "Monsignor Jones," just "Hi! I'm Jack from St. Louis" or "Phil from Escondido." To all appearances, then, I was one of them. And while the delegates were more than understanding as I explained again and again that I am not a priest but a writer, I still felt a little like a party crasher being found out. Considering that over the next year I intended to spend a lot of time in the company of priests, this didn't strike me as a terribly auspicious beginning.

By that evening's opening session, however, my anxiety was receding, in large part because most of the priests had changed into their clerical black. In a room meant to accommodate maybe two hundred people in comfort, more than three hundred of us were packed in, 737-style, sitting on those unyielding stackable chairs that hotels apparently are required by law to use. Glancing about, I noted maybe six women in the room: one or two reporters, a handful of religious who were participating in the convention, and some escapees from the booths along the back, which, as at meetings of other professional associations, beckoned conventioneers with books, tapes, and pamphlets for pension funds and insurance plans. Otherwise it was wall-to-wall men, most contentedly chattering away. Then suddenly, from behind us, a tall crucifix at the head of a procession seemed to part this black sea, and the talk abruptly died away.

After the opening prayers and remarks, the night's keynote speaker took the podium. Cardinal Joseph Bernardin of Chicago was plainly tired, even haggard. He'd been on the road for days, he explained, and had just arrived in San Diego that evening. In his speech he would quote John Wesley's memorable self-description of his preaching style—"I set myself on fire, and people come out and watch me burn"—but this evening the cardinal appeared to have little fuel to give. Soft-spoken anyway, he was finding it difficult to summon the energy to put across what he clearly intended as a major address. Though I sat near the front, I found him at times hard to hear.

Nonetheless, the speech was a good one, thoughtful and well crafted, and worth a measure of ear strain. Bernardin conceded that morale in the priestly ranks had taken a bruising in recent years but did his best to cheer the clergymen by reminding them how, as ministers, they have unique roles, not to mention opportunities. "My brothers, people are starving today for mystery, the power that grounds, suffuses, and surpasses all things, that ever-present yet elusive reality which Jesus called the kingdom of God," he declared. "As a result, our souls are withering from underuse and lack of nourishment."

Bernardin suggested two ways that priests should treat this anomie. First, he urged them to be "mystagogues"—that is, the bearers and translators of mystery. "Simply put, the priest must be an authentically religious leader," he said. "He must be, in the richest sense possible, spiritual director, mystical guide, shaman. It would be a great mistake to turn the priest into psychologist, sociologist, social worker, counselor—anything but a uniquely religious leader." With more and more priests occupying just such professions, Bernardin quickly added that he wasn't disparaging them or their missions. He only wanted to remind his fellow clerics that being "the bearer of the mystery of God is incomparably rich and carries with it its own justification."

Second, Bernardin said, priests must be "doctors of the soul." In unsettled times like our own, he said, people have a sickness "that no psychologist or physician" can hope to cure. A priest, on the other hand, can treat them with "the good news and the power of the Incarnation."

The cardinal's inspirational message seemed to buck the men up. For a few moments, he swept away worries about leaky roofs and ugly headlines to remind them why they had become priests in the first place. Bernardin's tonic effect on the conventioneers wasn't surprising; he had long been one of their heroes. With Cardinal John O'Connor of New York, Bernardin was paramount among America's recent Catholic churchmen. But where the conservative O'Connor is a tough, take-no-prisoners swashbuckler in a purple cape (and Pope John Paul II's favorite American cardinal), Bernardin always came across as more the diplomat, conciliatory and cerebral. In a time of conservative rule and political division in the Church, currents not unlike those abroad in America at large, Bernardin's was a voice of moderation. For its part, the NFPC—the national assembly of local priest councils that exist (ostensibly) to advise their bishops—is a child of the turbulent sixties and the Second Vatican Council, and in the beginning was an aggressively liberal outpost of the faith. And while today the NFPC's politics are considerably more mainstream, most of the men at this convention would probably describe themselves as left of the political center. They are priests who worry about the current pope as much as they love him, and in Bernardin they recognized their strongest high-ranking ally this side of Rome.

So in this room Bernardin received not simply the respect due a prince of the Church but the honest affection of friends. As such, it was easy to detect an undercurrent of concern for his health. If little was said openly, everyone in the room surely was wondering what kind of toll, physical and emotional, the travail of the preceding year and a half had taken on him. Bernardin's had been a lightning rise to the top—auxiliary bishop of Atlanta at age thirty-eight; archbishop of Cincinnati; archbishop of Chicago; a cardinal's purple cap at fifty-five—with no whiff of scandal. Then in 1993, Steven Cook, a former seminary student in Cincinnati, accused Bernardin of sexual abuse that he maintained had occurred nearly twenty years before. Bernardin vigorously denied the charges, but coming as they did amid the veritable cascade of like allegations being leveled against priests, who could be sure? In December 1994 Cook recanted, saying that his memories, which he originally said had been repressed, instead were inventions. Even so, as the lawyers are fond of reminding us, you can't unring a bell.

Not long after Bernardin's appearance in San Diego—this was in the spring of 1995—he announced that he was suffering from a grave form of pancreatic cancer. He was operated on immediately and underwent a regimen of radiation and chemotherapy. By September he was back on the job. That very month, in Cincinnati, thirty-six-year-old Steven Cook died of

AIDS, having sought, and received, forgiveness from the prelate he had falsely accused. Then in the fall of 1996, Bernardin disclosed that his cancer had returned; the following year it would kill him.

So it was that the cardinal's fatigue and drawn appearance that night in San Diego more likely stemmed from the cancer than some other cause. Still, his long ordeal under the cloud of accusation, his own Via Dolorosa, served to remind all the priests in the room that if someone of such universal esteem could be laid low by a single unsubstantiated charge, it could just as easily happen to them. That realization tempered any comfort or inspiration they otherwise might have derived from the cardinal's pep talk. In a sense, Bernardin had become a symbol of the trial that the contemporary priesthood has become.

In the United States today, there are sixty million Roman Catholics. For many, I daresay most, the priest remains a powerful mythic presence, reaffirmed every time he commands the pulpit, not to mention every time *Going My Way* or *Boys' Town* resurfaces on late-night cable. Well beyond symbolism, however, he continues to exert a real-world impact. Andrew Greeley, writing not as a novelist but a priest-sociologist, has said that the parish priest, a figure the culture still finds "irresistibly fascinating," has the greatest influence of anyone, save parents or spouse, in shaping a Catholic's spiritual life.

Even so, after centuries of veneration as a kind of superman in black, the priest today is off the pedestal. And while clerics generally will tell you that's fine, that they never wanted to be up there in the first place, the brusqueness of this dislodging has been unsettling all around. The sober truth is that, in modern times, it has never been more difficult to be a priest. Consider a glum litany, realities that for the most part didn't exist even twenty-five years ago. In the wake of the pedophile scandal, the average priest has had to endure the suspicions of even long-standing parishioners; he dare not hug a child lest he unleash rumors and fears—or lawsuits. For many, this imposed reticence feeds a loneliness already exacerbated by the growing number of single-priest parishes and rectories. Today's priests must minister to a renegade flock greatly at odds with Rome. They are caught between parishioners who feel the Church is not progressive enough and those who believe the reforms of Vatican II have gotten well out of hand. In one inner city they grapple with exploding Hispanic and Korean constituencies, while in another they shutter white-elephant churches and schools. They are forced to compete with the United Way and Jerry Lewis for the charitable dollar. They spar with formidable bureaucracies, and they preach morality in a culture that seems to have buried the concept. Their parishioners demand pastors of rectitude who are also great preachers and top managers—"Jesus with an M.B.A. and perfect pitch," one priest wrote—and if they don't get them they'll shop around, or "church surf," in a way that used to be unthinkable for Catholics. Most alarming, the clerical ranks are thinning so fast that the priest is becoming the ecclesiastical equivalent of the spotted owl. Yet John Paul II has emphatically said the Church will not even consider ordaining women or permitting priests to marry, a stance that means if nothing arrests current trends, within a generation there may *be* no more priests.

It is estimated that by 2005 the number of American Catholics will have swelled by a fourth, to seventy-four million. At the same time there will be only about twenty-one thousand active diocesan priests to serve them, down from twenty-four thousand in 1997. (The total current number of American priests, including retired and men in religious orders, is about fifty thousand.) Beyond the raw numbers are troubling trends: the priests who remain will be much older, serving twice as many parishioners, even as seminary enrollments continue their free fall. As it happened the shortage was a major theme of the San Diego convocation, where sociologist Richard Schoenherr, a former priest and co-author of *Full Pews and Empty Altars* (a 1993 book that brought the dilemma to broad attention), was a featured speaker. He had recently completed an exhaustive survey of American priests, the results of which he used to project the shape of the clergy into the next century. When Schoenherr told the delegates that the book based on that research would be titled *Goodbye, Father*, appreciative but mordant laughter rippled through the room. To me, as provocative as Schoenherr's numbers were his conclusions: he found that the Church's insistence on mandatory celibacy was directly responsible for the shortage and that the policy—as well as Rome's prohibition of women priests— would fall beneath the pressing demand for more clergy. He portrayed the Vatican as an institution that, like most institutions, clings to traditions more out of self-interest than logic. "Preserving compulsory celibacy in the Catholic Church is a smoke screen for preserving the patriarchy and all that goes with it: fear, hatred, and domination of women," he declared. Considering Rome's rather unambiguous and prickly views on these questions, I thought the delegates might consider such pointed rhetoric troubling, or at the very least awkward. I was mistaken. The priests, who after all are living the reality of Schoenherr's statistics, were nonplused. Many nodded their heads in agreement. (Another morbid convention footnote: eight months after San Diego, Schoenherr, too, was dead, age sixty, of a heart attack.)

All in all the situation is enough to induce priestly depression—and *that* subject was on the convention agenda, too. James Zullo, a clinical psychologist and member of the Christian Brothers order, dissected each of the aforementioned crises and warned how increasingly they are eating away at priests' mental well-being. The situation is serious and goes far beyond a question of overwork or declining numbers, Zullo believes, to something more emotional, something as fundamental as their own identity. "I think many men are grieving the loss of the priesthood as they have known it for the last forty or fifty years," he said.

As a Roman Catholic, I have gradually taken in these developments with alarm and, more to the point, surprise. Like most Catholics, I have known priests all my life, but also like most I was largely ignorant of the scope of their plight. As long as a parish has a priest—and more and more small ones do not—it tends to take him for granted. And let's face it, the clergy is about the only segment of society that hasn't turned up whining to Geraldo or Montel. So it wasn't until a few years ago that I began to be aware of what today's priests are up against, not to mention the dire implications for a sacramentally based Church that is running out of sacrament bearers. The catalyst for me was the United Nations conference on population in Cairo, held in the summer of 1994. There the Vatican was so intent on keeping any abortion language out of the final report on population control that papal delegates were cozying up to such outlaw regimes as Iran and Libya for support. For millions of American Catholics, even those who endorse wholeheartedly the Church's war against abortion, this was an unseemly spectacle. Then I wondered: if I were a pastor and a parishioner pressed me about the morality of allying oneself with murderous tyrants, no matter how high-minded the cause, what would I say? Once again, as we have seen with birth control, divorce, the role of women in the Church, liturgical language, and other contentious issues, I would have found myself smack between my pontiff and a goodly percentage of my flock.

Then again, I might have welcomed a diversion—*any* diversion—from the other ecclesiastical topic of that particular moment: the pedophile scandal. That same summer I went to the library and pulled out the *Reader's Guide to Periodicals* for 1993. Checking under the heading "Priest," I found sixty-five articles listed; fifty-seven dealt with some aspect of the pedophile and sexual abuse scandals. Aside from the moral and human toll, which cannot and should never be underestimated, that's a monumental public relations problem. What a turnabout: in a single generation priests had managed to go from saintly icons—if you squinted you could just

about make out the halos—to the targets of sidelong glances and the nasti-
est sort of innuendo. Parents found themselves asking grown sons if thirty
years ago Father So-and-So ever, *you know*—unable to bring themselves
even to say the words.

I could take refuge in more pleasant memories. I thought back to Father
Kilfoil, pastor of my boyhood parish in Indiana. Now there was a *priest*,
right out of central casting. Tall and well-spoken, with wavy silver hair always brushed back in an immaculate pompadour, Father was the kind of
man some would call autocratic, but that's not quite the right word. Aristocratic is more like it, I think. There was a positively regal bearing about
him. For one thing, he always wore the cassock, or black robe, cinched
snugly at his trim waist. In all the years I was around him, I don't recall
ever seeing him in slacks. (I must have, but early impressions are made in
indelible ink.) He came from money (or so we had heard), had an iron
grasp of finance, and conducted himself with a certain sense of noblesse
oblige in our workaday, blue-collar parish. It was simply inconceivable to
imagine Father Kilfoil attending a seminar based on Steven Covey's *Seven
Habits of Highly Effective People*, which was yet another offering at the
San Diego convention.

At a remove Father seemed austere. What a happy surprise to find out
later, at close inspection, how funny and gregarious he could be. My fond-
est memories of him are of listening to the jokes he swapped with Mr.
Miller, the funeral director, in the limousine on the way to the cemetery.

That, of course, was one of the perquisites of being an altar boy—getting
out of class to serve for funerals. Becoming a server was my first real accomplishment, in fact, as I memorized the entire Latin Mass as an eight-
year-old to pass muster. *Dominus vobiscum. Et cum spiritu tuo.* The Lord
be with you. And also with you. It nearly broke my tender heart when, the
very next year, in accordance with the modernizing reforms of Vatican II,
we pitched out the Latin and I had to learn the Mass all over again, this
time in English. (A dubious exchange, some of us felt at the time; after all,
Pater Noster sounded like something that could get you to heaven, but Our
Father was what you said five of after Father heard your sniveling, inept
confession.) Still, there were so many altar boy responsibilities, to be carried out impeccably in front of all those people: lighting the impossibly tall
High Mass candles at the back of the altar with a wick holder twice as long
as you were; ringing the bells during the consecration of the bread and wine
(not too long, not too short); holding the gold-plated paten beneath the
chins of communicants so that a fumbled host would never hit the floor (I

think in six years of service I made three total saves). And I recall the smug sensation of being the only person in church who knew how far along Father Kilfoil was in his sermon, since we altar boys were uniquely placed to see him tracking his way down the neatly typed, single-spaced text with the edge of that Sunday's bulletin.

Touchstones of a Catholic youth, they were, like your first scapular, or the smell of burning incense, or the May crowning of Mary, or the black-bordered prayer cards we all got back in 1963, our own *annus horribilis*, when we Catholics lost both Pope John XXIII and President John F. Kennedy.

Another of the acolyte's privileges was getting to witness, before Mass, what few others ever do: the priest donning all those garments, in an elaborate protocol, as he methodically transformed himself from mere mortal to someone capable, and worthy, of divine communion. First, over his black street clothes, went the floor-length, long-sleeved alb, a baggy robe of white linen. Then came the amice, a patch of white cloth worn across the upper back and tied about the neck. Then the stole, a long, narrow cloth that drapes around the neck and hangs to the knees. Then the cincture, a simple rope tied like a belt to secure the alb and stole. Then the maniple (used when I was a boy but seldom today), a kind of handkerchief curiously deposited over one forearm. Finally, over all the rest, came the chasuble, the great cloak whose color represents the theme of the day's Mass. The colors are dictated by the liturgical calendar. Thus violet, which symbolizes penance, is worn throughout Lent; white, the color of purity and joy, is seen at Christmastime and on the Marian feast days; and so on. (Green, the color of life, is for "ordinary" times and therefore is worn most often.) Centuries ago every element of this regalia had some practical purpose. Now the garments are symbolic, and watching the priest carefully add each totem you could almost feel the spiritual power welling up in him.

Heady stuff, that, so when we altar boys began to hear the standard entreaties about vocations, somewhere along the fifth or sixth grade, we paid attention. After all, a few older boys we knew, held up as examples, had taken the seminary track into high school. Two of my own cousins were seminarians. Yet to the extent I ever had the bug I quickly got over it. Hormonal considerations, as is their wont, elbowed aside spiritual ones. Girls turned up on the radar screen, then marriage, then family. Like so many Catholics, especially those of the baby-boomer, Vatican II generation, my own observance has waned and waxed over the years. My concerns about the Church and its policies are unresolved, even as my respect for its tradition, core values, and moral courage deepens. A believer is just that, even if he knows there will always be things he doesn't agree with, and certainly things he will never understand.

One thing that does become clear as you get older, however, is that priests aren't gods, or even saints, but human beings. Some are brilliant, some are dullards, and a few, as we now know, are dangerous. In this regard they are not unlike every other segment of society. But in most other regards they remain apart, literally and imaginatively, objects of our enduring curiosity. In an age without mystery they are mystery men. Most priests don't *mean* to be mysterious, mind you, but since so few people, Catholics included, really know what their lives are like, they can't help it. The vast majority of priests are no more monsters than they are latter-day Barry Fitzgeralds. They are people trying to do a difficult job armed with their conviction, their example, and the eternal power of the Word.

But who are they? Why do they do what they do? How does it feel to be a priest today? What does it mean? If they're no longer patterned after the Father Kilfoils of my memory, the benevolent dictator model—and they're not—what model are they? I resolved to find out, and I figured the best way was simply to ask. One can scope out the lurid headlines about priests or pore over scholarly research; heaven knows there is an abundance of each. (Sociologists joke that priests must be the most surveyed group in America, given the tempting subject matter, their manageable population, and their conscientious willingness to fill out nosy questionnaires and mail them back.) But these are only incomplete and unsatisfying glimpses of the picture. I determined a far more interesting approach would be to listen to them.

Which is why I was in San Diego, in the company of priests and at the beginning of a kind of journey. I wanted to make sense of a profession that has become so tangled that in one room an expert could urge the men to protect their mental health by forming more lay friendships, while in another a second expert was advising pretty much the opposite, arguing that getting too close to the people he serves compromises a priest's clinical distance. Samuel Beckett couldn't have been more confounding.

Still, for all the daunting problems and apocalyptic predictions in the air, I was pleasantly surprised to find that when they get together, priests talk about essentially the same things other working stiffs do. They worry about life insurance, rising health-care deductibles, and how hard it is to put a few bucks away. In fact, there was a lot of talk about money generally. At my table everyone chuckled when a priest brought up the fifty-dollar-a-month "bonus" one gets in his diocese for being a pastor. And when a guy from

Chicago said he made "only" fourteen thousand dollars a year, he was hooted at by dozens of others who will never earn that much in their dreams.

Over cocktails and canapes they compared notes about their long hours and how they try to fend off burnout. They also groused about another universal bane of the human condition: bureaucracy. For instance, years ago the Church dropped its rule against eating meat on Fridays—or I thought it had. I would learn from a priest acquaintance that the Vatican recently reminded its clerics that they are not to consume more than four ounces of meat on Fridays lest they be in a state of sin—not venial sin, mind you, but *mortal* sin, the big hammer. "I've found that if you cut both ends off a hot dog, you're usually all right," he informed me. I couldn't tell if he was kidding.

Groups always prompt grumbling, of course. When I chatted with the delegates individually I was much more likely to hear that, all in all, they enjoy their lives. Most said they would be ordained again in a heartbeat. True, they are tremendously worried about what's happening to their ranks, but personally they seem gratified by the priestly life, especially when they actually get to be spiritual ministers instead of mere fixers or problem solvers. Many even see a silver lining in the priest shortage, in that it has, of necessity, pushed the Catholic laity into positions of greater responsibility and involvement in religious affairs. The Church is its people, they reminded me.

Over the next year I would meet hundreds of priests, and I formally interviewed dozens of them, as often as I could on their own turf. I wanted my survey, while in no way scientific, to be as representative as possible, since one truth you quickly learn is that there is no such thing as a monolithic priesthood any more than there is a single "black community" or "typical Republican." So I tried to hook up with men from all over the country and running the gamut of age, ideology, and experience—which is to say not just parish priests but teachers, administrators, monks, social workers, canon lawyers, even a physician who is an AIDS specialist. What follows are the experiences and views of some of them. If their stories erase a bit of the mystery, I hope they also convey a collective sense of what the contemporary priesthood is really like, with all its frustrations, yes, but also its gratifications. (Incidentally, I have written about these men and their circumstances—ages, jobs, locales, etc.—as of the time I visited. In the intervening months one has died and several have been reassigned.)

On the whole these priests struck me as thoughtful, committed, and articulate but above all pragmatic. They care about theological issues, often passionately, but in their vocations they deal with real life, in all its messy incarnations, as it unfolds. Their work is about the hungry, about schools, about fund drives, about marriage and divorce, sickness and death, confusion and fear. It's about finishing up a homily ten minutes before Saturday's five o'clock Mass. To do this work they rely enormously on their faith, and on prayer. That includes where their own future is concerned. In conversation after conversation about the problems of the priesthood, I heard variations of this sentiment: "I don't know what's going to happen, but I have to trust that whatever does is the work of the Holy Spirit according to God's plan."

Before Cardinal Bernardin addressed the San Diego convention, we all stood and, after singing some hymns to limber up, chanted the Our Father, the way priests once routinely did at Mass but seldom do anymore:

> *Our Father, Who art in hea-ven, hal-lowed be Thy name . . .*

The clergymen were not tentative. Three hundred robust male voices merged as one and the sound reverberated in the small room. The effect was chilling—otherworldly, actually—and for a moment it was easy to imagine we were not in a sterile California conference room but in the soaring sanctuary of a medieval abbey.

Not long after, revisiting some of the essays of C. S. Lewis, I came upon his elegant effort to sort out the conundrum of prayer. ("It may be a mystery why He should have allowed us to cause real events at all; but it is no odder that He should allow us to cause them by praying than by any other method.") It was essential for God to leave himself some discretion where the answering of prayers is concerned, Lewis argues, lest he spend all his time being asked to sanction the ambitions of tyrants, "the horrible state of things envisaged by Juvenal: 'Enormous prayers which Heaven in anger grants.'" Juvenal was a first-century Roman satirist (some would add spoilsport), and in that passage he was decrying the ruthless likes of Crassus and Pompey. Yet as my mind fixed on that phrase "enormous prayers," I began to consider it in a different context. I thought back to that powerful and heartfelt Our Father, and then I thought about the entreaties those same priests, on their own, send up every day, asking for guidance and strength. These are enormous prayers, too, ones I suspect they are pleased to have Heaven answer, whether in anger or otherwise.

◙ Father
Benedict Groeschel

NEW YORK

On a dismal Saturday night, we are southbound on Interstate 95, about halfway between New York City and Providence, Rhode Island, and moving at a crawl. I am at the wheel of Father Benedict Groeschel's vintage yet sturdy station wagon, trying to divine the pavement in a driving rainstorm. Father Benedict himself is in the passenger seat, asleep, after a grueling twenty-four hours in Providence, where he had conducted a parish retreat. Father Benedict is a founding member of the Franciscan Friars of the Renewal, or the Gray Friars, as they call themselves after the gray monk's robe they wear. About ten miles back he had simply pulled the hood down, like a small tent, over his head—"Now you know what this thing is for," he said as he did it, grinning—and proven to me what he had asserted earlier: he can sleep anywhere given half a chance. A cassette of Puccini arias is losing out to the din of the storm. After a while the gale-force rain pounds the windshield with such vehemence that Father Benedict awakens, sizes up the situation, and exclaims, "Oh, St. Jude!" He says that a lot, and it can be an expression of glee, alarm, or disgust, depending on the provocation.

In the distance we spot the flashing lights of emergency vehicles. "I just want to see if this is an accident," Father Benedict says as we approach. "I stop for accidents." Through the rainy windshield he tries to discern what is happening. "It doesn't look like an ambulance. Oh, it might be, there's a fire engine. Yeah, there was an accident. Oh, brother."

I pull the station wagon onto the shoulder of the road; Father Benedict throws on a windbreaker and steps into the rain with an umbrella. From the rear of the car, he retrieves a small case that contains everything he needs to administer the sacrament called anointing of the sick. Father Benedict is prepared to comfort anyone, of course, but if an accident victim is Catholic and badly injured or killed, the priest will be ready with the last rites. "They don't like you to carry the holy oils unless somebody is in danger of death," he tells me, "but when you live in New York there is always somebody in danger of death."

Five minutes later he reemerges from the mist and slides back into the car. "A minor accident," he reports. "Nobody hurt, thank God." And we resume our drive back to New York.

Well, not New York, exactly, but Larchmont, in suburban Westchester County. This is where Father Benedict spends about half his week as director of spiritual development for the archdiocese of New York. In this capacity he works at Trinity Retreat, where priests, former priests, deacons, and Catholic laity come for retreats and prayer. The other half of the week he can be found at St. Crispin's Friary in the South Bronx, where he and forty other Gray Friar priests and brothers live and minister to the downtrodden in the Melrose neighborhood (a place known more familiarly, and notoriously, as Fort Apache), and in Harlem.

Father Benedict's two worlds represent an almost absurd dichotomy. Trinity Retreat, in affluent Larchmont, is a large, sunny residence that was bequeathed to the Church by its former owner, a doctor. It is situated on a tranquil cove of Long Island Sound; on the flagstone terrace, as geese glide past, you half expect to see Jay Gatsby walk up to borrow a cup of sugar. The South Bronx, on the other hand, is pretty much as advertised, a razor-wire landscape of burned-out buildings and vacant lots. The area is a collection point of latter-day scourges—poverty, violence, drugs, AIDS. Yet amid the destitution there is an undeniable vitality to the place. On a Sunday morning Prospect Avenue bustles with couples and families, and the shops are busy. The Gray Friars have become familiar figures on these streets, too, and they are committed to helping their neighbors break the grip of despair. It is a gratifying existence, Father Benedict maintains—"life where it is most real."

The friary, a converted Catholic church and rectory on East 156th Street, hums with activity. Here and in adjacent buildings, the friars run a homeless shelter and residence for eighty-five men. Nearby is a residence for homeless mothers, a part of Good Counsel Homes, an agency the friars substantially support. The men of the order distribute food to the poor and pay calls on the neighborhood's shut-ins. The parish hall has become a gym for local youngsters. (In their mission the Gray Friars are assisted by a small group of their sisters—the women live in a convent behind the friary—and several dozen lay volunteers.) But St. Crispin's also is a place of prayer. Several hours a day are devoted to quiet and contemplation. True to their vows, the Gray Friars lead lives as spartan as their wardrobe. Meals are communal and chores are shared. The men sleep on bedrolls in compact rooms that might contain a dresser, a crucifix, and little else.

Indeed, the Franciscan Friars of the Renewal came into being about a decade ago because Father Benedict and a handful of associates, at the time Capuchin Franciscans, decided that forming their own order was the only way they could truly devote their lives to the poor. "The whole group of us were very anxious to try to return to as authentic an observance of the Franciscan life as we possibly could," Father Benedict says. "That included the observance of poverty and working with the poor, which is what St. Francis of Assisi did. We were anxious to do that, and we feel that many religious orders have accidentally become overly middle-class in their lifestyle." St. Francis was also a Church reformer, and the Gray Friars consciously employed the word "renewal" in naming their order to make a point. "We believe there has to be a renewal, or reform, of the commitment to the gospel, of the commitment to the truths of faith and the Catholic tradition," he says, "a reform in many aspects in the life of the clergy."

With his slight stoop and almost gnomish countenance, Benedict Groeschel looks like you expect a monk to look. He has twinkling eyes and a snow-white beard that constant tugging has pulled into a point. He came from a middle-class home in Jersey City, just across the Hudson River from New York, and for all his acclaim as a psychologist and thinker he still sounds like a guy from the neighborhood. Now and again, usually for effect, he lapses into the broad patois that renders coffee as "*kaw*-fee" and lets you know "You're out of Shlitz" (which is to say, out of luck). As a speaker he holds listeners rapt as he moves effortlessly from history to philosophy to ethnic cuisine, all delivered with authority and borscht belt timing. During a homily back in Providence, he mentioned how one man suggested to him that heaven might be like one endless church service. "I've *been* to endless church services," the priest cracked, rolling his eyes. "And I truly became convinced that they are purgatorial."

Now sixty-three, Father Benedict says he knew at age seven that he would be a priest. Not only that, he knew specifically that he wanted to work with the needy, after being inspired by Longfellow's poem "The Legend Beautiful," about a monk who is visited by a vision of Christ. The monk is reluctant to leave the sacred apparition but does so to feed the poor beckoning at the convent gate, and Christ rewards him for his selflessness ("'Hadst thou stayed I must have fled!'/That is what the Vision said"). Benedict Groeschel became a Capuchin novice at seventeen. Ordained at twenty-six, he was appointed chaplain of Children's Village, a home for emotionally troubled children in the wooded hills above Dobbs Ferry, New York. He was there fourteen years, during which time he obtained a Ph.D. in psychology from Columbia University. Shortly after that, in 1974, New York's Cardinal Terence Cooke asked him to open the Office of Spiritual Development at Trinity Retreat. This was at a time when priests, in that great collective soul-searching that followed Vatican II, were still leaving the vocation in droves. Father Benedict's work with priests at Trinity involves counseling and psychotherapy, as well as conducting retreats and interviews. He considers one of his greatest joys helping return nearly eighty men to the active priesthood.

In 1987 Father Benedict secured approval to establish the Gray Friar order, but not at the expense of his work at Trinity; thus his divided schedule and untold miles logged on the New England Thruway. But it doesn't take much time in Father Benedict's company to mark him as a classic workaholic. He wouldn't know what to do if he weren't overwhelmed. In addition to overseeing Trinity and St. Crispin's, he is a prolific author and produces tapes about prayer and Church issues, sales of which help support the Gray Friar mission. He appears regularly on the Eternal Word Television Network, or EWTN, the Catholic cable channel, by himself and with the formidable personification of that network, Mother Angelica. Along the way Father Benedict has become something of a celebrity, in growing demand for speaking engagements around the world. He tries to fit in these appearances around his other obligations—he travels eight to ten days a month—and estimates that he works more than a hundred hours a week. "But that's including time to pray," he hastens to add.

In many ways, then, Benedict Groeschel must be considered a thoroughly modern priest. He writes, he travels, he appears on television, he markets. He's a reformer who welcomed the cleansing breeze of the Second Vatican Council. He's a psychologist who helps fellow priests hold their lives together.

Yet Father Benedict is a throwback, too. He walks through the world in sandals and a gray friar's robe, living simply, giving away what little material wealth he has. He preaches, and practices, traditional devotion to the sacraments, to the pope, to Mary. He believes the well-intentioned reform spirit of Vatican II was co-opted, became change for change's sake, with the result that the American Church, at least, seems to have lost its bearings. "This is the most difficult time in American Catholic history, no question about it," he says. "For the first time in two hundred years we find, as [Cardinal John Henry] Newman said, 'The enemies of the Church are not outside the Church, but inside the Church.'"

In short, he strikes me as an ideal figure with which to begin an examination of where priests have been, and where they are going.

❖   ❖   ❖

Offerer of sacrifice, shaman, liaison between the natural and supernatural worlds: the figure of the priest has been an essential part of civilizations around the world and across time, as humans have tried to reconcile themselves to those prodigious forces beyond their control and understanding. To a great extent the roots of today's Catholic priesthood, like those of the Church itself, reach back to the Judaic tradition into which Jesus of Nazareth was born. The priests of ancient Israel were the teachers and interpreters of law, proclaimers of divine will, and ritual presiders of offerings and sacrifice. More broadly, they were the righteous representatives of an entire nation of priestly people, whose very lives were meant to be offerings to the God of Israel. The Catholic Church likewise holds that all the baptized constitute a priesthood, a tenet reinforced by Vatican II, and that its ordained priests are men uniquely called to serve the faithful through teaching, personal witness, and sacramental ministry.

The precise origins of the priesthood, however, like so much about the turbulent early years of Christianity, are murky. The word "priest" derives from the Greek *presbyter*, which means "elder," and it is known the term was not applied to the apostles or their immediate successors, who were carrying Christ's teachings across the Mediterranean world. Rather, they were considered bishops, at the time the exclusive presiders over the Eucharist (the ritual re-creation of the Last Supper) and overseers of the first Christian communities that for the most part were concentrated in major cities, such as Jerusalem, Antioch, and Alexandria. This loose organization of believers, comprising Jew and Gentile alike, sufficed for the infancy of the movement, which by the early second century was being referred to as the Catholic (from the Greek for "universal") Church. But the spread of the faith into outlying regions, the growing problem of renegade preachers, and the continuing persecution by Rome necessitated a more fixed structure if Christianity was going to survive. With a laying on of hands—a tradition that continues to this day through the sacrament of holy orders—the bishops began to ordain lieutenants, called presbyters, and conferred on them certain powers, including celebration of the Eucharist and preaching of the gospel. The presbyters in turn were assisted by deacons and, less well known today, deaconesses. These latter were women whose role seems to have varied from region to region but who were ordained essentially to minister to other women. Though they were not to teach, they did perform baptisms and tended to the sick and indigent. It would be several hundred years before deaconesses officially were removed from the Catholic ministry.

By the time Constantine sanctioned Christianity throughout the Roman Empire, early in the fourth century, the Church organization had begun to adopt and even supplant the imperial government structures. (Church provinces are still known as "dioceses" after their secular Roman namesakes.) This development marked the first real ascendance of the priest-administrator class over the priesthood of all the faithful, the laity. This same period also witnessed the rise of the monastic movement, which would be so influential not only in the continued spread of the faith but in the future of its clergy. For instance, as monasticism took hold, so increasingly did certain of its mores, including the rejection of wealth and the discipline of celibacy. Priestly chastity long had been valued in certain regional traditions, or rites, but it would not become required of priests in the dominant Latin Rite until the twelfth century.

By the Middle Ages the Church had clearly and consciously divided into two classes: the clerics, who were concerned with spiritual matters and Church rule (sometimes state rule, too), and the laity, who presumably were occupied with their more mundane problems. The Church was becoming the religious manifestation of Europe's princely states, with lay noblemen and Church leaders inextricably bound up in one another's political aspirations and intrigues. Such activity regularly provoked internal calls for reform; these backlashes often originated with, or resulted in, some of Catholicism's most venerable religious orders (e.g., the Cistercians, Dominicans, Franciscans, Jesuits). But in the sixteenth century, when Luther, Calvin, and the other great Protestant reformers rattled the Church to its foundations—challenging among other things its clerical culture and the sacramental powers reserved to ordained priests—the Vatican's reply was the landmark Council of Trent. In recasting and clarifying Catholic dogma specifically to rebut the Protestants, the Church not only reaffirmed the priest and lay castes but its entire hierarchy—a pyramid with the pope on top, the lay faithful at the base, and the various clerical ranks in the middle. Trent likewise reinforced the unique ability of priests to consecrate the Eucharist, forgive sins, and perform other sacramental duties. In short, it fixed the blueprint for the modern Catholic priesthood. As theologian Richard P. McBrien asserts in his book *Catholicism*, "This view of the priesthood was passed on within the Catholic Church without criticism or essential change all the way into the middle of the twentieth century."

The first Catholic priests in the Americas were those missionaries who arrived with the colonizing European armies, and who in their zeal to convert the indigenous populations also helped settle the New World from Florida to California. But it was the immigration of the nineteenth and early twentieth centuries that truly shaped Catholicism in the United States. Transplanted Irish, Italians, and Eastern Europeans increased the number of American Catholics exponentially; sending sons into the priesthood not only was essential to serve that burgeoning population but was an expedient avenue to social respectability. Between the world wars America's seminaries were so crowded that some graduates didn't make the cut for ordination; the Church was in the enviable position of taking only the best. By the mid-sixties there were still nearly fifty thousand men in training for the priesthood here. (By contrast, in 1996 there were fewer than five thousand.) Beyond the numbers, this wealth of priests made possible (in larger churches anyway) the familiar parish construct: an entire staff of priests, with a pastor who ruled more or less by fiat and three or four associates to handle the routine. Come dinnertime, a rectory cook had prepared a bounteous meal, and the table was crowded.

Then came the watershed event in modern Catholic history. In 1962, when Pope John XXIII convened the Second Vatican Council, he was not responding to some internal crisis or heretical threat, which prompted past conclaves. His aim was more proactive. Coming at the height of the cold war—as it happened, the opening session would coincide with the Cuban missile crisis—Vatican II was charged with exploring how the Church could do more to promote peace, to end human suffering and discord, to reach out to the world's other great faiths and affirm their common ground. At the same time John invited discussion of a wide range of internal Church issues. When the Curia, or Vatican administration, attempted to keep these colloquies narrow and tightly controlled, John rebuked the powerful bureaucrats and sided with his bishops. This pope, whose great humanity radiated from his round, grandfatherly countenance, was throwing open the windows in a breathtaking fashion.

In four sessions over four years, the council went a long way toward achieving Pope John's stated goals. (After John's death in 1963, his agenda was carried forward by another progressive, Paul VI.) The Church declared that its mission must involve working toward peace and social justice. It said the "Church" includes all Christians, not just Catholics, and held that salvation may be found in other religions. It reaffirmed the principle that the priesthood comprises all the baptized, not just its clerics and hierarchy, and that the laity are likewise charged to participate equally in its mission. And it recognized the integrity of individual parishes, in effect saying they were more than small cogs in a very large machine. Among the most immediate and visible consequences of Vatican II was a stunning transformation in the liturgy. Latin was out and English (or whatever the vernacular) was in. The altar was moved closer to the congregation, and the priest, who before presided with his back to the people, turned around. For the first time, communicants could chew the host and partake of the sacramental wine. Laypersons turned up as lectors. Guitars supplanted pipe organs. This new liturgy in fact would have looked rather familiar to the first Christians, but to twentieth-century Catholics it was nothing if not strange.

Just as significant were the unforeseen consequences of the council and its modernizing sensibilities. Vatican II represented such a sea change for Catholics that, three decades later, we're still trying to steady our legs. In its wake long-held aspects of Catholic dogma were questioned by the Church's own theologians. Many traditionalists, in both the clergy and laity alike, considered the new liturgy common; they felt something beautiful had been discarded, something mystical lost. The seeds of ideological division were planted. Increasingly, bishops became hostile to Rome, pastors hostile to bishops, parishioners hostile to pastors. The American Church especially, arguing with itself over such emotional issues as birth control, divorce and remarriage, abortion, homosexuality, and women's roles, at times seemed on the way to schism. And the priests? They were scarcely immune from the turmoil. In fact, where they were concerned, Vatican II not only changed all the old rules, it didn't bother to give them the new ones.

❖   ❖   ❖

The story of St. Patrick's Church in Providence is so familiar that it could be emblematic of the great urban parishes of the Northeast—at least to a point. The church, situated almost literally in the shadow of the Rhode Island statehouse, was founded in 1851 to serve the city's burgeoning Irish community. This it did with distinction for more than a century. By the time of Vatican II, however, those fully assimilated Irish Americans had moved up and out of the inner city, and the once proud parish had to be shuttered. Today there's a parking lot where the church used to be.

Happily, St. Patrick's departs from the script in that the parish is still alive. Indeed, despite its modest means it's probably one of the most vibrant Christian communities in Providence. Twenty years ago a handful of local Catholics active in the charismatic movement and looking for a permanent home resurrected the place. The old elementary school was reopened, first with volunteer instructors and later with a dedicated if meagerly paid staff. Parents remain very involved in the instruction, and today St. Patrick's, with only one hundred twenty-five pupils, has achieved wide recognition for its enterprising approach to education.

The neighborhood is low-income and multiethnic, and so is St. Patrick's congregation. (Out front a sign welcomes you to Iglesia Catolica San Patricio.) But because it is charismatic—a niche church, if you will—it draws Catholics from all over greater Providence, and on this weekend the congregation had invited Father Benedict to lead them in a parish retreat, or "mission." Snarled traffic outside New York caused us to be late in arriving Friday night, but several dozen team leaders listened enthusiastically as the priest gave them a ninety-minute sermon-cum-pep-talk. After that he signed books and greeted well-wishers for another half hour. This kind of give-and-take is his favorite part of the job. "I am a people's priest all the way," he admits. "I love people: poor people, rich people, crazy people, sane people, atheists, agnostics, as long as I am doing something religious. If I am praying with agnostics, I am having a ball."

On Saturday nearly four hundred people, some from other parishes, show up for a packed schedule of workshops, lectures, and prayer, capped with an evening Mass. To create a new sanctuary the parish some years ago converted the school's former gymnasium. The space is laid out on an east-west axis, giving it the opposite feel of a traditional nave church, and is dominated by a startling, larger-than-life-size crucifix.

As in some other denominations, the services of charismatic Catholics are emotional and exuberant, with people singing and dancing and sometimes speaking in tongues. Father Benedict, like many mainstream Catholics, is not entirely comfortable with all the charismatic trappings—he warned the participants beforehand that his Mass might be a relatively tame affair by their standards—but he has great affection for the people of St. Patrick's and respect for the enthusiasm with which they profess their faith. At one point, complimenting their own pastor, Father Ray Kelly, Father Benedict mentioned an observation from St. Gregory I, a sixth-century pope: "There are many priests but few apostles."

The Catholic charismatic movement is yet another surprise offspring of Vatican II. When the Church reached out so demonstrably to the laity, it paved the way for an explosion of opportunities to express their individual spirituality. These expressions run the gamut from the orthodox Opus Dei to the gay activist organization Dignity, with a little of everything sprinkled in between. This big-tent phenomenon has reinvigorated the Church even as it has irked and confused many Catholics who no longer seem to recognize the religion of their upbringing.

As a freshly minted priest when Vatican II began, Father Benedict was delighted by it. He was certain the Church needed to reach out in many directions, not just to its own people but to other denominations. He was one of those many priests happy to see the liturgy become less about the celebrant and more about the congregation. Father Benedict says proudly that he was the first priest in New York City to say Mass facing the people.

Somewhere along the line, however, that liberalizing spirit of reform grew out of control, he says, unwittingly became a Pandora's box. The combination of an energized laity and the Church's willingness to examine some of its traditional positions led to a questioning of everything, he says, including core values that were never meant to be under the microscope. An example Father Benedict raises frequently is present-day observance of the Holy Eucharist. From the time of the Council of Trent, Catholic dogma—based on ancient traditions—has held that when the priest consecrates the bread and wine at Mass, the elements, in a process called transubstantiation, become the substance of Christ's body and blood. Yet surveys consistently show that a great majority of American Catholics, two-thirds or more in some samples, today consider the Eucharist a purely symbolic ritual. On this subject Father Benedict can become visibly upset; he is as protective as a parent defending a child. "I love the Eucharist," he declares, saying belief in the communion transformation goes to the very heart of what it means to be Catholic. "Unfortunately, we can't all be partly right" in interpreting Catholic teaching, Father Benedict tells me as we discuss a particular theologian he considers "very cavalier" with dogma. "If I am right, he is wrong."

Many people also are inclined to blame the priest shortage on Vatican II, but that's not quite accurate or fair. It has been shown, for instance, that World War II interrupted vocations, and that afterward the GI bill opened secular doors for many young men who before might have become priests. (It's true the fifties did see the greatest number of vocations in American Church history, but the growth rate already was slowing.) Still, it's not altogether coincidental that from the day Vatican II ended in 1965, the number of American priests has steadily fallen. Thousands simply left the vocation, those in earlier cohorts retired or died, and as was indicated earlier, the number of seminarians began to plummet.

At Trinity Father Benedict has studied this phenomenon and interviewed hundreds of men who have left the priesthood. He cites a variety of factors for the exodus, only one of which is the general disorientation that followed Vatican II like a hangover. Father Benedict says the council tended to deal with changes on theoretical and theological levels but didn't always anticipate how they would affect people, either clergy or laity. For instance, pastors were suddenly asked to abandon their patriarchal model and begin sharing authority with lay parish councils. This was a huge adjustment; many didn't make it, and even those who did received little in the way of guidance or support.

But Father Benedict ticks off other reasons for the falloff. One is the broad secularization of society itself, and with it a perceived decline in the estimation of clergy. Another is celibacy, an always difficult lifestyle made all the more challenging, even ridiculed, in a culture fixated with sex. And a critical but seldom discussed factor is a change in the men themselves. "You know, a Catholic population which was almost entirely blue-collar workers and farmers in fifty years became a population of middle- and upper-class people," Father Benedict explains. "And the clergy got caught in that gigantic thing. The needs, psychological and otherwise, of priests in the 1930s who had come from industrial or farmer homes [were different from] priests in the 1970s and '80s, who were like everybody else in the United States—much more psychologically aware, much more aware of their needs, much more complex. If you will, much more neurotic. There was a difficulty in coping with that. I wouldn't say that the Church didn't try. A tremendous amount of effort and interest was given to psychology, but psychology itself was often grasping at straws and feeling its way along."

Then there is good old-fashioned stress. This is especially true for parish priests, who are men in the middle—trying to reconcile Church teachings and policy with parishioners who want to be upright Catholics yet often lead lives less tidy than the guidebook would have them. The Church must recognize that and adjust its expectations of those in pastoral work, Father Benedict argues. Parish priests "have to be careful. They have to meet people where they are. You've got to be patient and gentle, and you can't bring the house down. Even when we preach, when we preach on abortion we have to be careful. There are women sitting in the church who have had them. So, you've got to be gentle—and yet very clear on the fact that abortion kills a child."

On the other hand, he continues, "We think that priests who are *not* in pastoral work and have the time to study should loyally defend the Church, and take prophetic roles as it now emerges as a countercultural force against the hedonism and materialism of the American society. I must say that we are very disappointing in that. Nonparochial priests have a fairly good reputation, well deserved, in terms of social problems and care of the poor. But we haven't done anywhere near as well in the defense of the Catholic faith against the inroads of secularism, skepticism, utilitarianism, all kinds of things that lead people to religious cynicism."

Back at St. Patrick's for that evening's Mass, Father Benedict, despite talking all day, stood and delivered a forty-minute extemporaneous sermon. His theme was how even amid life's afflictions, to love God is to be grateful for his gifts. He told about a visit he once paid to a ninety-four-year-old black woman in rural Alabama. The woman, who was blind, seemed full of grace, he said. She took communion every day, and Father Benedict had brought her the sacrament. "As I was getting ready to leave, I told her, 'Christina, I want you to pray for priests, because I work with priests,'" Father Benedict told the congregation. "'Pray for priests who have left, to help them find their way. Pray for priests who are in trouble. Pray for priests who work hard on the job and are overwhelmed. Pray for priests who are dog tired, priests who are discouraged.' And she smiled and she said to me—remember, she's blind—she said, 'Father, I'm here all day by myself, and all I do is pray. And there passes before the eyes of my soul all kinds of things, and all kinds of folks, and all manner of things seen and unseen.'" Father Benedict paused and shook his head in wonder. "The way she said the word 'unseen' sent a chill through me. Seen and unseen. This blind woman I think saw things that we never see."

After Mass, on our way to the car, we have a hard time taking our leave of the many well-wishers. Even as we're about to pull away from the parking lot one last man pokes his head in the window to say good-bye to Father Benedict. Then he says to me, "He's a saint!"

Father Benedict, embarrassed, nods farewell and rolls up the window. "Oh, St. Jude!" he mutters. He hears that saint business often and calls it "ridiculous." Yet the fact is, the people of St. Patrick's and countless like them *do* consider Father Benedict something of a saint, or at least a patron saint. He stands for what they believe in, articulates what they can't always—which is that the Church must return to its values of long standing. To Father Benedict, these people represent Catholicism's great middle ground, ecclesiastical analogs of Nixon's silent majority. They defy facile labeling, he warns; for instance, they are conservative on many issues, yes, but also dedicated to progressive social legislation and care of the poor. Given all the commotion on the far left and right flanks of the Church, it is a constituency too easily overlooked, he says. "How do you find the middle of the road in an earthquake? The forgotten people are the devout."

Father Benedict himself, however, is hard to overlook as he imparts his views, clearly but bluntly, on television or at a retreat or in a car in a rainstorm. He thinks too many Catholic schools, even seminaries, are doing a "lousy" job teaching basic catechism. He insists on much greater allegiance to the pope and devotion to the sacraments. He understands and is sympathetic to women who aspire to the priesthood but maintains that the Church doesn't have authority to permit their ordination any more than it could replace the Eucharistic bread with some new offering. "If women could be priests, I would be perfectly in favor of it," he says. "But the Church teaches that the sacraments were established in their essential form by Christ. He had his reasons. Why should we argue with him? And the Church has always maintained that it cannot change the nature of the sacraments. But I still understand why people are disappointed."

Mostly, though, the Bronx friar carries a broader message, that Christianity is not a spectator sport. As we creep along the New England Thruway, he tells me about a friend, Father Walter Ciszek, a Jesuit who spent decades doing ministry in the former Soviet Union. Much of his work took place in Siberia, where conditions were appalling and he was regularly beaten and imprisoned by the KGB. For years, the man's friends thought he was dead, but it turned out he was simply busy. "We were called to be Christians in this time," Father Benedict says. "Don't sit around bellyaching that you lived in a bad time. You know, fight the good fight."

Monsignor J. Joshua Mundell

WASHINGTON, D.C.

In the dining room of the rectory at the Church of the Immaculate Conception, I am having a genial chat with the man in charge, Monsignor J. Joshua Mundell. Actually, I am munching tasty finger sandwiches of chicken salad as Mundell tells me stories, methodically works through a ration of Marlboros (at easy reach in a small silver cup), and flexes his charm. At seventy-six, Mundell has blue eyes that are as animated as his wit is deadpan. Were he smoking cigars instead of cigarettes, you might think you were in the presence of an ecclesiastical George Burns. Recalling for me the surprise his family and friends registered when he told them of his intention to become a priest, Mundell said, "No one thought it would ever last."

It has. For half a century, in fact. In a city full of institutions, Mundell is one made of flesh and bone, and no small measure of starch. For the past thirty-two years, he has been pastor at Immaculate Conception in Washington's grim Shaw neighborhood, which is maybe two miles from the Capitol but might as well be on another planet.

If Benedict Groeschel embodies a new priestly model, Monsignor Mundell, his floor-length black robe bisected at the waist by a wide scarlet sash, strikes me as one of the last lions, a pastor like those of my youth. Running things in a benevolent, no-nonsense fashion, well connected in a town where connections count for so much, he has become the walking embodiment of Immaculate Conception. In turn, he uses that authority and a daunting will to bring hope to a part of the world so many others have written off.

Fact is, the cruel reality of inner-city Washington is never far from Mundell's thoughts. As quickly as he can get you laughing—as he did me by recounting how one of his young student helpers, after a wedding, tried to pick up a carpet of rose petals with a vacuum cleaner—the levity can vanish. "Tomorrow morning we're going to have a funeral here," Mundell abruptly announces. "I dread it. I've been through it too many times. One of our boys at the school here. He was bright. He used to work around here on Saturdays when he was a young boy. He got on drugs, selling drugs in the neighborhood. In the last ten years he had been in and out of jail. On Christmas Day he called me up from jail, and that was the greatest present I received. It really touched me."

Mundell's "boys" and his "girls," which they remain however old they become, are any of the several thousand students who have passed through what the priest calls Shaw's "shining star," the Immaculate Conception elementary school. Mundell began the school, which has one hundred and twenty pupils in pre-kindergarten through grade six, after his arrival in 1964, and he has kept it going against absurd odds. Even so, for all Mundell's efforts and those of the faculty—not to mention the brave determination of the kids themselves—there are so many malevolent forces working against young people here, so many traps waiting for them, that sometimes they meet unhappy ends. In this instance the young man was in his late twenties. I ask what happened.

"Last week he was beaten to death," Mundell says. "Eleven o'clock in the morning, about five blocks from here. Three boys beat him, killed him with a baseball bat."

There is resignation in Mundell's voice as he is relating this, but at the same time he is matter-of-fact. This is life in the Shaw neighborhood, he seems to say, which is not much of a life. I ask if the killing was about drugs.

"Oh, yes, he probably owed money to the guys. I don't know. I don't ask. But I dread it, because I know how they will be screaming. 'Oh, my Ryan, Ryan! Jesus save us!' I'll be washed out tomorrow afternoon, I can tell you that. I dread it."

The majestic red-stone church and its adjacent school have been fixtures at the corner of Eighth and N Streets, Northwest, since Abraham Lincoln was president. For a century, the congregation of Immaculate Conception was white, even affluent. By the time Mundell arrived in the mid-sixties, he found a congregation still mostly white—longtime parishioners who had moved away but came back on Sundays—while the surrounding neighborhood was predominantly black. Shaw was still vibrant, however, a community of single-family homes with lots of shops, markets, and theaters. Then came the riots. In 1968, after the murder of Martin Luther King Jr., the area went up in flames. As Mundell watched in horror, whole blocks of storefronts and row houses were devoured. About the only thing spared was the complex at Immaculate Conception. Mundell has no illusions why. "That wasn't the goodwill of the church," he says. "It was the school."

Survey the neighborhood today and you'd never guess this apocalypse occurred three decades ago. The damage seems too fresh; so many buildings still gutted, so many lots vacant. After the fires Shaw became infested with drug activity and prostitution, and family life inexorably declined. These days the neighborhood is unsettling by day and just plain dangerous by night. In this milieu Mundell is, to say the least, an unlikely presence. With his silver hair neatly combed back, a lined face, and an easy, aristocratic carriage, he looks like he got lost on the way to the Senate cloakroom.

In fact Mundell is a Washington native, born into a solid, loving family. "My mother and father practiced their religion," he says. "They weren't like—" He begins to mention a prominent politician, then thinks better of it. "You know, always talking about their faith. They set a good example. It meant something to them." He was just another guy, interested in girls and sports, neither particularly intellectual nor a religious "goody-goody." There was nothing about him that bespoke priest material. In prep school and then at Georgetown University, however, he was exposed to a number of Jesuits whose lives and work he admired. Toward the end of his college career, he began to consider a vocation, and upon graduation he entered the seminary. He was ordained in 1947.

At the urging of a priest friend, Mundell spent the next five years working in rural North Carolina, where Catholics were about as rare as Communists. "When I left there weren't many more," he says with a laugh, though he thoroughly enjoyed the experience. Returning to Washington, he became an associate pastor at the Sacred Heart parish, which at the time had the largest Catholic population in the city.

He stayed until the archdiocese summoned him to Immaculate Conception, and his marching orders were unusual. Not only were Immaculate Conception's parishioners mostly Sunday commuters, but almost all the students at the school, which then was a boys' junior high, lived in far-off neighborhoods. Additionally, Immaculate Conception was located between two long-established black parishes, Holy Redeemer and St. Augustine's. As a result, almost no one who actually lived in Shaw had any involvement with Immaculate Conception. But the archdiocese felt the church could, and should, be a resource for the troubled area. "Take care of the people in the neighborhood," Mundell says he was told, "because the people in the neighborhood do not feel free to come here." That's been his goal ever since.

I met Mundell on a springlike Sunday morning in February, after the eleven o'clock Mass at Immaculate Conception. At the front of the splendid old sanctuary is an illuminated statue of the Blessed Virgin, which is incorporated into an elaborate marble altar. Nothing could be more traditional. Then again beside the altar, on a crucifix, hangs a black Christ. At this service, one of four weekend Masses, there were perhaps a hundred people, all but a handful African American and everyone dressed neatly in suits and prim dresses—what people used to call their Sunday best. The liturgy itself, seventy-five minutes long and full of ritual, pleasantly reminded me of the old High Masses of my pre–Vatican II youth. There was an elaborate blessing, with incense, of the offertory gifts; bells rang out at the consecration of the bread and wine; and the Lamb of God, or Agnus Dei, was sung in Latin. And there were processions—lots of them. One such parade was just prior to the Gospel, when Mundell led his deacon, acolytes, lectors, and choir members around the sanctuary and back up the broad middle aisle.

The Gospel passage concerned the devil's temptation of Christ in the desert, a theme Mundell easily yet artfully developed. His homiletic style is the unhysterical, authoritative voice of a patriarch. Mundell told the assembled that they should not only have the willpower to resist temptations that are sinful but to give in to temptations to do good, to live right. "Temptation is not a *bad* thing," he declared. "Our character is built upon it."

Toward the end of the service, I was startled when Mundell invited everyone with February birthdays to come up to the communion rail. He offered them a special blessing, after which the congregation serenaded the group with a hearty rendition of "Happy Birthday."

Usually after Sunday Mass Mundell likes to invite a few parishioners for coffee or a casual lunch. Today, however, he had a baptism to perform. When that was done and we finally sat down to chat, I asked him about the birthday blessing. He told me it's something he's been doing for years at Immaculate Conception. "Most of these people would not have a celebration at home," he explains. "These are really poor people."

He estimates that only a small fraction of the children in the school—ten percent, maybe—live in homes where the father is present. Yet when the pastor leaves the subject of their surroundings and discusses the kids themselves, Mundell turns enthusiastic, animated, as if an inner light has switched on. Immaculate Conception has done other concrete things for the community—built a high-rise for low-income renters, for instance, and a four-block garden apartment complex—but clearly it is the school that Mundell regards as his chief accomplishment. It's not simply a question of giving needy children a good education. The school is also a haven, albeit a temporary one. And it's a place where the kids might just acquire the tools to help them fight off those destructive temptations just beyond the iron gates.

With only a few exceptions, the students come from Shaw. That's the point, Mundell emphasizes. "If a child moves from [the neighborhood] in the third grade, and the teacher and the principal feel that that child needs us, we'll keep the child. But if the child comes from a house where there is love and concern, we say go find another school. One of the older boys serving on the altar this morning moved out of the parish and we kept him because we thought he needed us. The majority of the children have no fathers, no man present. It's really sad. The mothers will have a boyfriend for six months, they get in a fight, the man leaves. Two or three or four months later another man comes into the house. Here we teach them one thing, and they see this. They know more about life in second grade than I knew in prep school. That's the truth. They see everything."

I asked Mundell about the challenges of being a white man ministering to a predominantly black congregation. He shrugs. "I never think of them as being black," he says. "If I like them, I like them. If I don't, I don't. I mean, they are just good people. We don't have quantity here, but we sure have quality. We really do."

Later, as Mundell shows me around the rectory, I notice in his office the photographs, warmly inscribed, of such friends as President and Mrs. Bush and former chief justice Warren Burger. It takes a lot of money to run a place like Immaculate Conception's school. Since Mundell doesn't rely at all on the archdiocese—"I just like my independence," he says mischievously—he must privately raise about one hundred thousand dollars a year to keep the lights on. He has some well-heeled benefactors, and every year hundreds of his "friends" hold a fund-raiser for Immaculate Conception. It is clear the monsignor is comfortable in these circles. He told me that earlier in the week he had conducted the funeral of an acquaintance who had sometimes come to his church. The woman was the head of the Heinz Foundation. "The church was packed," Mundell said. "There were eight or ten senators here, the Heinz family—Teresa Heinz, who is now married again to Senator [John] Kerry." He smiles. "It killed me that you couldn't take up a collection."

Mundell has succeeded in making the church a part of its community, but he admits to less success in involving his Shaw neighbors in the church itself. Their reticence doesn't surprise him. As he put it, "If you apply for membership to a club today and they turn you down, then two years later they are hard up financially and they come to you and say, 'We would like to have you as a member,' what are you going to say? 'When I wanted to become one you wouldn't accept me. Forget it.'" Still, most of Immaculate Conception's parishioners are converts to Catholicism, and Mundell slowly builds the rolls by cultivating relationships and making visitors feel welcome. He often holds receptions in the courtyard between the church and rectory, a small oasis where classical music gently washes over you and where a person can momentarily forget the horns and hurly-burly out on Eighth Street.

"It really has not grown like I thought it would," he says. "At times I think it's the best-kept secret in the city. Like today, one of the friends at the baptism came up to me afterward and said she had been thinking about becoming a Catholic, and she liked it here. She'd been coming to Mass occasionally and asked me to direct or guide her. I told her to call me up tomorrow and make an appointment. One person."

Mundell formally "retired" a year ago, at the archdiocese's mandatory age of seventy-five. By special arrangement, however, he remains on the job. "I may wake up tomorrow with a letter in the mail saying thank you for staying on, but now we found someone. I told [Cardinal James Hickey] if he found someone who wants to come in, I will not put up any fight. I will get out gracefully, as gracefully as I know how."

As he says this, Mundell sounds like he doesn't think it will ever happen.

⬙ Father
J. Saul Madrid

PHOENIX

Two thousand miles away from Washington, St. Anthony's Church glints in the harsh Arizona sun. The building might well have been plucked from a Tuscan hillside and deposited into this tumbledown neighborhood just south of Phoenix's downtown business district. Here, within a few jarring blocks, the Sun Belt prosperity evident in the city's office towers and new sports arenas gives way to palpable poverty: row after row of small, shambling homes, many of which almost seem to be wilting in the heat. Though it was still early May during my visit, the temperature already was reaching one hundred degrees by midafternoon. A friend reported that a few days after I left it hit one hundred nine.

J. Saul Madrid is pastor at St. Anthony's, which looms above its humble surroundings like a great terra-cotta mother ship. The exterior brick seems freshly scrubbed, the barrel roof tiles lending a classic Mediterranean finish to the basilica-style structure. The neighborhood, largely comprising Mexican American families, surely was more prosperous (at least relatively speaking) when missionaries of the Claretian order built St. Anthony's back in 1948, yet I wonder if there is significance to the way they situated the church at a forty-five-degree angle on its lot. The effect is to turn its back on the bourgeois of Central Avenue, Phoenix's main thoroughfare, while its front embraces the proletarian homes of the neighborhood.

Stepping inside, I found a glorious, ethereal space. Morning sun flooded the sanctuary, illuminating a long Easter linen draped across the stolid rafters high overhead. Below, the plain oak flooring seemed recently sanded. Then it dawned on me that the reason I noticed the floor at all was because there were no pews. Instead, folding chairs were stacked all along the perimeter. But for the stained glass windows the space might have been an elegant gymnasium. There was definitely an unsettled air about the place, something that didn't make sense. That is until Father Madrid told me about the fire.

Emerging from his living quarters having just washed the morning's dishes, Saul Madrid extended a damp hand to greet me. But he clearly was in something of a rush. After he had invited me to come by, it turned out that at the same time a crew would be at the parish hall next door, installing a new sound system. They had done some prep work but now were ready to fix the speakers in the suspended ceiling—if we could just get a few decisions from Father, said the crew chief.

Madrid is a man of average height and the wiry, athletic build of a runner. He had just turned forty, but with his dark, wavy hair and handsome bronze complexion he looks younger. Clad in chinos, sports shirt, and Italian loafers (no socks), he could easily fit in with the crowd across town having breakfast that very moment beneath the orange trees at the Arizona Biltmore. Instead he and I are trolling the parish hall, ducking dangling wires and studying the black holes where tiles have been removed from the ceiling. With the recent heat, unusual for early May, Madrid was rather quickly forced to move St. Anthony's services from the church, which isn't air-conditioned, to the parish hall, which is.

"Oh, by the way," says Madrid, "can you fix it so that this system won't pick up any radio stations?" It seems the previous Sunday the temporary sound system was sporadically treating the congregation to some decidedly unliturgical programming.

The crew chief, a pleasant young man with long blond hair and a beeper hooked to his blue jeans, snorts. "Lemme guess—it was a country station. Or maybe rock."

"No, it was more a New Age sound," replies the priest, a little mischievously. "Like that alternative jazz type of music. It would come in and out, and actually it wasn't entirely inappropriate as a kind of accompaniment. I just joked about it. When I was giving my sermon and it started up, I said, 'All right, I get the message.'"

St. Anthony's not only is the religious center of its community but the social hub. It sponsors dances and festivals, has operated a senior center, and through the years offered a variety of popular youth programs. Life here is always hectic. The discombobulation I was witnessing, however, was the continuing fallout from a disaster that nearly destroyed this proud symbol.

On December 11, 1994, the third Sunday of Advent, Madrid had just finished the noon Mass, his fourth and last of the day. The priest, who had been assigned to St. Anthony's only six months earlier, was greeting people outside the church. When someone asked if he might make an appointment to see the pastor, several parishioners who were selling food outside the church told Madrid to go ahead, they would close up for him. Madrid thanked them and headed to his office in the rectory. It was about one o'clock. Unfortunately, the parishioners didn't realize that, high above the altar, the church's Advent candles were still burning.

The candles had been incorporated into an Advent wreath, a large (more than four feet across) adornment the people of St. Anthony's had crafted themselves by interlacing vines, pine boughs, and other natural material onto a steel frame. The wreath was suspended from the rafters about ten feet above the wooden altar. When the candles burned down far enough, they caught the wreath on fire. The burning wreath, in turn, dropped to the altar.

About four-thirty that afternoon, the exhausted Madrid was roused from a nap by the doorbell. Alarmed neighbors had come to report seeing smoke cascading from the church rafters.

Madrid rushed up the church stairs and hurled open the doors, finding the sanctuary filled with thick smoke. Forgetting the elementary rules of fire safety, he waded in to discover an even more horrifying sight—the altar in flames.

At this point in his recounting, Madrid pauses for a moment, and I ask him what such an image must mean to a priest. Madrid lowers his head, searching for words. But even now, a year and a half after the event, this is difficult for him. "For a priest . . . ," he begins, then trails off. "I would imagine for many people, but for a priest. . . . To see an altar up in flames, it is an indescribable event. Because our lives are so intimately connected to the altar. It is the source of everything—in many ways, for me and for many others, it really is the source of priestly identity. So, when you see that up in flames. . . ." He pauses again. "And the fire department leaves and it's just a pile—literally a pile of ashes. It's a very powerful experience."

To add injury to insult, in all the tumult Madrid fractured his foot. His first reaction on seeing the smoke—"before I realized it was not a fire-extinguisher kind of fire," he says with a self-deprecating jab—was to rush downstairs to find one of the devices. Moving hastily in the smoke, he missed a step and wrenched his foot. He didn't know until hours later, after the fire was put out, that the foot was so badly broken that he would be in a cast for five months.

The church structure survived. But flames consumed the altar and portions of the floor, and smoke damage was pervasive. Icons, important to all

Catholics but particularly so to the Hispanic faithful, were a major casualty: paintings were ruined, and the sanctuary's many statues of saints were black with soot. The estimated physical cost of the fire was in the realm of two hundred thousand dollars. The psychic toll, however, was beyond figuring. In a community where people had never had much, they had always had St. Anthony's. Now, as the firefighters rode off, it was entirely possible that what was left wouldn't be worth saving.

The next morning Madrid was lying in bed, his foot throbbing, when suddenly a terrible vision made him shudder. "My room is upstairs and I can look directly out to most of the church building," he says. "As I lay there and looked at it, it really looked like a coffin. I really had the sensation that it was—a very powerful sensation of death."

❖   ❖   ❖

Buildings that evoke such emotional responses, the best buildings, are those that insinuate themselves into our lives. For half a century St. Anthony's has been a touchstone for the people of the neighborhood, the place where they have come together for baptisms, first communions, confirmations, marriages, funerals. It's the kind of church where even those who move away from the neighborhood come back to Mass on Sundays, because it's their spiritual home. Indeed, despite the area's economic anomie—Madrid says St. Anthony's is "one of the poorest parishes in the diocese"—religious life remains robust. The parish serves some seven or eight hundred families, Sunday Masses (one in English, three in Spanish) are crowded, and Madrid performs fifty or sixty baptisms a month. St. Anthony's was the first parish in the diocese to use mariachis, traditional Mexican musicians, in the liturgy, as well as the first to embrace the Cursillo lay-activist movement.

As it turned out, the fire was scarcely evident from the outside. Inside, however, the church was a smoky, charred, hellish mess. For insurance and safety reasons, parishioners were not allowed inside to see the damage, so Madrid had a photographer document the scene; a half dozen of the images were blown up to poster size and hung in a kind of ghastly exhibition. The church called in several grief counselors, who spent a week helping parishioners come to grips with what they were experiencing.

Only after that initial period of mourning could they turn to the essential question: What now? Although he was the pastor, Madrid knew the decision about what to do with the burned-out church was not so much his as the congregation's. So a "restoration committee" of a dozen or so parishioners was formed. "We really began to [discuss] what is this experience about," recalls Madrid. "As I saw it, and I shared with them, this was an opportunity. It was a tragedy, but it was an opportunity as well. I think we began to uncover together a very powerful spirituality about that—the spiritual dimension of tragedy and hope, death and resurrection, which is the Christian experience. We began to say this is not just about rebuilding a church. This is about renewing and rebuilding a community."

Of course, as any property owner knows too well, renewing and rebuilding take a lot of money—money neither the church nor the congregation had. (The church was insured for much of the damage, but that was only a fraction of its replacement cost.) There was good news: with a few structural repairs the shell itself could be salvaged. But the bad news was that such an extensive overhaul would require upward of half a million dollars. One might reasonably wonder whether it is fair to prevail on poor people for that kind of money. But Madrid urged them to think in terms of the church's legacy. "Many people, some of whom are still in the parish, labored intensively to build this church," Madrid told the committee. "They built it a brick at a time, and they gave us a church that has been useful for fifty years. Now it's on us to set it up for the next fifty years."

Without knowing where the money would come from, the committee decided not merely to return St. Anthony's to the way it was but to make it better.

First, however, came the cleanup, which seemed endless. The church was aired out, the walls were repainted, the oak floor was reinforced and repaired where the incinerated altar had burned through. Overhead, the chocolate brown paint that muted the space was blasted away to reveal beautiful pine planks, which have been left exposed. The statues were sent out for cleaning and repair. The parish hall was set up to accommodate the church services, and engineers and contractors began pawing through the debris-strewn basement to assess the building's systems. They were, in a word, terrible, and had been long before the fire. It was obvious that all the electrical would have to go, as well as the old lighting. And a new heating and cooling system was penciled in, so that for the first time the church could be habitable even in the dead of Phoenix's wicked summers.

As the physical activity progressed, Madrid seized the opportunity to focus his flock on spiritual renewal, too. With the help of a liturgical consultant, he had parishioners for the first time discuss their worship needs and the kind of church they wanted St. Anthony's to be, both in design and spirit.

Madrid says that when he arrived at St. Anthony's he found a welcoming but traditional parish. He sensed a certain isolated quality about it, he says, and a kind of spiritual complacency. The past decade has been a time of great change in the Catholic world, and he felt part of his mission was to awaken the people of St. Anthony's, gently, to that change. He began to broaden the liturgical ministries—where laypeople act as lectors and distributors of communion at Mass, for instance—and he introduced the Rite of Christian Initiation of Adults (RCIA), which invites non-Catholics to join the Church (and "lapsed" Catholics to become reengaged). At the same time he's been trying to reach out to the community at large. For instance, he influenced the formation of a neighborhood business alliance and has interested developers in building new homes near the church. And St. Anthony's recently joined forces with the other institutional anchor of this part of town, Phoenix Memorial Hospital, and the nonprofit Phoenix Revitalization Corporation in getting unsafe and unsightly buildings razed, planting trees, and generally endeavoring to regain some control of what's happening to their neighborhood.

Madrid says all these steps are meant to show parishioners how, in the spirit of Vatican II and in an age when priests and nuns are becoming endangered species, the laity itself is being called to be more responsible for parish affairs. "Part of my leadership in the parish is to make sure that I help them come to understand that, what happens if I am the last resident pastor of St. Anthony's?" he explained. "Will St. Anthony's disappear, or will St. Anthony's continue to be a viable, credible, Christian community that teaches its children the faith, that prepares people for marriage, that encourages our young people, comforts the sick, and feeds the poor, without a priest? I think we have not yet begun to do that with our community."

To the extent that the fire sent the people of St. Anthony's on an unintended journey of introspection, it was a pilgrimage their pastor had already made.

Madrid was born in the state of Chihuahua, in northern Mexico, in 1956. Raised in a devout Catholic family, he considered the priesthood when he was young but didn't pursue it. Instead, at age eighteen he made his way to the Phoenix area as a migrant worker, picking fruit in the orange groves of the East Valley. Madrid learned English and got a job as a janitor at a Catholic church in Mesa. There he came to the attention of the diocese's director of vocations and began thinking about the seminary again. But he went on to college in New Mexico, graduating with a degree in criminal justice, and his career very nearly took an unclerical turn. "I almost joined the Dallas police department," he says with a grin, recalling how persuasive recruiters were when visiting the campus. In the end, though, the Dallas cops were no match for the Ultimate Career Counselor, and this time Madrid listened to the call.

He was ordained in 1985 in Phoenix and there landed an attractive assignment at the cathedral. To all outward appearances a promising career was taking shape. Inwardly, however, Madrid says some doubts were arising. It's not unusual for Catholic clergymen to ask themselves whether they really want to be priests; indeed, in the sixties and seventies thousands answered no. Madrid says his questions were different. Coming to the calling from such unorthodox and humble origins, he wondered whether he was worthy to be a priest in the first place. Would he measure up? And what would people think of him if he didn't? "What would my parents say? What would my friends say? What would my bishop think? You know, all of that."

It was guilt, of course. "There's sort of a Catholic strain to that," I suggest, speaking from some experience.

"A very *strong* Catholic strain to that," he laughs.

Determined to work through his anxieties, Madrid plunged into parish work. He moved through a variety of assignments with increasing responsibilities, including his first pastorate at a small church in Buckeye, Arizona. Along the way he got a better sense of his capabilities, which improved his self-esteem, which eventually banished his doubts. Now were he to set down the collar, he says, he could do so and feel a sense of accomplishment rather than failure. Yet he has no intention of doing that. Madrid admits having other personal issues to deal with—he has yet to become a U.S. citizen, for instance, even though he concedes "home" is now Arizona, not Chihuahua—but the priesthood isn't one of them. "I would be ordained [again] next week," he says confidently. "I could very easily kneel before my bishop and make the same commitment."

Which is not to say the job isn't occasionally exhausting (in addition to St. Anthony's, Madrid tends to a small "mission" church nearby, St. Pius X). The increasing workload has required some lifestyle adjustments. He gets more sleep and tries to get more exercise, jogging several times a week and playing racquetball. Mostly, he's regulated his pace. "For the first time after so many years, I really feel that I need to take care of myself," he says. "I need to slow down. I need to take time. I need to approach things with less a degree of urgency. Not everything is an emergency. Even the restoration of the church, you know."

Nonetheless, the pace of the restoration has been brisk. The congregation regained limited use of the church by the first anniversary of the fire. More substantive repairs and systems work continued all through the relentless summer and into the fall of 1996. The parish received professional donations for such things as mechanical and structural drawings. Then, too, it sponsored regular "days of work," in which all able-bodied parishioners were invited to pitch in on certain dirty but necessary jobs, such as clearing out the basement. Everyone was pressed into service, not just because sweat equity is economical but because it feels good. Says Madrid, "When it is finished, I want every single family in the parish to be able to say, 'We helped rebuild this church.'" Parishioners later told me that if the fire had a silver lining, it was in pulling them together toward this common goal.

Of course, donations go only so far. Since insurance covered less than half the cost of the refurbishing, the parish launched a fund drive to come up with the rest. Madrid has been appealing to charities and local businesses, but inevitably much of the money must come from the parish members themselves. Outside Sunday Mass, they can often be found selling homemade pastries and coffee. Fund-raising dances are being held, and parishioners are raffling off their own donated jewelry.

The challenge for such a poor parish is daunting. "Some people think I need to have my head examined," Madrid admits. The official theme of the fund drive was inspired by the city itself: like the phoenix, this church is rising from the ashes. The inspiration, however, comes from medieval times, when tiny villages sacrificed almost everything to erect those towering edifices that reached into heaven. "Sometimes now we consider them scandalous," Madrid concedes of those extravagant undertakings. "But through the mist of tremendous poverty there stood a magnificent cathedral, which gave people a glimpse of a better life. I think it is very real here in this community."

The December after my visit, on the second anniversary of the fire, Saul Madrid said Mass at a temporary altar, in a glistening new sanctuary, as the people of St. Anthony's came back to their church. Much work remained to be done, but once again the joyful light of candles danced overhead. And while the Advent season anticipates Christ's birth, the atmosphere doubtless felt more like Easter, which is to say rebirth. There were smiles, tears, and prayers of thanksgiving. And when Mass was over, no one forgot the candles.

Father
Robert Lacombe

GREENVILLE, RHODE ISLAND

Back in Rhode Island I had come upon a priest who outwardly would remind me a great deal of Father Madrid. Father Robert Lacombe, associate pastor at St. Philip's Church in Greenville, a well-to-do western suburb of Providence, is also young, energetic, committed, multilingual, and possessed of a certain worldliness. Only in conversation do their differences really emerge.

Our visit this Saturday morning would have to wait, however, until Lacombe finished up the baptism of tiny Eric Thomas Gentile, who was commendably sanguine as the priest anointed his forehead with the holy water and oils. Earlier that day Lacombe had presided at a funeral; awaiting him that afternoon was a wedding. Actually, this was comparatively light duty. Lacombe told me the previous weekend's schedule had begun with Saturday morning's eight o'clock Mass, followed by a noon wedding, a one-thirty wedding, a three o'clock wedding, a four o'clock baptism (of his own godchild), the regular five o'clock Mass, and two receptions. Then on Sunday he had three additional Masses, one more than a priest technically is supposed to say on the Sabbath. The bonus Mass was for twenty members of the Denver Broncos football team, which that afternoon would play the New England Patriots in nearby Foxboro, Massachusetts. Lacombe has conducted services before for the Patriot players, and the hospitality director at the Broncos' hotel had called to see if this time he might accommodate the visitors. "I anticipated going up there and having a lack of enthusiasm on the part of the congregation," Lacombe said dryly. "But much to my surprise they were among the most responsive participants at Mass that I have ever experienced. I even commended them on that. I said, 'There is no question in my mind but that you will beat the Patriots by a long shot because of your response being so much better than theirs.' They laughed about that and proceeded to beat the Patriots, thirty-seven to three."

Robert Lacombe says he can't imagine being anything other than a priest. A handsome, dark-headed man of thirty-one, he grew up not far from here in the small town of Lincoln. He came to St. Philip's immediately after his ordination in 1991, and by his own admission it has been a priest's dream assignment. With three thousand families, St. Philip's not only is active but affluent enough that money isn't a constant headache. St. Philip's energy level is such, Lacombe told me, that parishioners were about to embark on a program of perpetual adoration of the Blessed Sacrament. In such programs, volunteers take turns praying in the presence of a single consecrated host (displayed in a tall, gilt holder called a monstrance) around the clock—twenty-four hours a day, seven days a week. That's a big coordination job, and an even bigger spiritual commitment by the members of the parish. "It's a great place to be," Lacombe says. "I would say this is one of the top ten parishes in the diocese, in terms of vitality, availability of resources, and people who are willing to be involved. It's amazing."

He's sipping coffee in the airy living room of the rectory, dressed in his long black cassock and white collar. Lacombe wears clerical black all the time, in restaurants, classrooms, theaters, airports—everywhere but the golf course as he gets in the occasional round with St. Philip's pastor, Father Gerald Beirne. He dresses this way purposely, even to the point of derision by some peers. Why? "I think it is projecting a witness and availability of the ministry," he explains. "I often say to priests, 'There is never a vacation from your vocation. You are never on vacation from being a priest.' And wearing the collar, I think, is a reminder of that."

Clearly Lacombe grasps the power of symbols, and his conviction about dress is merely one indication that he belongs to a resurgent new breed of Catholic prelate. Some call them the Church's neoconservatives, some John Paul's soldiers, since they have come of age during his pontificate and its commitment to orthodox Catholicism. For his part, Lacombe eschews "liberal" and "conservative" labels as being simplistic and freighted with bias, especially as they've been manipulated by the political system. "Conservatism usually implies a narrow-mindedness, a lack of openness to new concepts," he says, adding that in his case such characterizations don't apply. "I would see myself as a more theologically informed traditionalist. But again, we have to be leery of stereotyping people."

In 1994 the *Los Angeles Times* published the results of a wide-ranging survey it conducted among America's Catholic clergy. The poll drew wide attention, in part for one of its most surprising findings: the Church's seminaries are turning out young priests who, as a group, are much more conservative in outlook than their predecessors. That headline was surprising, that is, to many lay Catholics. To priests, especially those of the Vatican II generation, the survey merely validated a trend they had seen developing for years.

The *Times* survey prompted some debate in the Catholic press about what really constitutes a "trend," especially considering that priests under age thirty-five account for only about six percent of the total priest population. Yet there's no disputing that these newly ordained represent a philosophical departure. The survey found that nearly forty percent of young priests consider themselves conservative, about twice that of priests age thirty-six to sixty. Two times as many young priests, compared to priests overall, were likely to identify with the Republican Party. The survey also found this younger cohort more closely aligned with the views of John Paul and generally in agreement with his handling of controversial Church issues, from his objection to married and women priests to his curbing of dissent. About the only issue where the young priests and the pontiff part company is artificial birth control; just under half agree with John Paul that it is a sinful practice.

What accounts for the neoconservatism? Many factors are suggested: the appointment of more orthodox bishops in the United States and their emphasis on vocations; a return to more traditional teaching in seminaries; and the resurgence of American conservatism generally, especially under President Reagan, who had a strong following on the nation's college campuses. But most experts point squarely to the influence of the pope, with his personal magnetism and unstinting efforts to swing back from what he considers the excessive change and plurality of the postconciliar Church.

Certainly Lacombe counts himself a big fan of John Paul, with whom he once concelebrated a Mass. "I have found his spirituality is so exemplary, so profound," he says. "This man has to be in conversation with the Holy Spirit." The young priest understands how the pope has been a powerful magnet for like-minded Catholics, be they laypeople or eager seminarians, and he is thankful for John Paul's unique standing as a moral leader. On the other hand, Lacombe says no one should hold convictions "just because the pope says so." He believes Catholics are obligated to study the Church's teachings, understand how they were derived, and then embrace them for their moral truth.

Indeed, Lacombe does not come across as an idealogue. He readily admits there are many prickly issues dividing the Church. He enjoys discussing those issues and believes there is room among "good Catholics" for healthy debate. What bothers him is when Catholics hold views contrary to Church teaching for inadequate or uninformed reasons (as examples he cites people who believe priests should be permitted to marry because they feel sorry for them, or who use artificial contraception merely as a sexual convenience). "My challenge to the faithful is, if you are going to espouse an opinion that's contrary to the Church, please pray about it, please inform your conscience," he says. "That's where some of the detrimental repercussions of the Vatican Council arise. The council documents emphasize that people employ 'freedom of conscience,' but no one has an *informed* conscience."

The exception to that, he says, is abortion, which he considers "one of my main apostolates, if you will," and a subject on which Rome can brook no dissent. Every year the Church proclaims a Pro-Life Sunday, and for four years running Lacombe has taken to the pulpit to decry abortion in the kind of blunt and personal terms that make many Catholics squirm. "I have said to people that if you are pro-choice, basically that's saying you are in favor of murder," he told me. "You can rationalize in favor of free choice, but that free choice leads to murder. I then said that if you are a proponent of abortion that you are not disposed to come forward to Holy Communion. More priests should challenge their people in this way." These intense sermons generate a lot of support, he says, but "I always have about three or four who walk out of the church as well. That doesn't bother me. That's the only area of controversy where I have been intolerant of discussion. I don't see any gray area."

This unyielding view is shaped in part by personal experience. Born to a single mother in Boston a decade before *Roe v. Wade,* Lacombe was placed for adoption and went to a loving home. "I can't help but think, and I said this to the congregation, if abortion had been a legal right in 1964, would I be here today? Irregardless of the convenience or inconvenience of birth circumstances, God has a plan for every human life."

Lincoln, where Lacombe grew up, has such a strong French Canadian heritage that French was the predominant language spoken in his household. (Today he is comfortable in seven languages.) He knew from a young age that he wanted to be a priest, being particularly influenced by a devout grandmother and the pastor of their tiny parish, a man Lacombe still calls "probably the holiest priest I have met in my life." After seminary, he was sent to do graduate work in biblical studies at the Pontifical University in Louvain, Belgium. Since Louvain is a well-known outpost of liberal theology, the experience was, to say the least, jarring for a young seminarian more grounded in the traditional upbringing, and a schooling in the doctrine of St. Thomas Aquinas, of Providence College. "It didn't change me from a traditionalist to a more liberal outlook, but at least it exposed me to different opinions and whether they were theologically sound or not," Lacombe says diplomatically. Louvain also toughened him up. There, as at most seminaries of northern Europe, it's customary for the priests-in-training to wear coats and ties rather than clerical black. Lacombe was the only member of his class who, once ordained to the deaconate, routinely wore the collar. That invited some hazing, but already he was making a statement. Lacombe felt that in the wake of Vatican II, priests had rather too successfully integrated themselves into the secular world—and that the vocation was suffering for it.

"I felt very strongly that a call to the priesthood was something whereby I could serve Christ and help to redeem the image of the priesthood and give the Church added credibility," he said when I asked what had gone into his decision. He felt Catholicism "would need articulate, clear, and intelligent spokesmen to defend the teachings of Christ and to represent his Church in the world. . . . I don't look upon myself as a savior of the Church. The Lord will do that through the Holy Spirit. Nevertheless, to a degree I can cooperate in that."

Lacombe wears the collar not only as a statement but an invitation. He recounted an incident that occurred when he was visiting the historic Cathedral of St. Louis in New Orleans. While Lacombe was walking along the Stations of the Cross, a stranger approached him, said he was Baptist, but asked if they might talk. They sat in a back pew, where the priest learned the man was greatly distraught over his sister, whose dissolute life had recently ended in suicide. "I spent about an hour talking with this man and answering his questions, some of which had no answers," he says. As they parted, Lacombe handed the man his card. Back in Rhode Island a few weeks later, the priest received a letter from him, saying that their conversation had finally given him some peace about the tragedy. "Now, if I wasn't dressed as a priest," said Lacombe, "he would have had no reason to come up to me."

Lacombe also applies his traditional outlook to the liturgy. His Masses are more solemn than most, with routine use of incense and the acclamations often given in Latin. Bells are rung at the consecration of the bread and wine. As a result Lacombe's Masses last a little longer than other priests', but he says people seem to like them—especially young Catholics, for whom Latin and High Masses are historical curiosities. Lacombe is convinced the enhanced ritual and sense of mystery help satisfy their hunger for the sacred. "I think that's what they are looking for."

Lacombe speaks in the clear, precise manner of a teacher, and his demeanor, while friendly, is also formal. Upon his arrival at St. Philip's, some people were afraid that he and Father Beirne—whose style is more gregarious and religious approach less orthodox—would make a clerical "odd couple." ("He's more an Oscar stereotype and I am much more a Felix stereotype," the younger man says.) But they became fast friends, not only playing golf but attending the theater and other social functions together. Lacombe says a third priest who lives there, a man in his forties who works in Catholic youth ministry, is less traditional in his ways, and though they coexist peacefully they have little interaction. The upshot, Lacombe says, is that St. Philip's parishioners get three distinct styles of liturgy, and they've gotten used to that diversity.

About the only concern Lacombe raises is his schedule. He does a lot of teaching—catechism classes in the elementary school; the weekly confirmation classes; a Confraternity of Christian Doctrine (CCD) program (religious education for Catholic children who attend public schools) with over a thousand students; and theology classes at Providence College. Beyond that, at St. Philip's the celebrants don't reserve homilies for Sunday Mass, as at most parishes, but give them every day. "One of my frustrations is that my tendency to be a perfectionist is challenged by the amount of work that I have to do," he says. "I do not like to go into sermons unprepared. I do not like to do anything unprepared. However, I find with the volume of liturgies that we have, the requirements of my teaching, et cetera, that I cannot always do things as well as I would like." To help find time and despite some late evenings, he rises daily at four-thirty (trying to squeeze in a twenty-minute "power nap" most afternoons). And as fond as he is of his parishioners, he says they're just "traditional" enough themselves that some have outmoded ideas about what priests do all day. These are the ones, he says, who "seem to think that we merely say Mass on Sunday and sit in the rectory waiting for phone calls."

These are niggling complaints, however, things he likely anticipated as he prepared for the job. Indeed, unlike those men who were already ordained when Vatican II transpired, today's young prelates followed the calling with their eyes wide open, fully aware of the worsening shortage, the long hours, the political divisions in the Church. I asked Lacombe whether, under the circumstances, he had experienced any trepidation making that commitment.

He thought for a moment, then said, "At no time did I feel that I was jumping on a sinking ship. However, I did know that the seas would be tumultuous."

Part of the tumult, of course, is the question of celibacy. At his Thursday night sessions with confirmation candidates, Lacombe invites questions from the students, and he gets all manner. One night he was asked, "Father, aren't you upset that you will never have children?" He replied that he had thought about that a long time before deciding to take his vows, then tried to explain to these curious thirteen-year-olds, in the throes of their own awakening sexuality, how he views chastity as a gift, not a rule or an imposition. "And that gift is to be used for the edification of the Body of Christ, the Church," Lacombe maintains. "I'm not trying to be pious about it. That gift has to be channeled in positive directions. Basically, celibacy can only be possible through the nurturing of very strong and intense prayer. You can't rationalize it. You can't understand it psychologically, because it seems to be so foolhardy psychologically. But when understood spiritually it makes a heck of a lot of sense."

To be a priest is to have a complete and demanding vocation, he says, and the same is true of a family man. Mixing the two inevitably would undermine one of those obligations, he feels, which is one reason why Lacombe thinks it would be a mistake to permit priests to marry—and particularly so if such a change comes about simply as an expedient way to end the priest shortage.

At the same time he warns that priests must take care not to "rationalize being lonely" or using celibacy as a "crutch" to keep from enjoying life beyond the rectory. A big basketball fan, Lacombe has season tickets to Providence College's games, and in fact tonight he and three married friends will be attending the school's annual Midnight Madness—a late dinner and pep rally followed by the team's first official practice. Even so, none of those friends calls him "Bob." It's always "Father."

"Someone asked me about that one time, a friend of mine who once studied to be a priest and is a married man now. He said, 'Why can't I call you Bob?' I said, 'Well, you could, it wouldn't upset me to be called by my name. But being Father Lacombe is part of who I am. I can never divorce that from who I am. You befriended Bob Lacombe, who happens to be Father Lacombe, and that's just the way it is.'"

Monsignor
William H. Shannon

ROCHESTER, NEW YORK

William H. Shannon, priest of the diocese of Rochester, is a teacher, scholar, and writer. For the past fifteen years, he has also served as chaplain of the mother house of the Sisters of St. Joseph, adjacent to the picturesque campus of Nazareth College. The building where he lives and works is situated in the leafy, affluent suburbs southeast of Rochester. The campus itself borders on Oak Hill Country Club, which only weeks before my trip here had hosted the Ryder Cup, the biennial contest between the best American professional golfers and their European counterparts. Monsignor Shannon, who is nearly eighty, is as intellectually vigorous as ever, but bad knees and a troublesome back cause him to use a motorized chair to navigate the wide corridors of the mother house. At that morning's Mass he wheeled to the sacristy but walked to the altar, where a tall, hydraulic draftsman's chair awaited him. From this perch he conducted the liturgy. Some sixty women religious, many of them retired, were scattered about the large chapel.

Shannon knows them all. He has been in their company, in one capacity or another, for half a century. "When I was assigned at the age of twenty-eight or twenty-nine to come to Nazareth College, an old pastor invited me to lunch," Shannon recalled for me. "We chatted a while, and he said, 'Now, I want to give you some advice. When you go out to Nazareth College, you will be involved with a number of women—older women who are teachers and younger women who are students in college. My advice to you is to treat them like the souls of purgatory—pray for them and stay away from them.'" Shannon chuckled. "I was very happy that I did not follow that advice. This has been an enrichment in my life, and I think it makes me much more sympathetic with the position that women have in the Church."

That position, in Shannon's view, is decidedly one of inequity, and he is sad about it. The scholar's office doubles as his living room, and books are everywhere, in places climbing the tall walls to the ceiling. On this late summer day, the window air conditioner is blasting away behind him, keeping the room chilly enough, it seems to me, to store lunch meat. "It's very interesting if you read the fifteenth chapter of First Corinthians, where Paul speaks of the witnesses to the Resurrection, you know. Where he says, 'I have news of Our Lord Jesus, how he suffered, died, and rose again. And he was seen by the twelve, by Cephas, by a hundred people, and by me, who was born out of due time.' He never mentions the women who were the first ones [to see Christ]. I think that's just one example how from the very beginning our theology, our understanding of the Christian faith, has been directed by a paternalistic, anthrocentric way of understanding God's revelation. I think women are beginning to challenge that, and I think that challenge is a very refreshing thing for the Church."

A smallish man with a kind face and white hair, Shannon looks like a chaplain. He does not look like a firebrand, but some would call him one. That description is not entirely apt, as Shannon is not the sort of person to raise his voice or incite others; he prefers reason to emotion, persuasion to exhortation. The fire one detects in him is simply the intensity of his convictions. He is one pole of that priestly paradox: where Father Lacombe is in the traditionalist (some say conservative) mode of many of today's young priests, Monsignor Shannon is one of thousands of senior clergy whose outlook is unabashedly progressive (some say liberal).

Born in Rochester, Shannon has never really been away for any length of time except to work on his doctorate in Canada. As a seminarian, he aspired to teach, and he was lucky; in the Church, as in the army, young recruits didn't always get what they wanted. "When I was ordained a priest, those were decisions that were made for you, not by you," he says. "I just went where I was told to go."

That was Nazareth, in 1946, where he would teach theology until 1980, when he retired and became chaplain at St. Joseph's. Beyond the campus boundaries Shannon is probably best known as a writer and an authority on Thomas Merton, the Trappist monk who wrote *The Seven Storey Mountain* and other popular books of poetry, meditation, and autobiography. Shannon, who never met Merton, says he stumbled onto the subject when he told some students one day that he'd like to teach a course about the monk; they kept at him until he did. Researching Merton, Shannon became so fascinated that he wrote a book about him. After that, in 1982, he was appointed general editor of Merton's letters, of which there are more than four thousand. Shannon brought out five volumes of correspondence, and in 1992 his biography of Merton, entitled *Silent Lamp*, was published.

"Silent Lamp" is English for "Mei Teng," the name Merton was given by a Chinese colleague, John Wu. It is a worthy name, Shannon wrote, given how Merton's insights continue to illuminate the spiritual lives of countless Catholics, including his own. In fact Shannon, inspired by his subject, has himself written several well-received books on prayer. He has also produced magazine articles about Church issues, especially as they have to do with the priesthood. His elegant writing, scholarly but accessible, has lots of fans but critics, too, particularly among those Rochester-area Catholics who regard his views as heretical. These opinions would include Shannon's support for the ordination of women and optional celibacy for priests, and his desire for less authoritarian rule from Rome and more aggressive leadership from American bishops (many of whom are "weaklings," he contends, when it comes to standing up for their local churches).

Shannon believes divergent views can be healthy for the Church if there is discussion, but what he sees instead is division. Too many Catholics follow the Vatican without question, he says, because it makes them feel secure, and it's easier than thinking for themselves. "It's something that keeps people who are Catholic perpetually immature. We don't want to be adults as Catholics. [Other people] want the pope to tell them how to live their lives. I want to let the Holy Spirit help me. I mean, I want to listen to the pope and what he has to say, and I want to take it seriously, but at the same time I want to be able to stand on my own feet and make decisions that I believe I have to make."

In Shannon's view, a Vatican hierarchy intent on recentralizing power in Rome and quashing debate is threatening the new "openness" that was the aim of Vatican II. With reluctance, he holds John Paul II accountable for that. "In spite of his charism, in spite of his wonderful commitment to what he considers his ministry, I think he has set the Church back," Shannon says. "I feel bad saying that, because I know the dedication of the man, how he must be absolutely exhausted, and yet he keeps at it and keeps at it."

As the monsignor ponders the condition of the Church, one of his gravest fears is that the Vatican's clinging to the traditional priesthood is actually jeopardizing the Holy Eucharist, the sacrament at the core of Catholicism. Because of what Shannon calls an artificially created priest shortage, more and more Roman Catholics are being deprived of the opportunity to celebrate the Eucharist. That's why he believes one day the Church will permit optional celibacy and women priests—though he would like to see such change not because emergency necessitated it but because Rome believed it was the right thing to do.

Because the Church's insistence on celibacy is essentially a question of policy, it could be altered rather easily, should Rome ever become so inclined. The ordination of women is much thornier, however, because the Church has always considered that a theological issue, a fundamental tenet—and therefore an impossibility. Shannon and many others have never found the Church's theological arguments against women clergy terribly persuasive. And lately, as Rome endeavors a delicate finesse—proclaiming the worth and equal status of Catholic women even as it denies them the priesthood—Shannon says Vatican theologians have themselves in a trap. "The basic teaching of our tradition for the nonordination of women is the nonequality of them—that they are in a state of subjugation by their very nature," he says. "Now the Church is saying, of course women are equal to men in the Church. They always have been. So they can't use the traditional arguments. So what they have to do is come up with some new ideas, like Christ didn't ordain women. The answer to that is that Christ didn't ordain *anyone* as far as we know. Or with the idea that the priest acts in the person of Christ, and a woman can't act in the person of Christ—which is not a very good argument because both men and women are in the image of God, as Genesis says."

The real issue, he believes, is one of inherent fairness. Then, too, he says Catholics must come to understand that they are empowered by their baptism, not their princes.

"When Pope John Paul II came out with his statement on women and the ordination question, and saying that it was not even to be discussed, I remember a young priest coming to see me. He was very upset about this. So we talked about it for a while, and finally I said to him, 'Paul, remember, you do not belong to the pope's Church; the pope belongs to our Church.' I think that's very good theology, because the only claim that the pope has to being a member of the Church is his baptism. It isn't his papacy or his bishopric or his priesthood that makes him a Christian. It's his baptism."

As for celibacy, Shannon believes the discipline can have great value, and he has no regrets as to his own experience. "I would hate to see it lost in the Church because I think it can be a way of witnessing to the kingdom," he says. "But I am not sure that disgruntled celibate priests, however many there may be, are witnessing to the kingdom. Because now, celibacy is forced on them." Shannon says he knows many young men who would like to be priests, and would be good ones, but want no part of the asexual lifestyle. Were celibacy optional, he contends, "I don't think that the good of it would be lost. But it would be something that would be freely chosen."

The change would also ameliorate the biggest problem Shannon sees among his colleagues in parish work, which is loneliness. As someone who has led a life surrounded by larger communities—faculty, students, women religious—Shannon says he has never had to do battle with it himself, but he says more and more priests must.

For all Shannon's concerns, when I asked him to tell me how the Church will look twenty years from now, he was ultimately upbeat. He said the question reminded him of a story told about Pope Pius VI when he was in the custody of Napoleon. "Napoleon was pretty brash with the pope, and said to him, 'I am going to destroy this infamous Church of yours.' The pope laughed at him. He said, 'We clergy have been trying to do this for eighteen hundred years and we haven't succeeded, and you won't succeed either.'" Shannon permitted himself a laugh, too. "I don't know whether it's a true story or not, but I think it's a valid story."

In 1993, when he celebrated the golden anniversary of his ordination, Shannon spoke to his guests about several spiritual insights that had been impressed on him over the course of a long life. At the request of friends, he had the talk made into a pamphlet, and he gave me a copy as I left him. One insight has to do with the true meaning of baptism and how it relates to ordination. "Ordination is a call from God to some of the baptized to serve all of the baptized," Shannon wrote. "But those who are thus called to the performance of certain functions in the Church are not higher or better than, or superior to the rest of the baptized. Rather they are servants of their sisters and brothers."

◼ Father John Beal

WASHINGTON, D.C.

In nearly two thousand years, the Catholic Church has accumulated a substantial and often confusing body of rules and regulations. I don't mean as to its theology, but rather the formal guidelines governing the activities of the Church and its followers. There are rules concerning the sacraments— who may administer them, who may receive them, and under what circumstances. There are rules governing the clergy. There are rules about the administration of Church property. There are rules concerning the liturgy and Church teaching. And there are rules for dealing with the offenders when the above rules have been violated. This amalgamation of internal guidelines and procedures is known as canon law, and the people schooled to make sense of it canon lawyers. One of these, Father John Beal, explained his job to me with an analogy: if the Church's theologians are like scientists, articulating what Catholicism is all about on a theoretical level, its canon lawyers are like engineers. "Now that a pure scientist has woven this elaborate theory," he says, "how do we take that and make it work? What are the structures to make it work? What are the processes? What are the rights and obligations of the various players in this situation?" Canon lawyers, in other words, translate Catholic theory into practice.

Beal, forty-nine, is a professor of canon law at Catholic University in Washington. Most of his students are other priests, but he also instructs deacons, women religious, and laypeople interested in pursuing Church work. Like their civilian counterparts, canon lawyers develop specialties, and Beal himself is versed in two of its thorniest fields—the annulling of marriages, and the rights of priests, especially where they pertain in cases of alleged sexual misconduct. As such, he was able to give me an insider's perspective on some of the most emotional issues to grip the contemporary American Church.

Beal was born in Titusville, Pennsylvania (somewhat better known as the birthplace of America's oil industry), and was ordained in the Erie diocese in 1974. After teaching high school for seven years, he was given the opportunity to work with the diocesan marriage tribunal, the judicial body that decides whether a Catholic marriage can be voided, or annulled. After demonstrating an aptitude for this uniquely sensitive work, Beal was sent to Catholic University to obtain a doctorate in canon law. In 1984 he returned to Erie as judicial vicar, the official in charge of the marriage tribunal.

Beal says that shortly before he first went to work for the tribunal, it was handling maybe six cases a year for the entire diocese, an area covering all of northwestern Pennsylvania. By the time he left, in 1992, it was adjudicating more than two hundred. That explosive growth can be laid in part to the soaring numbers of failed marriages in the population as a whole (at forty percent, the American divorce rate remains the highest in the world). Primarily, however, the surge resulted from a change in the Church's attitude toward annulments, and a subsequent easing of their availability. Even twenty years ago, annulments—sometimes called "Catholic divorce"— were a kind of oddity. They were hard to come by, and to the extent they were discussed at all it was in a whisper. Annulment, like bankruptcy, came with a certain stigma. And like bankruptcy, when that stigma was removed the numbers took off.

Non-Catholics may find the distinction between divorce and annulment puzzling or curious, but to a Catholic—especially an observant one—it can make all the difference in the world. To understand this, one first must appreciate the Church's position on the sacrament of holy matrimony, which is that a man and woman really do marry "till death do us part." Marriage is deemed a sacred covenant and therefore one not lightly sundered. So if a divorced Catholic remarries, he is considered in a state of grave sin—adultery, actually—because the Church still recognizes the first marriage. Among other sanctions, this person is not allowed to partake of the Eucharist. On the other hand, if that earlier marriage is annulled, the Church in essence declares that it never existed because it wasn't valid in the first place. The man and woman are free to remarry and participate fully in Church life.

This pain of spiritual exile has historically made divorce, traumatic enough under normal circumstances, even more agonizing for Catholics. At the same time, it creates some of the most vexing dilemmas a parish priest can face. If a remarried Catholic comes up for communion at Mass, should the priest cause a scene by withholding it? When a divorced parishioner, someone the priest knows as an upright person or maybe even as a friend, asks him to sanction a second marriage, what's he supposed to say? These are people, after all, who desperately wish to be in the Church's good graces. In his book *Bending the Rules*, author Jim Bowman surveyed priests, in confidence, about how they handled the sensitive areas where Church teaching and real life often collide. Though his list covered such dicey issues as birth control, abortion, and homosexuality, Bowman concluded that for the priests "marriage and divorce is the chief rule-bending arena." In the case of remarriage, most priests reported that they first try to steer the couple to the annulment process. If annulment isn't possible or the couple simply won't pursue it, the clergymen often fall back on what they call the "internal forum," which is to say they privately counsel the couple and deal with issues of "sinfulness" in the confessional. In any event the priests follow their consciences and endeavor to be compassionate, trying to hew to the Church's forgiving spirit at least as rigorously as to its rules. One of Bowman's priests seemed to speak for many colleagues in describing how he once agreed, reluctantly, to sanction the marriage of two people in their seventies. The woman was Catholic, but the groom was a Protestant who had been married several times before, so annulment wasn't an option. After careful consideration, and after making sure the bride's family didn't object, the priest finally shrugged and said, "I am willing to perform the marriage and let God figure it out."

Beal can sympathize. After a decade of sorting through the detritus of failed relationships, he well knows how complicated a marriage can be. And each is unique, especially to someone who has to determine whether the union ever should have occurred in the first place. There are so many variables. What if, twenty years ago, a woman had a brief, impetuous marriage as a teenager and now wouldn't even know how to find her ex-husband? What about a man who was married and divorced but much later converts to Catholicism? What about a woman whose first marriage was so traumatic she can't bear to revisit it, even in an effort to have it expunged? Though he's no longer in the annulment business, Beal says he still fields inquiries from other priests seeking guidance on the tough calls.

Until the mid-seventies it was quite difficult to obtain an annulment because the process essentially was designed to prevent it. "Part of our problem was our inherited law," Beal says. "The 1917 code [of canon law] had looked at what people consent to when they marry primarily as giving each other the right to potentially procreate in sexual acts. That's not a very pretty theology of marriage, and it wasn't what we preached from the pulpit or what we told people in marriage preparation. In that canonical notion of marriage, love simply didn't figure in."

As it did with so much else, Vatican II prompted a wholesale reconsideration of marriage, including the notion of what made one valid. Says Beal, "Once you start looking at marriage not simply as a contract for having sex and babies but as a commitment to a loving relationship that encompasses the whole life, then a lot more is required for that to be a genuine marriage."

That includes, the Church decided, that the principals possess the emotional maturity to make a permanent commitment. So in the United States especially, tribunals began to take into account the psychological dynamics behind a couple's decision to wed. If either partner was coerced or was deemed too immature to know what he or she was getting into or was otherwise unable to provide informed consent—was unaware, for instance, of a fiancé's latent emotional problems—an annulment could be granted.

"There are all kinds of horror stories," Beal says. "Like high school kids who get pregnant and have a shotgun wedding. Under those circumstances can they make a prudent choice about a marriage? The tribunals began saying no, they are too immature to realize what they are doing. There's too much pressure being put on them to make a decision that they are not prepared to make." He described other circumstances he encountered as judicial vicar. In the early eighties, for instance, tribunals began to notice a growing number of collapsing marriages involving Vietnam veterans who married when they returned stateside. It turned out many were suffering from what came to be understood as post-traumatic stress disorder, a condition that might not become apparent for several years, so the tribunals began to consider that a mitigating phenomenon. In a quirkier example, Pennsylvania tribunals suddenly got a rash of cases involving young couples who all had attended one particular college. A little spadework revealed they had been through the same family-life course there, one whose curriculum included a book advocating open marriage.

One of the most difficult aspects of tribunal work—and the hardest for petitioners to understand—is that the events of a marriage itself are not a primary factor in determining whether it should be annulled. What the judges must ascertain is what was going on between the two people *when they married*. Tribunals routinely see cases where a man and woman came from solid backgrounds, had children, and seemed happily married for twenty years until one of them (usually the husband) had a midlife crisis and ran off. Tragic as that is, Beal says, it's not grounds for annulling what was clearly a valid marriage. Then again, he says, "you find twenty-year marriages that were hell on earth from the beginning." These cases typically involve physical or emotional abuse or both, and such marriages generally are annulled. "Say it was the woman's dependent personality and her helplessness that made her stay in, and he eventually walked out on her. But the fact that it lasted twenty years, it's amazing."

Even given the Church's about-face on policy—looking for reasons to approve annulments rather than reject them—the process still is no picnic. Cases obviously without merit are tossed out immediately. Those that move on to the tribunal can take a year or more to adjudicate, even without complications, which there usually are. For instance, in at least half the cases a petitioner already has remarried, and the ex-spouse either can't be found or isn't interested in cooperating. And judges are obliged to dig into the most intimate and often uncomfortable aspects of married life. In part, Beal says, that's because the tribunal judges, at least in Erie, were trying "everything in our power" to find grounds for approval. "But if it looked like we couldn't, we wanted to make sure we scraped the bottom of the barrel for the last bit of evidence before we told them there was no way."

Of course, some traditionalists believe the Church has become altogether too efficient in granting annulments. The ease or difficulty in acquiring one has varied widely from diocese to diocese, depending to a great degree on the philosophy of the bishop involved. In recent years the Vatican has insisted on strict compliance with annulment protocol, including an automatic review by another court. This has had the effect of slowing the process, as have the declining number of religious available to deal with cases and, in some dioceses, financial constraints. The resulting backlog makes a long ordeal even more tedious and annulment an even less appealing venue than it was to begin with.

Beal's tribunal escaped many of these problems, but there were other drawbacks to the job, not least being that it's an emotional wringer. "Yes, one of the standard pieces of office equipment is a box of Kleenex," he acknowledges. "We never hear happy stories in the tribunal. You only see the sordid side of marriage." To keep his equilibrium, not to mention his faith in the institution of matrimony, Beal insisted that while he served on the tribunal he be allowed to live in a parish, where he could interact with couples who had more functional relationships than those in his case files. "If I hadn't been in that atmosphere I don't think I could have survived eight years" on the tribunal, he says.

Even so, the "steady daily diet" of matrimonial misery finally prompted Beal to seek a change. In 1992 he returned to Catholic University as a professor of canon law. As it happened, that was precisely when another emotional Church issue was exploding across the nation's consciousness—the

sexual scandals involving Catholic priests. Since one of the responsibilities
of a canon lawyer is to advise his bishop on legal matters, it became part of
Beal's job to train students about the Church's rights and options in such situations, as well as the priest's. In the latter case, it turns out, there are few.

◈   ◈   ◈

The tawdry spectacle of clergymen caught in sexual scandal has been a
grave blow to American Catholicism, and it will be years before the true
toll, emotional and financial, is known. Already, though, we are cognizant
of its tragic consequences for everyone involved: the victims, their families,
and the Catholic community at large, all of whom experienced a devastating betrayal of trust. It's a tragedy, too, for the offending clergymen, not
just in terms of ruined lives but because so many never got the help that
might have mitigated their behavior.

Of course, to the extent the Catholic establishment responded to any of
these troubled men at all, it did so the only way it knew how at the time.
Until very recently, the Church considered sexual perversion not so much a
sickness as a sin, and like all sin it could be forsworn, even redeemed. Many
problem priests were simply ignored, and those who couldn't be were sent
for some counseling before being quietly shuttled off to new assignments,
with no one—least of all their new congregations—the wiser. By the mid-
eighties, as society became more educated about the scope and causes of sexual abuse of children, complaints about individual priests began to mount
and for the first time turned up in the press. Rather than sympathize with
the victims, American bishops, still in denial about the extent of the problem
and already running short of parish priests, generally took a hard-line response. The veracity of accusers was questioned, and lawsuits often were
met with countersuits for defamation. At the same time, in cases where guilt
was patent, Church officials were authorizing substantial cash settlements,
desperately trying to keep the burgeoning scandal under wraps. Some experts estimate the total payoffs at upward of half a billion dollars.

But by 1991, when a handful of the more lurid pedophile cases transfixed
the national media, containing the scandal was no longer possible. Hundreds of victims, many of whom had hidden their shame for decades, were
emboldened to come forward. Television and magazine exposés were suddenly de rigueur, one more salacious than the next. A disgusted nation grew
all too familiar with monsters like James Porter and other priests who used
their positions of trust to prey on children. And it wasn't only pedophilia.
Bishops in Georgia and New Mexico resigned after their affairs with

women were divulged. In my own hometown in Indiana, the popular pastor of a large congregation was abruptly removed after he was caught ordering videotapes of child pornography.

The scandal probably reached its nadir in late 1993, with the accusation lodged against Cardinal Bernardin. Conversely, when his accuser, Steven Cook, recanted a year later, it was a sign that the hysteria was fading. After intense criticism, the bishops helped calm things, too, by reversing field; they began to receive accusers with compassion instead of combat. (They also quietly instituted aggressive psychological testing of seminary candidates to weed out potential problem priests.) Fresh cases still surface; as I write this, the Tampa Bay area is reeling from three separate revelations of clerical scandal in three days, including that of a pastor who was secretly married for fifteen years and another who paid a man more than two hundred thousand dollars from parish funds to buy his silence about their sexual relationship. Yet most of the priests I spoke with believe the worst of the scandal has passed. That includes Beal, who says, "What I see now reported in the press tends to be old cases that are still being litigated."

As often happens in such highly charged stories, in the settling dust it's becoming clear that the panic was overblown, at least in terms of raw numbers. According to Beal, when the archdiocese of Chicago decided to find out the true scope of its problem, it examined the status of every priest who had served there in the previous twenty years. It found that just over one percent of these men had had a charge made against them, while verified charges amounted to less than one percent. Then in late 1995 a Penn State professor of religion and sociology, Philip Jenkins, a specialist in contemporary "moral panics," published a book called *Pedophiles and Priests*. He, too, concluded that the scandal, arriving amid broader national debates about child abuse and the validity of "repressed memory," not to mention the political wrangling within the Church itself, was inevitably exaggerated. He figured the actual percentage of priests accused of some kind of misconduct was 1.7 percent, not the six or seven percent commonly reported in the press. Instances of true pedophilia (that is, molesting of prepubescents) were rare, as most cases involved boys or girls age fifteen or older. Perhaps most significant, Jenkins found that the incidence of sexual deviance among Catholic priests was no higher than among clergy in other denominations. But since Catholic priests outnumber their counterparts in other faiths and given their special place in the American mythos, it was the Catholic episodes that figured in the headlines and fired the public imagination. While none of this excuses the crimes, the perspective is instructive.

Beal understands that so harsh a spotlight generates a lot of heat. But he is concerned that the Church, in finally trying to be responsive to victims, has moved too far the other way. Where once a charge against a priest may have been ignored or covered over, he says, today it carries a presumption of guilt. "Now we have come to the other end," Beal says, "where the bishop calls the priest in and throws the book at him"—sometimes without even the most cursory investigation as to the merits of the allegation. Priests suddenly summoned to administrative hearings (as distinct from criminal or civil proceedings) for alleged misconduct have few rights before their bishop and are on their own even to find counsel.

As an adviser to bishops himself, Beal recommends a more "measured" response to such accusations—not only to avoid scaring congregations but in the interest of fairness to the priest. Beal says that's because more and more allegations, as in Bernardin's case, are proving untrue. Yet child molestation is the kind of charge that tends to stick, the facts notwithstanding. As Beal says, "Once a priest is pulled out of a parish in the dead of night and the parishioners are told Father's been accused of molesting children, even if he is eventually found to be innocent his reputation and probably his effectiveness as a minister are ruined."

He tells me about a case in which a priest who taught at a high school was accused by a fourteen-year-old female student of giving her a French kiss. The man was summarily removed from his position and sent into treatment. "Finally someone bothered to ask the fourteen-year-old, 'Just exactly what did Father do?'" says Beal. "Well, it turned out she had seen an old movie with Charles Boyer where he gave [a girl] a peck on the cheek, and she thought that was what they must mean by French kissing. Maybe that was inappropriate [behavior for the priest], but it certainly wasn't what they had acted on. By the time they were in a position to try to redress the thing, the priest was so devastated that he was in clinical depression, and he hasn't been able to minister ever since. It's a horrible example of what can happen if you overreact to accusations before you have the facts."

In the past year, just in the vicinity of Washington, Beal says he is aware of at least three priests who committed suicide after being accused of sexual misconduct. A less sensational but still unfortunate result of the scandal is the distance priests are putting between themselves and young people. From his own years of working with teenagers, Beal says he knows that when they really want to talk about personal matters—problems at home, say, or a possible vocation—they don't schedule an appointment. "They'd come up to you when you were watching a basketball game and say, 'Could we talk during halftime?' It was that being available outside of business hours that was often where you did the most effective ministering. They would sort of feel you out to see if they could trust you, and then in a casual way get into a conversation about what they were concerned about." For fear of false accusations, Beal says, fewer of those off-hours conversations take place these days.

He is reminded of his own high school encounters, back in the seventies. "I remember one group, one class, where I referred to the girls as the 'touchy-feely' group because they couldn't see you without giving you a hug. There were hugs all around. I don't know how many times I got hugged in the four years they went through the school." Today he would avoid that kind of contact, Beal tells me, a little sadly.

▩ Father John J. Dreese

NEW LEXINGTON, OHIO

It's one thing to deal with the clerical sex scandal on a procedural basis, as Father Beal does, but something else to live and work in its ugly shadow. Priests by and large reacted to the lurid revelations as did most other Catholics, with shock and outrage. Yet among the clergy there is another emotion uniquely theirs: discouragement. The scandal tarred them all, the innocent with the guilty. Bishop John J. McRaith of the diocese of Owensboro, Kentucky, who for several years monitored clerical attitudes for the National Conference of Catholic Bishops, told me, "I don't think we have any idea how devastating this has been to the morale of priests." For one thing, living with the scandal means having to withstand the stares of strangers and friends who wonder if you're a closet pervert. And it means being robbed of even the most innocent expressions of affection. One afternoon when I was visiting with a group of pastors, longtime friends who get together once a month for lunch, shoptalk, and personal reflection, I asked them about that. One, a burly man in his forties, admitted with some agony, "You have to be *so* careful. You're afraid to so much as straighten an altar boy's surplice if it's crooked without someone else being in the room." As he said this, every other man in the room nodded his melancholy assent.

Another problem for the innocent men is that no one actually expects them to vent these frustrations; after all, they're *priests*, not whiny quarterbacks or petulant rock stars. That's why, in my research of the priesthood, I was taken by an unusually forthright article on the scandal's fallout in *Commonweal*, a Catholic magazine. The author was a pastor, and the piece a full-throated cri de coeur: "My anger is mixed with sadness. My sadness comes from the strong strain of selfishness, self-interest, revenge, vindictiveness, and sensationalism that lingers in the air after every new report. Priests who have not committed the crimes are deeply hurt. A heavy pall hangs over the life of the priesthood. Priests find their duties to be difficult and joyless. Some are ashamed to wear a Roman collar."

I decided to pay a call on this man, who runs a small parish in rural Ohio. Father John J. Dreese told me that he sat down one day and wrote the article out of sheer frustration, saying that the revelations about new cases were beginning to affect him like Chinese water torture. Though his article was intended as a personal statement, Dreese felt sure he was speaking for countless of his brothers. As one exasperated friend had told him, "I want to wear a sandwich board that says, 'I'm not one of them.'"

John Dreese is a funny, self-effacing man. Shaking hands with him, you notice his powerful arms, and when he said he was sixty-three I would have guessed at least ten years younger. As pastor of St. Rose of Lima Church in New Lexington, a town about fifty miles southeast of Columbus, he is back in the parish where he was born after a career that has taken him around the world. He grew up with one brother and eight sisters, most of whom still live in and around New Lexington and attend St. Rose. "We have penance services twice a year," he says, "and they always manage to go to the other priests." Of the one hundred fifty pupils in the church school, thirteen are Dreese's grandnieces or grandnephews. "Whenever I see a kid in school, I ask them what their mother's maiden name is."

New Lexington is situated in that part of Ohio where the agricultural plains give way to the hillocks of the Appalachian Plateau. St. Rose itself sits atop Straight Hill, the derivation of which becomes apparent as you drive straight up to reach the top. New Lexington is an unprepossessing community of five thousand people, the only city in Perry County. Garrison Keillor aficionados will note that it has an honest-to-goodness Chatter Box Cafe, while a historical marker informs you that it also is the home of Januarius McGahan, a gadfly journalist who is remembered—here, anyway—as the "liberator of Bulgaria."

Perry County is rural, poor, and getting poorer. It's one of those out-of-sight, out-of-mind pockets on the American landscape where economic development means a new video store, and national news reports about low unemployment read like taunts. Aside from agriculture, the county's traditional industry has been mining, but Peabody Coal pulled out several years ago and the area has never come out of its tailspin. As Dreese says, "The big day here is the first day of the month, when all the black lung checks come out, the Social Security checks, pension checks. Then you need a traffic cop uptown." In five years only two families have moved into the parish. The only "move-outs," he says, "are by way of either going to the cemetery or going to the city to get work."

Dreese's job is like that of many rural pastors, which is trying to keep Catholicism vibrant in a place where energy and resources are draining away. This involves overseeing the school, consolidating and closing tiny outlying parishes, refereeing squabbles among the congregation, visiting the sick, covering for vacationing colleagues, and trying to keep his liturgy committee together ("eleven women and me; I can't keep men on it"). Just now St. Rose is raising funds for a desperately needed parish center. The previous Sunday, Dreese confessed to me with some exasperation, "I preached on money for the first time in thirty-five years."

In other words, Dreese has enough on his plate that he could be forgiven for letting others wring their hands over the clerical sex scandal. But it kept eating at him because he took it personally. He considered it an immense and inconceivable betrayal of all priests, past and present, by a handful of troubled and selfish men. "If I identify with the Roman Catholic priesthood," he wrote, "I must be ashamed, saddened, and sickened by it all."

When the first rumblings of the scandal were heard a decade ago, Dreese's first impulse, as was the case with so many other Catholics, was to deny it. Then as the revelations mounted, he began to wonder whether he should have been more aware of the scandal's potential. He thought back to certain priests he knew who always managed to be in the company of boys or young men. In fact one of these, a "guru to teenage boys," would be convicted of sexual abuse and sent to prison. But Dreese knew him decades ago, when all of us were either more innocent or more naive and no one wanted to believe his darker suspicions about a colleague—especially a priest. "In today's climate I would confront the man," Dreese wrote. "In 1963 I gave him the benefit of the doubt, and, as far as I know, so did everyone else."

Gradually, of course, the reality that crimes had occurred became inescapable. Dreese told me about an occasion some years ago, in a previous assignment, when an elderly man came up to him and asked whether a certain priest they both knew was still alive. Dreese told him no, the clergyman was long dead. The old man then shared a secret he'd been carrying for more than half a century: when he was a boy that priest had sexually abused him. "He never said anything to anybody—no one," Dreese said, shaking his head. "He said, 'Every time I see those things on TV, I think that could be true.' So he came and talked to me. He just had to tell somebody and talk it out. But he carried it all his life, an old man in his seventies. It's just awful."

In this newfound awareness Dreese grew angry—at the abusive priests, at the Church hierarchy for its clumsy handling of the situation, at the media for their fascination with the subject (and their almost exclusive focus on Catholic clergy as opposed to those of other faiths), and at private investigators and attorneys who seem intent on digging into the history of every man who ever donned the collar. He decries the "fishing expeditions" into records of priests long dead and thinks there should be a reasonable statute of limitations for filing charges against them. But for those culpable priests still alive Dreese has no sympathy. "I have no problem at all with guys going to the slammer," he declares. "Every time one goes [to prison], I say that's fine. Maybe the message gets out."

Dreese fears that aside from creating problems of morale and squandering the inheritance of trust generations of priests have built up, the scandal will have other far-reaching consequences. These include a deleterious effect on the already skimpy number of priest vocations. "Any young man who's thinking about going into the priesthood today is going to get a lot of, you know, strange looks by his peers," he says. "Sure, are you one of them? Are you gay? Are you a pedophile? Are you crazy? There aren't a raft of people lined up as it is."

Back in the late fifties, when Dreese himself was deciding whether the priest's life was what he wanted, he nearly decided it wasn't. For him the issue wasn't sexual scandal, but sex, period: Dreese didn't know if he could be celibate. He always enjoyed the company of girls and of course had grown up with eight sisters, so he had a pretty good idea what he'd be giving up. He wrestled with that through twelve years of seminary, all the way up to the point of no return. And there, he says, "I decided I wanted to take a year off and think about it, because I wasn't sure I wanted to do this. So I called a halt to the whole ceremony of ordination three months before it was to happen." Today the Church builds in just such a preordination period for that kind of introspection, but at the time Dreese's decision was wholly unorthodox. "That's kind of like calling off your wedding after the invitations are sent out. It wasn't done much in 1958."

"I didn't know whether I wanted to be celibate," he continues. "I didn't know whether I could be. My God, this was scary. I couldn't understand how so many of my classmates could readily step forward. My best friend, who had no problems at all, couldn't understand why I was holding up. Eight years later I'm saying good-bye to him as he leaves [the priesthood] to get married." In the intervening year Dreese taught high school in Colum-

bus, and in 1959 he went ahead with his ordination. But without that sabbatical to make sure of himself, "I would have checked out long ago."

That belated decision opened up a career of extraordinary variety and,
Dreese says, gratification. Once ordained, he did more teaching and a ministry that included parish work and a stint as a prison chaplain. Dreese then
was sent to Rome to do graduate work in biblical studies, after which he returned to Ohio to teach seminarians in Cincinnati and work on his doctorate at Hebrew Union College. Then it was back to Columbus, where he and
another priest served as co-pastors of a large parish. "Oh, God, it was awful," he remembers with a sardonic laugh. Dreese likened the experience to a
five-year marriage, and apparently it was a miracle it lasted that long. "We
survived it because we used to have our secretary do our marriage counseling. We'd get in awful fights. I'd say, 'If you don't do this I'm leaving.' He
would say, 'If you don't do this *I'm* leaving.' She was a kind of referee."

Dreese left to become administrator of the cathedral in Columbus, the
bishop's home base. That's the kind of job that can put a priest on an executive fast track, if he's so inclined. But given his propensity for bluntness and
reputation as a boat-rocker, Dreese knew he would never be a bishop and
says he wouldn't want to be one in any case. "You are never really free as a
priest until you decide that you don't want to be a bishop," he says. "Really,
think about it. The guy that wants to be a bishop is crazy. You've got to go
to every dog fight and bless the dogs. You're a politician." (Later on, when
Dreese and I were discussing the priest shortage, I asked him if he'd thought
about writing an article on that subject. Laughing, he said he had considered
it, but all he had come up with was a title: "No Shortage of Bishops.")

Dreese's next move brought him back to Perry County, to take over a
small parish in Crooksville, about ten miles from New Lexington ("and
where I had no relatives," he says). After six years there, the standard pastoral term in the Columbus diocese—pastors here usually have the option
of re-upping for another six years if they choose—Dreese was approached
about the possibility of teaching in Africa. The Catholic Higher Institute
(now Catholic University) of Eastern Africa in Nairobi, Kenya, was estab-
lishing a program to allow African priests to do postgraduate work without
leaving the continent, and Dreese was invited to spend a semester there
teaching scriptural studies. Just before he left, however, the pastorate at St.
Rose came open. The diocese prevailed on Dreese to take it, but with so
much family there his first reaction was, he says, "Count me out." The
bishop was persistent, as bishops usually are, so when Dreese returned
from Africa, in 1989, it was to New Lexington.

St. Rose is the largest parish in the area, but as generations of immigrants—Welsh, Italians, Germans, Poles, Slovaks, even Lebanese—arrived to populate Perry County's farms and mines, parishes sprouted up in a dozen of its smaller communities. The eighties and nineties, however, have been about decline. The tiniest parishes are gone, and the survivors, with their atrophying congregations and the dwindling number of priests available to serve them, have been pulled together into a county "consortium." The idea is that more efficient management will keep open as many as possible, even though there are not enough pastors to go around. At sixty-three, Dreese is the youngest priest in the county; his colleagues are seventy-five, seventy-four, sixty-eight, and sixty-five. The bishop has already determined that by the year 2000 there will be only two diocesan priests to serve all of Perry County.

Until recently, Dreese, in his role as pastor of St. Rose, also administered the consortium. As such, he had the melancholy task of closing several of its least viable parishes. That's an emotional business. A church typically is one of the last remnants of a dying town's identity, something that binds a community after its commerce has evaporated and the local school has been swallowed by the consolidated facility miles down the highway. Certainly that was the situation when Dreese closed the parish at New Straitsville, in the county's southern end. By then the congregation was down to forty active parishioners; it was so poor and so small that the annual collections *totaled* only five thousand dollars; a large suburban parish will take up that much in a single Sunday Mass.

Things there came to a head when it became clear that several repairs to the creaky church building could no longer be ignored. Dreese had an estimate that it would take seventy-five thousand dollars simply to fix the unsafe roof. When parishioners came together to discuss how they might raise that kind of money, they all sat in silence for a few moments, pondering what was essentially imponderable. At last a middle-aged woman said hopefully, "We'll have bake sales."

Dreese worries about these people, and not only because losing a church means losing a piece of one's self. It also means getting less access to the sacraments. To demonstrate his point, he goes to a bookcase and pulls down a thin leather volume published by the National Conference of Catholic Bishops. The title: *Sunday Celebrations in the Absence of a Priest.* It's a handbook for conducting what you might call self-serve Sunday Mass, except it's not a Mass. It consists of scriptural readings, perhaps a homily by a parish administrator or visiting deacon, and distribution of communion hosts that have been consecrated elsewhere. Many Catholics don't even know such services are possible; for millions in marginal communities, they're becoming a regular occurrence.

Dreese does not strike me as by nature pessimistic, but as he surveys things he sees little room for optimism in the Perry Counties of the world. "We'll probably end up with one Catholic church in virtually every [rural] county," he says. "We'll become more and more about nonpracticing Catholics." Or about congregationalism. Dreese applauds the empowering of a lay ministry, but he warns that if it's done in desperation, primarily to fill the void left by departing priests, the movement comes with serious risks. "I think we have a certain number of Roman Catholics who unwittingly want to become congregationalist," he says. "But if we become congregationalists, whatever else we are we are not Roman Catholics." Dreese pauses, then smiles. "But I'll be in my grave when it plays out."

Father
Roger Griese

KETTERING, OHIO

Down the road in Kettering, just below Dayton, it is a bitterly cold February day when I meet up with Father Roger Griese. The seventy-nine-year-old priest lives in a retirement community, where he is also chaplain. His studio-like apartment—bedroom, kitchen, living room equipped with a compact altar—is cluttered with papers and crowded with a lifetime of keepsakes. Photographs on the wall: of Mother Cabrini, the first U.S. citizen to become a saint; of Griese's 1942 graduating class from Mount St. Mary's seminary in Norwood, Ohio; and of Griese posing with presidential candidate Pat Buchanan, a picture taken at a Cincinnati rally, the two Catholic conservatives having been introduced by mutual friends. Griese was such an enthusiastic supporter of Republican Buchanan that he donated eight hundred dollars to his campaign. This from a man whose pension is three hundred a month.

The last name is pronounced in two syllables, the same as quarterback Bob Griese; "he's my son," the priest tells me with the hearty laugh that is one of his trademarks. The once vigorous Griese has been in shaky health for most of his retirement, which was imposed on him a few years ago, and just now an ulcerated leg has him moving slowly. There is nothing infirm about his opinions, however, which he delivers with the same vinegar and enthusiasm he always has. Former parishioners have used adjectives like "brusque," "gruff," "cantankerous," "brutally honest," but also "beloved" to describe Griese. It doesn't take much effort to imagine what a handful he must have been in his prime.

Still is, really. As he holds forth on the lamentable shape of American Catholicism, Griese takes aim at such high-ranking prelates as Cardinals Bernardin and Roger Mahony of Los Angeles for succumbing to the sin of "pride" and fostering wholesale "disobedience" to Rome. "Some of the bishops are the worst enemies of the Church," he allows. "I often say there's only one thing wrong with the Catholic Church in the United States:

that's ninety-five percent of the bishops. Their faith isn't very strong, or they've lost their faith." And Griese is a man who acts on his convictions. He once had special buttons made up and sent to a number of "disloyal" American bishops. The buttons, featuring silver lettering against a black field, read: "Judas Iscariot Society: Member."

I can see how over the years Roger Griese might well have been a Church bureaucrat's worst nightmare: an opinionated, uncompromising man with a flair for getting attention. As we visit, my host constantly shifting in an easy chair trying in vain to get comfortable, I suddenly realize he reminds me of another curmudgeon of more familiar acquaintance, my late grandfather. With snow flurries dancing outside the window, I make a note to myself: here's a lion in winter, all right.

Griese came from the heavily Catholic west side of Cincinnati. After ordination he obtained a master's degree in sociology from Catholic University. The archdiocese of Cincinnati put his expertise to use in Dayton, where for several years Griese was both the assistant director of Catholic Charities and assistant chaplain at an orphanage. On the side he did chaplaincies at a state mental hospital and several other social agencies. Of those days he recalls, "We worked our tails off, whew! Dear God!"

Eventually he returned to Cincinnati for a succession of pastorates on the city's traditionally non-Catholic east side. In the late fifties and early sixties, anti-Catholic sentiment there was still pervasive. He worked to break it down, but it wasn't easy. "When I first got there, if I walked down the street there were people who would get off the sidewalk until I passed by," he says. "That wasn't for me personally; that was hatred for the Church." Then again, at one of those parishes he discovered that the biggest headaches were *internal*. "It was probably the worst parish in the archdiocese," he says. "I think when I went in there I should have had a general exorcism. There were a few good people there, but some of them were so *nasty*."

In 1968, Griese returned to Dayton for the assignment that would define his career. For twenty-two years he presided at Sacred Heart, a venerable parish in the heart of downtown. As was the case for many inner-city parishes, Sacred Heart's most robust years were long behind it. (The archdiocese actually closed it in 1996.) But when Griese arrived it was still kicking, and his fondness for the place is evident. "I think it's the most beautiful church in Dayton," he tells me. "They didn't put up a plaster barn. We had a real church."

Griese has always had a knack for being in the middle of things (he was a prolific and stern letter-writer to Dayton's newspapers, for instance), and his visibility at Sacred Heart facilitated this talent. There was that memorable Sunday morning in the early seventies when a band of militants stormed Sacred Heart during Mass to protest the Catholic Church's alleged "exploitation" of Dayton's inner-city residents. Griese had been tipped off to the possibility of trouble, so when the protesters tried to read a statement he simply cued the choir loft. "They came up with 'Holy God We Praise Thy Name'—all the stops," Griese recalls. "So you couldn't hear a thing these people said. We kept up the organ music and the singing until they were ready to leave." Griese insisted the ringleader be prosecuted—until he had extracted an apology from him. Much favorable publicity ensued. "After all, the Catholic Church is in the business of showing mercy," he says with a knowing smile. "That went over big."

About this same time, with much less fanfare, Griese instituted a dress code at Sacred Heart. This was in response to the cutoff jeans, tank tops, micro-miniskirts, and bare midriffs he was starting to see in church, which he deemed inappropriate. "Respectful conduct, respectful dress" was his motto, and signs about proper attire went up all around the building. Miscreants were called aside and sent away to change. Most were teens and young adults, but not all. "I even had a religious brother from Louisville visiting up here—*he* was in shorts," Griese recalls, shaking his head. "I invited him to leave. He was very upset. He wrote me a snotty letter, as if I were the abuser."

In any event Griese says the people of Sacred Heart, long accustomed to his no-nonsense positions and nature, took the dress code in stride for more than a decade. In 1989, however, a young man—Griese still refers to him variously as a "clown" and a "troublemaker"—decided to challenge things. He showed up one Sunday morning in shorts; when he refused Griese's invitations to leave, Griese refused to give him communion. This scenario played out for several Sundays in a row, Griese says, until at last the young man finally came to Mass dressed in slacks, and with his mother. Griese gave him communion.

Nonetheless, the confrontations were widely reported, and Griese's dress code became something of a southwestern Ohio cause celebre. Of course, the headstrong pastor of Sacred Heart already was well known to Cincinnati Archbishop Daniel Pilarczyk, not just as a priest of the diocese but as someone who had written him privately to criticize certain of Pilarczyk's policies and decisions. When Pilarczyk appealed to Griese to relax his enforcement of the dress code, Griese refused—and then excoriated his archbishop from the pulpit. Pilarczyk responded by taking the extraordinary step of removing Griese from Sacred Heart. Griese, then seventy-two and three years shy of retirement, countered by appealing his removal through Church channels. That, he says, "infuriated Pilarczyk no end. See, he couldn't move me while the appeal was in Rome. So I had him by the tail. He didn't think he should be appealed. It was going to give him a black eye over in Rome, and he was expecting to be a cardinal—that was the big deal there." Griese chuckles again, heartily. "I hope I prevented it."

In the end Griese's appeal failed. He still feels he was right rather than insubordinate. As he recounts the story, he shows me a photograph of a sign posted outside St. Peter's Basilica at the Vatican; it instructs visitors on appropriate dress for admittance: no shorts on men, no miniskirts on women. Griese maintains that what's good for Rome is good for Dayton, and his lingering disappointment is palpable. He tells me that at one point during the contretemps he wrote Pilarczyk, "and I quoted the fourth chapter of Galatians: 'Have I become your enemy because I have told you the truth?' He didn't answer."

By late afternoon we decide to finish our conversation at one of Griese's favorite restaurants, a Chinese place in a nearby shopping center. We are the only customers there, and over piping hot wonton soup the priest holds forth on other religious issues. Most of these observations are variations on a theme: how American Catholicism is being undone by its own: bishops and priests and nuns and lay interest groups intent on doing what they want rather than what they should. When I ask him to describe his own religious ideology, he fires back, "Orthodox. I'm a Catholic, and right down the line I believe everything the Catholic Church believes and teaches. And the Holy Father is the head of the Church, and he has complete authority for individuals and all groups in the Church. The rules and orders he gives, those must be obeyed, because he is the divinely instituted head. He's the only one who has the authority. Some of these clowns"—he cites Hans Küng and a handful of other liberal theologians—"are just heretics. We've got a couple bishops now who are heretics, but nobody's correcting them.

"I'm not a troublemaker," he continues, but adds, "I've never been accused of being a coward. I don't do these things arbitrarily."

As dinner wears on, I sense the steam going out of his remarks; he is clearly tiring. He climbs back into his Chevrolet and drives me back to his apartment. Then, in the parking lot as we are saying our good-byes, he surprises me: unprompted, he blesses me and offers a prayer for my safe trip home. It is an unexpectedly sweet gesture from a lion, and I appreciate it.

⬚ Father William Dietsch

PETERSBURG, INDIANA

Sts. Peter and Paul Church is small and compact, and Father William Dietsch, who goes a husky six-foot-four, is not. When he makes the short walk to the altar from the sacristy, just off to the side, he looks like the imposing male lead making his entrance from the wings of a tiny community theater. This Tuesday morning there are five other souls besides me at his eight o'clock Mass, which takes twenty minutes. Afterward, Dietsch and I head over to the Fish Hut, a onetime gas station-turned-restaurant, where he tucks into a heaping plate of biscuits and gravy. We sit down at a table with about eight other men, most retired, who gather at the Fish Hut every day in a kind of breakfast social club, or what many southern Indiana residents of German ancestry still call a kaffeeklatsch. The group's composition changes throughout the morning: early birds, especially the active farmers, start rolling in about six, and colleagues come and go until about ten, but at any given time you're apt to find about ten of them there, drinking coffee and smoking cigarettes. Most aren't Catholic, but Dietsch joins them often enough that if he misses a few days they'll tease him about his whereabouts. The Fish Hut men gossip and joke or talk about things that matter around here, like farming, mining, fishing—and weather. They talk about weather a lot. Last night, in fact, there were storms in the area and a tornado warning was broadcast on television. "I went outside to look around," one man says. "I saw all my neighbors outside, all looking at the sky, too."

Everyone nods. For people who live around Petersburg, a rural community of about six thousand, weather remains close to the bone, especially in springtime. Six years ago on a Saturday night—ironically, the eve of Pentecost, when the Holy Spirit descended on the apostles amid a rush of wind to empower them to preach to all peoples—a funnel cloud roared through this town like a giant road grader. The twister leveled a half-mile-wide swath of Petersburg from one end to the other, killing six people, injuring hundreds, and rendering many times that number homeless. Petersburg's Nazarene church was destroyed. Its Free Methodist church was destroyed. Its Wesleyan church was destroyed. Across Eighth Street from Sts. Peter and Paul, a sparkling new United Methodist church now stands because the wooden buildings in the old complex were so battered they had to come down. Yet a few yards away, Sts. Peter and Paul, the only Catholic church in Pike County, escaped with negligible damage, a testament to nature's maddening serendipity.

Bill Dietsch was spared, too, and like so many others here he would come to feel both grateful and guilty about that. The fifty-two-year-old priest had arrived as pastor of the small parish only months before the storm hit. That afternoon he had presided at a wedding in Petersburg, and the reception was twenty miles away, in Jasper, Indiana. Dietsch was tired and disinclined to go, but the wedding party implored him, and he knew it would be a good opportunity to get better acquainted with some of his new parishioners. And indeed, he had such a good time that he stayed hours longer than he expected he would. Then on the drive back, heading west, he got behind some slower vehicles, further delaying his return home. So it was that Dietsch was still a few miles outside Petersburg when, shortly after eight-thirty, he encountered one of the worst storms in his memory. Huge hailstones pocked his car with dents, and he could make out the tops of funnel clouds against the frightening horizon. He rushed the rest of the way to Petersburg, only to find half of it strewn about like giant jackstraws. "You know how as a kid you used to imagine atrocities happening, like bombings?" he asks. "It was like that."

As he surveyed the devastation, Dietsch remembers being filled with the sensation that the events that had kept him at a safe remove—the out-of-town reception, the unexpected conviviality, the unusually slow drive home—were more than coincidence. "I came away from there with a very strong feeling that divine providence kept me out of town—got me out of town and kept me out of town," he says. He would spend the next five or six hours checking out the church and rectory and wandering the town helping out where he could. Then, still in a state of shock and with no power in the rectory, Dietsch left to spend the rest of the night with his brother. "We drove back to Petersburg the next morning, that Sunday morning, and I went through an incredible experience," he says. "I said to myself, 'Bill, you dreamt this thing. You know it didn't happen.' But I got back in town and said, 'My God, it really did.' I didn't want to believe it."

Because Sts. Peter and Paul was one of the few churches left standing, it became "a natural gravitation point," he says. "People were traumatized and disoriented, and they didn't want to stray very far away from their buildings and their property. It was all they had left, and they wanted to keep an eye on things." As the community's disenfranchised began showing up, so did food. First it was individuals dropping off covered dishes, then local supermarkets and wholesalers donating meat and staples in bulk. Within days the members of the tiny parish—there are perhaps one hundred fifty families at Sts. Peter and Paul—had launched an impromptu soup kitchen, an operation that would continue for the three months or so it took Petersburg to get back on its feet. Dietsch likens the phenomenon to the biblical story of the loaves and fishes. "I could take you down there and show you this little kitchen," he says, "and we served between fifteen and twenty thousand meals during that time on a stove that has only two burners that work, and the oven didn't work properly. They'd bring in their crock pots, their Fry Daddies, their griddles."

Those months passed in a blur. Like the community's other clerics, Dietsch practiced the ministry of expedience, helping residents cope with the trauma whatever it took. When he wasn't coordinating the church's food operation, he was helping victims deal with the Red Cross or the Federal Emergency Management Agency or their own insurance companies. He consoled those who punished themselves for surviving when loved ones hadn't. It was the priest's first brush with a natural disaster of such magnitude, and while it turned out that none of his own parishioners had died, everyone knew the people who had. He well understood this as the kind of swift, unpredictable tragedy that can shake people's convictions. "I was afraid that was going to happen," he says. "The strange thing is that, more than anything, it probably led to a strengthening [of faith]. It helped me and many others realize just how fragile life is. We are not in control; it's not in our hands. The other thing is that as bad as this disaster really was, God can make good things happen. To me, that's always been one of the unbelievable things about it. The incredible strength that people showed. That God can work wonders, sometimes through human frailty and weakness. I don't think God sought to punish us or anything; I certainly don't believe in that. But I think [this helped us] to realize the value of human resources."

As it turned out, that kind of affirmation couldn't have come at a better time for Bill Dietsch himself.

The pastor of Sts. Peter and Paul is the kind of funny, easygoing person everyone likes. For such a big man, he has a slight, high-pitched voice that takes you by surprise, not unlike the effect Mike Tyson's squeaky voice has on people the first time they hear it. Dietsch grew up as one of seven children in an isolated farm community with a deep Germanic heritage; even now you can detect a faint German lilt in his speech. The Dietsches were observant Catholics and no strangers to religious orders. Several of Dietsch's cousins were priests. One of his brothers tried seminary for a while, one of his sisters a convent. Involvement in parish life was a given. "My mom kind of had this rule that when the church doors were open one of us needed to be there," Dietsch says. "It was almost literally true."

Still, after high school Dietsch opted not for the seminary but the navy. Stationed first in Maine, then in Virginia, he took a lot of ribbing from fellow sailors for eschewing their wild off-duty ways ("Guys there pretty much thought I was a freak," he says). But he says that once they accepted his more spiritual mien some actually encouraged him to try the priesthood. The navy experience, while not especially pleasant at the time, "toughened me up," Dietsch says, adding that he doesn't think he'd have made it through the four-year rigor of Rome's Pontifical North American College without it. Ordained in December 1971, he returned to Indiana to begin his pastoral work.

Dietsch tells me he is looking forward to his impending silver anniversary as a priest. Even so, he admits that only in the last several years has he known for sure he made the right decision. For a long time, he was in emotional turmoil, an ordeal that finally culminated with "my big fight with the Lord."

At issue was celibacy. Not whether it was right, but whether it was right for Dietsch.

※   ※   ※

For as long as humanity has been suspicious of, even ashamed of, its impulse for sex, the forgoing of that particular pleasure has been regarded as spiritually meritorious and ennobling. The tradition of sexual chastity reaches back to Rome's vestal virgins and ascetics like the Essenes of Christ's time. As Robert Barron, a Chicago priest and professor of theology, has written, "Celibacy is unreasonable, unnatural, and excessive, which is why it has been chosen, across cultures and throughout history, as one of the ways in which lovers of God have traditionally expressed their love."

For the first several hundred years of Christianity, there were no rules as to priestly celibacy, but it was not uncommon. Through the Middle Ages the practice became not only more widespread among Catholic priests, thanks in part to the influence of the monastic orders, but practically expected of them by many in their flock. (Spiritual considerations aside, this may also have had something to do with the irritating little problem of married clergy's sometimes trying to pass along Church property to their heirs.) Against this backdrop the Lateran councils of the twelfth century made celibacy official policy for Western priests. This didn't apply to the Eastern rites, however. To this day the Eastern churches in union with Rome, such as the Byzantine Rite, permit the ordination of married men. Eastern bishops, however, must be celibates, which means they tend to come from monastic ranks rather than from parish priests.

Celibacy is not intrinsic to the sacrament of holy orders but a sacred vow taken in conjunction with it. Indeed, there *are* married Catholic priests— former Protestant ministers who converted to Catholicism and received the pope's permission to be ordained—as well as men who became priests after being widowed. But the great majority of Catholic priests are men who never married and voluntarily forswore sexual activity. Through the centuries the Church's primary rationale for this demand has been that it promotes a holier life and that by giving up a family of one's own a priest can more fully devote himself to the faithful. The perspective was summed up this way by Father Theodore Hesburgh, former president of the University of Notre Dame: "By not belonging fully to somebody, a priest can be called 'Father' by all, and all can expect loving compassion, understanding, and forgiveness from him. If this is not true in the life of a priest, he is just a selfish bachelor."

Most of the priests I encountered would concur with that assessment. Indeed, the *Los Angeles Times* survey found that while nearly sixty percent of Catholic clergymen favor allowing priests to marry, only a fraction—four percent—said they would definitely get married themselves if they could. (Another thirteen percent indicated they "probably" would.) For thousands of these men, then, the celibate lifestyle holds real merit. One priest will tell you that celibacy is a gift *to* God, something of extraordinary personal value offered up to him; while another will describe it as a gift *from* God, a lifestyle that can be maintained only by constant devotion and prayer. None of them will tell you, however, that it's easy.

Bill Dietsch stands as poignant testimony. His own wrestling with the matter very nearly prompted him to leave the priesthood. Candid as he is, it remains a difficult subject for him to discuss; as he does so his voice is low and halting, and you get the sense that he's still hard on himself for reacting so emotionally to a dilemma that other priests seem to take in stride. Yet it was finally deciding to talk about it with other priests that eventually led to

Dietsch's self-discovery and, in the end, spiritual contentment. (He also learned that, appearances aside, the discipline is a battle for almost every priest.)

At the heart of Dietsch's problem, frankly, is his sensitive and affectionate nature. While those are fine attributes for anyone, priest or otherwise, Dietsch learned to his dismay that in his case they make it all too easy to fall in love. On several occasions in past assignments, he found himself emotionally drawn to some women parishioners. The women weren't married, and while Dietsch didn't deny his feelings he didn't act on them either. Betraying his vow of celibacy was unthinkable. But living with it was intolerable, because he had never really been persuaded of its value or need. His prayers to the Lord became anxious supplications. "I'd keep saying, 'Why do you make me so vulnerable? I am so easy,'" he recalls. "I didn't want to believe that anyone, let alone myself, could be happy and truly joyous as a man, a very virile person, and not have the ordinary things that men do have."

In time supplication gave way to the occasional explosion. "It was rage and anger and cursing, and I did this aloud in church a few times" when he was alone, Dietsch concedes, shaking his head almost mournfully at the memory. "I know a lady—I was there in church one day and I happened to look out the sacristy door and here she was walking by. *Ohhhh!* She never alluded to the fact that she overheard. [But] she *had* to hear me, because it was loud."

Eventually Dietsch concluded that if he was experiencing longings priests aren't supposed to have, perhaps it was God's way of telling him he should leave the priesthood. He even investigated what was involved in obtaining a dispensation, but he could never make himself follow through. "I think if I didn't love the Church so much in the first place, I probably wouldn't have got this angry," he says. Finally, at a retreat with thirty other priests, he decided to confess his torment. He was scared, afraid his friends and colleagues would be shocked, or at least disappointed in him. Instead they empathized—and apparently had a better sense of Dietsch's anguish than he had realized. "They said, 'What took you so long? We knew you could do it.'"

That experience gave Dietsch the courage to confront his dilemma squarely, in one last conversation. The priest calls it his "mountaintop experience."

"I finally went to church one day and said, 'Let's have it out.' I said, 'You know as well as I do that [celibacy] is a man-made law. You know that I really believe that this law could and should and probably *will* change someday. What if this law changes in my lifetime and I am still young enough to want to do something about it? What is this going to mean?' The Lord said,

'It may well change in your lifetime, and you may well have something you want to do about it then, but it won't make any difference for you. I want you just the way you are.'"

Dietsch smiles. He relates the story to explain how at least one man came to see the worth of celibacy, what it can mean to a priest who believes in it and channels that incredible commitment into his ministry. Suddenly, Dietsch says, he saw how he had been called to a celibate life all along, and for a reason, but only then had begun to listen.

I tell him the whole experience sounds like a crucible. "Yes indeed," he says, nodding. "And I think that's just the way the Lord wanted it. The Lord was using my background, and my priesthood, as the pry bars to get me to hear. Strangely enough, now this is where I feel I found my witness. This is where I find my real self. It's also where I get my perspective for day-to-day living." One result of his newfound peace is that he's no longer afraid to be close to people, including women, because no one misreads his intentions. "I mean, women especially know when you've got it together or if you don't."

Even so, if Dietsch is now sold on the value of celibacy, he continues to be troubled by its mandatory application for Catholic priests. His own experience has persuaded him that in order for the discipline to have real value it must be honestly embraced. "I wanted the Church to see that I was making a willing choice," he says, "and they're saying, well, you are only doing what we expect of you anyway." As long as candidates are presented an ultimatum—sexuality or the priesthood, but not both—he fears the situation will continue to breed resentment in some men, thereby doing more harm than good. He says he doesn't have the answer—perhaps a "tiered" priesthood, like the Eastern churches have, which recognizes the "kingdom value" of celibacy but doesn't require it of all clergy—but he has great concern about the status quo.

Dietsch may have resolved his own doubts, but life as a small-town pastor never gets easier. The demands are endless, and the better known you become, the more people want you on their committee. Repeatedly during our visit the rectory phone rang and he excused himself to answer it; at Sts. Peter and Paul there is no one even to do that for him. "You run the whole show here," he says. "You're the chairman of the board and the trash collector." The problem with that arrangement is that things, and people, can fall through the cracks. He relates a recent example. He had been away for a few days, and when he returned he had a message that an older parishioner was in the hospital and wanted him to visit. It wasn't urgent, and for one reason or another he didn't get by to see her. "Several days later I called her when she was home. She was not easy on me," Dietsch says. "She basically said, 'I was deeply hurt, Father.' She wasn't angry, she was hurt. She had an expectation that I didn't meet. I didn't pretend with her. I said I goofed."

But he points out that with the declining number of priests those situations will become more frequent. That's why he believes the Church must put a premium on involving the laity in active ministry. Priests should increasingly spend their time being "ministers to ministers," he believes. "I really think priests ought to work like they're working themselves out of a job."

With that, Dietsch scrunches himself into my car so that we might drive around town and examine the tornado's impact on Petersburg. What look like suburban subdivisions have sprouted, improbably, in the middle of town, replacing longtime neighborhoods that were leveled. From a hill southwest of town, we can look back and discern the diagonal swath the twister cut. Hours later that same day a tornado would touch down west of Petersburg, moving in roughly the same northeasterly direction as its deadly predecessor. This one skirted the city, and no one was hurt.

⬢ Doctor Jon Fuller

Dr. Jon Fuller, assistant director of the Adult Clinical AIDS Program at Boston City Hospital, has just finished his examination of a patient and is scribbling out a sheaf of drug prescriptions for the young man. The small exam room is furnished with a tiny desk and two plastic chairs. The walls are equally spare. On a bulletin board there are informational fliers in English and Spanish about safe sex and a lone *Far Side* cartoon. In the cartoon, a shlub is exiting a restroom as a sign goes off over his head, flashing, "Didn't Wash Hands."

As Fuller scribbles, the patient, an African American man in his early twenties, asks warily, "Did you say something about needing blood?"

"I need some blood," Fuller says without looking up.

"Ah, man."

"Well, it's been a couple of months," Fuller says. "We need to check. These are strong drugs."

The patient nods. He has been coming to the clinic for about a year. He tells me that when he originally got sick he didn't believe it could be AIDS. He took drugs, he admitted, "but I didn't use a needle and I *definitely* ain't a fag." I would learn later that the young man is a recovering addict who is in the latter stages of AIDS, which means he is one serious infection away from the grave. His hale appearance belies this, however, and Fuller says he has a positive outlook and has been taking better care of himself. In fact, the man moved to Boston in the first place to escape the drug influences of his hometown in western Massachusetts.

The patient attributes much of his improvement to Fuller. Like many of Fuller's patients here, he didn't know for some time that his doctor is also a Jesuit priest. Indeed, Fuller wears many hats: he is a nationally recognized expert on HIV, a lecturer at Harvard Divinity School, a professor at the Boston University School of Medicine, and a leading advocate for Church outreach to those affected by HIV and AIDS, including some of its own clergy. Around here, though, Jon Fuller is better known as a physician of extraordinary capability and, more important, compassion. Another of his patients, a white man in his thirties who bounced around a variety of institutions and doctors until he came under Fuller's care, told me, "You break your arm, any doctor—Doctor Bob, Doctor Jim—can fix it. But I need someone who can help me fix my *life*."

Which is not to say the doctor-priest administers sermons with his shots. Quite the contrary, he doesn't bring up his clerical identity to new patients; they tend to learn about it later, second- or third-hand, if they find out at all. Fuller doesn't want to make any of his patients self-conscious—many people who come to the clinic are anxious enough as it is—and besides, preaching is not his style. Fuller simply uses medicine as his own vehicle for Christian witness. "Medicine is something I'm good at, and I love it," he says, "but it's a tool. You know, I don't presume I will always be doing it, and to the extent that I can use it to do what is really the major work in my life—which is to try to follow the Lord in the Society [of Jesus]—then it works."

Indeed, despite his decade-long commitment to the clinic, Fuller considers his "real focus" to be the work he does outside it: educating Catholic hierarchy, clergy, and policymakers about the facts of the AIDS epidemic and promoting a healthier pastoral approach to its casualties. It is sensitive work, more suited perhaps to a diplomat than a doctor, because Catholics are conflicted on the issue. As Fuller puts it, the Church is reaching out to the AIDS community as never before, but "how do you be compassionate to people whom you have judged to be immoral in their personal lives?" That is, the Church wants to be pastoral without condoning gay behavior, which it has always held to be sinful (but which it continues to evaluate in light of new scientific and medical insights into the origins of homosexuality). Fuller's liaison work involves regularly meeting with bishops and priests at their conferences, lecturing at diocesan AIDS awareness days, and sponsoring his own seminars. He says it's imperative not only for the Church to keep the subject of AIDS alive but to consider it apart from its traditional views of sexual behavior. "The transmission of fatal disease is not addressed in *Humanae vitae*, for instance," he says, referring to Pope Paul VI's 1968 encyclical reaffirming the ban against artificial contraception.

Still, if Fuller has a base of operations, the AIDS clinic, located in Boston's only public hospital, is it. City Hospital (now part of Boston Medical Center) is in the south end, a hard part of town where recent efforts at gentrification have yet to chase away the prostitution, drug activity, and other crime. Its patients are a poor, polyglot clientele; the hospital has translators available in half a dozen languages, from Creole to Chinese. Working here definitely has its occupational hazards. A colleague had her computer stolen while she was with a patient, Fuller says, and "one of the surgery residents woke up to somebody trying to slit his throat in an on-call room."

Fuller is here two days a week, seeing dozens of the more than seven hundred and fifty late-stage patients who come to the AIDS clinic (another several hundred people with less advanced cases get primary care elsewhere in the hospital). Most of the AIDS patients are adults, but there are plenty of children on the premises as well. (They are treated at the pediatric AIDS section next door.) The clinic endeavors to create a family-friendly and helpful environment, because if a child has AIDS the mother usually does, too, and simply getting them to the hospital at all is a challenge. "For people coming in here, AIDS is not the biggest problem in their lives," the doctor explains. "Getting food on the table, or a warm place to stay, or evading crime in your neighborhood is much bigger. So social services are a huge part of what the clinic provides, both because it needs to be provided, but it's also the entree to convince people to get care. Turning on their gas or their phone, or getting them food, may be the way to really get them into care or drug treatment."

Fuller's non-clinic work takes him around the country and occasionally, given his involvement with international Catholic charities, around the world. When I dropped by the clinic, he had just returned from a monthlong stint at a mission hospital in Uganda, where he estimates that up to sixty percent of the patients are HIV-positive. He was still visibly excited about the trip, which he called a valuable learning experience—despite picking up a case of malaria and coping with the exigencies of Third World medicine. "Just simple things," he says, "like they take bandages out of a wound and they wash the gauze and put it on the line and use it again and again. Needles are reused until they just bend out of shape. Even paper surgical masks get washed and reused. You just do it by the seat of your pants."

Fuller is a wiry, energetic man of forty-three. Studying a clipboard as he goes, he navigates the hospital's familiar hallways so intently and quickly that it's all you can do to stay in his wake. There is always another patient to see, another doctor to consult, another family member to console. During a rare lull in appointments, I ask him if he decided to become a doctor after having committed to the priesthood. "No, actually medicine was the thing I was always going to do," he says. "It was really the priestly thing that came very, very late."

Growing up in Los Angeles, Fuller attended a Jesuit high school there, and by his senior year he already had been accepted to college in pre-med.

"Then this sort of idea came from nowhere, which I really wasn't trying to entertain," he says. "It just kept getting stronger and stronger."

Part of the lure was the example of his Jesuit instructors. "I think it was just the impact of seeing this order of priests who seemed to be having a very stimulating, happy life together and doing work which was exciting," he says. "But then it gradually became a much more focused thing on a personal relationship with the Lord, and a real sense of a personal call." Even so, he admits that the idea of pursuing the priesthood, especially after having his heart set on medicine for years, "was a tremendous leap into the unknown that was very uncharacteristic of me." Yet when the call refused to abate, "I just decided I have to trust this to some degree and see where it goes."

Jesuits, the great ancient order of Ignatius of Loyola, Isaac Joques, Teilhard de Chardin, and Robert Bellarmine, are known primarily as teachers and missionaries. They occupy many other professions, however, and about two dozen in the United States are medical doctors. Upon applying to the order, Fuller told his superiors of his desire to likewise practice medicine. "The Jesuits were very clear that that's a possibility but you can't enter with that as a condition or an expectation," he remembers. "And actually, it *was* a bit of a rocky road. I talked about it for years and eventually began to make formal applications. And for a brief period there was real tension, when some of my superiors questioned where my fundamental loyalties were."

Looking back, Fuller believes that tension was a good thing, in that it helped convince him that he could operate effectively in both worlds. When at last he convinced his superiors, too, he set off on his divergent educations. After minor seminary—essentially the equivalent of undergraduate college—and two years of teaching high school, he veered to medical school at the University of California at San Diego, where he obtained his M.D. in 1983. Wanting to work in an inner-city program where he could keep up his Spanish, Fuller embarked on a three-year, family practice residency at San Francisco General Hospital. After that he returned to seminary to finish his theological studies, and he was ordained a priest in 1990.

Fuller originally pursued family practice because the Jesuits figured it would dovetail with missionary work, especially in developing countries. But in 1983, shortly after his arrival in San Francisco, the hospital established the world's first in-patient AIDS unit. Like the rest of us, Jon Fuller was about to be introduced to a fearsome new plague.

"When this thing just blew up," he says of the burgeoning AIDS crisis, "my sense of it was, well, I can either avoid this or I can see this as kind of a providential experience." Not only was it a fascinating and scary phenomenon for a doctor, but for a minister-in-training it was "obvious from the very beginning what convulsions this was putting the Church through. To see bad pastoral care being delivered, and people wounded by pastoral care, and to see even within medicine how people were being judged and mocked behind their backs—it made it obvious that this was not just a clinical problem. Since then my focus has been entirely AIDS."

Moving cross-country in 1986 to attend the Weston Jesuit School of Theology in Cambridge, Fuller immediately began working at the newly opened AIDS clinic at Boston City Hospital. Over the years he picked up more and more responsibility for its operation. For all his administrative and teaching abilities, Fuller seems happiest working with patients. Once he has conducted a physical exam, Fuller sits down across from a patient, almost knee to knee, to find out how he's doing—*really* doing—by listening. As the patient pours out his problems—a strained marriage, a lost job, fear of a recurring infection—Fuller moves imperceptibly from physician to counselor as he tries to ascertain how he might help. A young gay man who has been coming to the clinic for eight years tells me that Fuller is his third AIDS doctor "and by far the best." The man checks in every five weeks and has been seeing Fuller for three years. A Protestant, he didn't realize for nearly a year that Fuller was a priest. "He never talks about it," says the man. "Now that I know it, I really like the fact that he's a priest. I think it kind of balances out the whole picture. I feel I have a more rounded view from him." I ask him what sets Fuller apart, besides his other calling. "His warmth, his sincerity, his manner. I trust his judgment."

Despite this patient's long HIV history, his health is good. Of course, for all the advances in the treatment of AIDS, most of Fuller's patients don't survive so long. (Within a year of my visit, the two patients mentioned at the beginning of this chapter were dead.) As a doctor who grows unusually close to these people, how does Fuller deal with their deaths? He upends my assumption. "In a funny way I think I'm reconciled [to their dying] as soon as I meet them," he says. "That's not true in a non-HIV situation." More important, he adds, is the enormous satisfaction he derives from helping patients live with HIV, as increasingly they do. And when they draw down, "It's also very satisfying to help people die well. I don't mean suicide, but help them decide how they want to do it—around family, [so] that comfort is maximized, that people don't do it alone. Dying is always sad, but it's also comforting to know that they're doing it the way they want."

That kind of compassion, not to mention his expertise, keeps Fuller in demand as a liaison between the Church and the AIDS community. Fuller is working not only to improve the Church's pastoral efforts, which he says are definitely on the rise, but to spur discussion where AIDS issues rub up against Church policy and tradition. "I think the Church needs to remember that it can't simply move from other issues like contraception or drug use and apply those to the epidemic, without understanding that some broader work needs to be done," he says. For instance, condom use, anathema to Catholic teaching, prevents the transmission of AIDS. So does needle exchange, but the Church doesn't want to be accused of promoting drug use any more than it would promiscuity. Dilemmas, Fuller concedes, but ones he says must be confronted, as the Church has done before. "I think there are analogies in history where we've had to face very hard-nosed, gut-wrenching realities, where both sides of the question were challenging our fundamental views," he argues. He points specifically to the American bishops' position on nuclear weapons. The prelates obviously opposed nuclear war but came out in support of American deterrence because they believed, given the situation, that was the only way to ensure nuclear weapons were in fact never used.

The AIDS crisis also has exacerbated the Church's dilemma concerning gay and lesbian Catholics, who weary of their alienation. For two thousand years, the Church has declared homosexuality evil, based on biblical injunctions and its own teaching that sexual relations are moral only between a married man and woman. In the wake of the gay rights movement, that community's fight for acceptance within the Church has at times been contentious, as seen in the Act Up! disruptions of Cardinal O'Connor's Masses and the now annual free-for-all over the right to march in New York's St. Patrick's Day parade. Yet beneath the acrimony it would seem some amelioration is occurring. Theologian Richard McBrien points out, for instance, that the new Catholic catechism, while maintaining that homosexual behavior is "intrinsically disordered," also says that gays and lesbians "do not choose their homosexual condition" and "must be accepted with respect, compassion, and sensitivity."

A less visible but equally important part of Fuller's ministry is working with priests who have HIV and helping the Church come to grips with that once "untouchable" subject. While it's not exactly the kind of thing statistics are kept on, Fuller estimates that in the past decade there have been one hundred to two hundred priests who have died of AIDS, have it now, or are HIV-positive. Fuller said he got into this area as an offshoot of his regular AIDS work and came to appreciate the particular concerns that confront the affected ministers. "Especially in the early years they were *really* on the outside," he says. "They were scared to death—afraid their superiors would find out, worried about what would happen to their health insurance, and so on." At some early conferences, he recalls, "ministers testified with bags over their heads, they were so terrified of being discovered."

That kind of fear has abated, though not completely, he says, and the Church is increasingly sensitive to the handling and care of these men. Fuller's efforts on this front include making sure the men are acknowledged and helped, trying to keep their situation from being lumped together with the pedophile scandal (they're two distinct problems, as most pedophiles aren't gay), fighting the impression that all HIV-positive clergy are gay, and helping develop testing policies and procedures. As for prevention, the doctor says the Church is doing a better job in the "psychosexual development" of its priests, but that an even greater priority must be placed on young men in formation, especially in "helping them grow into and sustain a healthy celibacy."

After a busy morning in his company, I ask Fuller if he ever feels schizophrenic. He says no, he does not view his two roles as contradictory. Indeed, he believes that *all* good doctors are spiritual in that they are interested in their patients' whole being. Still, doesn't the AIDS scourge ever shake his faith in God? Again, no: "I think if my faith were going to be shaken," he says, "it would be by the enormous poverty in the world, not by AIDS. This pales in comparison. So if I can live with that . . ." His voice trails off, because he hasn't meant to imply we *should* live with poverty, only that, as Christ said, we apparently always will.

Before I leave the hospital, a woman physician who works with Fuller makes a point of pulling me aside, discreetly, to make sure I am aware how much his colleagues cherish him. She tells me that he's an inspiring teacher who created a valuable primary-care model for doctors working with AIDS. She then tells me that one of their colleagues at the clinic had recently died, of AIDS, and that "Jon conducted the memorial service with the same kind of sensitivity that he does everything else." After a bit more unsolicited testimony about Fuller's dedication and his apparently inexhaustible energy, she says simply, "He's my hero."

◈ Father Charles Fuld

Rare as it is to find a priest who's a physician, it's perhaps even rarer to encounter one with grandkids.

After a decade as a priest, Father Charles Fuld might have figured the novelty of his story would have worn thin by now, but judging from the number of people who continue to ask him about it, that's not so. "I've gotten used to the interest people have in a grandfather priest," says the man who turned to the cloth after raising a family and putting in twenty years with the navy. "I see myself not as a curiosity but as a sign of hope and acceptance to the many others who find themselves at a crossroad." Fuld says he knows there are other widowed priests out there; he's met one or two, and besides, the day I talked to him he had received E-mail from a colleague proposing they get up a kind of club—informal, if by definition exclusive.

Fuld, sixty-three, is pastor of the Church of the Resurrection in Escondido, a growing community north of San Diego. To help deal with the large (twenty-six hundred families) parish, he has a church family that includes a newly ordained associate pastor, three deacons, a parish council, and numerous active committees. As for blood kin, Fuld has two daughters and a son—all in their mid-thirties, all married, all living close by. And those grandchildren? There are five, Fuld says, each one a joy.

In fact, the hardest part about a job Fuld otherwise relishes is the limited time he has for them. "I think the thing that I miss most [about the lay world] right now is the sense that my grandkids are growing up. Very often I'm so committed here that I don't have time for them," he says. On weekends, a normal time for other grandparents to indulge the grandchildren, Fuld generally has a full schedule of Masses, baptisms, and weddings. "I think families need grandfathers. I never had one, and I don't want to be an absentee."

Fuld is an articulate man with a ready, self-effacing wit. (He allows, for instance, that being a priest provides convenient cover for his spotty memory for names: "I always tell people, 'You really don't want a priest who remembers *everything* you tell him, do you?'") As it happens he came to his Catholicism in as roundabout a fashion as he did the priesthood. Born in New York City, Fuld was raised in a foster home by a German immigrant family in the Bronx. They formally adopted the boy when he was nine— shortly after the United States had entered World War II. "They spoke German at home," Fuld says of his parents, "and the one thing I knew was that I didn't want the other kids to hear me speak with a German accent." Deciding he'd better learn to "speak American," he hung out at the movies and patterned his speech after the actors on the screen. Indeed, there is no trace of Germany, much less the Bronx, in his speech, which is the firm, flat voice that might belong to a television broadcaster.

The Fulds were nominally Catholic if not especially devout. Charles Fuld would not really begin to practice his faith until he married in 1956. His wife's name was Elaine. "We met in the Loews Paradise Theater in the Bronx, where she was an usherette and I was an usher," he tells me. "The problem came up when I decided to get married to this young lady. She was Irish, and her mother was *very* Irish. So I came back to the Church largely to marry my wife. I think I learned more about my faith for my wife and my children."

By then, Fuld, who had graduated from New York University, was a freshly minted ensign. After washing out in an effort to be a navy pilot ("At that stage of my life, I had never even driven a car," he admits), Fuld moved on to ships. He would spend most of the next two decades in positions of increasing responsibility, eventually commanding salvage ships off Southeast Asia during the Vietnam War.

Chuck and Elaine Fuld had three children in quick succession. They were a close family even though Fuld spent literally half his military career at sea. Then, in 1969, as Fuld was on the verge of leaving for another tour of duty, tragedy struck. Elaine, thirty-five, suddenly developed an ailment that baffled her doctors. "When my wife was complaining about pains, the bottom line was they could find nothing wrong," Fuld recalls. "The night before she died, her lead doctor said 'It must be psychological,'" because Fuld was about to ship out. To this day he doesn't know what killed her. All these years later there's a slight quaver in his voice as he revisits her memory. "When my wife died, I discovered she had saved all my letters," he says wistfully. "I still have them. Every letter I ever wrote."

Fuld shipped out after sending his children, then ages six, eight, and nine, to live with their aunt and uncle back in New York. When that tour ended, he returned to California and brought them home. "We learned how to cook and take care of each other. It wasn't easy," he says. "That's why we've always been very thick, my kids and I."

Fuld reached a crossroads of a different sort in 1975 when he retired from the navy and faced the prospect of what to do next. He had become more involved with the Church, enough that one option that unexpectedly occurred to him was the priesthood. He tried to dismiss the idea—"That would be trading one uniform for another," he told himself—but it persisted. He decided to let the possibility marinate for three years, during which time he worked as a district executive and newspaper editor for the Boy Scouts of America. Meantime he took a few classes in religion and theology at the University of San Diego, a Catholic college, to see how they felt. Finally he decided to apply to the local seminary. He was forty-five at the time. "They were rather mixed about the whole thing," he says. "They had never taken on an older guy before. It took me a while to get accepted."

And what did his children think? "By then the kids were starting to do their own thing," he says. "I figured that I'd shown respect for what they'd wanted to do, that they could do the same for me. And they did." If there was some mild surprise on their part, they were so tied up with their own career decisions that no one made an issue of his, unorthodox as it seemed. "I remember my son asking me, 'What shall we call you—"Father Father"?' We laughed and I said, 'No, just "Dad."' He said, 'OK, Father Dad.'"

Fuld was ordained in 1986. He was fifty-three, an advanced age even in a time when more Catholic men than ever are coming to vocations after long civilian careers. As a new priest, Fuld tackled five jobs in his first six years, including editing the San Diego diocesan newspaper, before coming to the Church of the Resurrection in 1992. As we discussed his transition from the lay to clerical life, I asked if it had been difficult deciding to give up intimate female companionship. He said yes, telling me that after Elaine died he did eventually see other women and nearly married again. "But it just didn't work out. I don't know why. Maybe the answer is I never stopped loving my wife. I still wear my wedding ring. More likely, the Lord had something else in mind for me."

Being celibate is difficult, he concedes. However, "I find living that commitment is a lot easier for somebody who's sixty-three years old than for someone who's a young priest. I frankly would find that to be very difficult, to become a priest at age twenty-four or twenty-five and make that kind of decision. I have tremendous respect for young men who make that kind of commitment. But it's a *commitment*. It's like saying I'll be a husband and that I'll be faithful to my wife for the rest of my life."

As that rare person who has lived both sides of the proposition, does Fuld believe priests should be able to wed? No, he says, he simply doesn't consider it a viable option. To those who argue that Protestant ministers marry, Fuld respectfully points out that they often have fewer demands and smaller congregations than many parish priests, and besides, more than a few of their marriages don't survive the strain. "I think the commitment to marriage is huge," he says. "The commitment to the priesthood is huge also. Combining them into one state would create an impossible situation. Now, I realize that it's a big stumbling block for [potential priests], the fact that they can't get married. But I can't see any way realistically that they could do both things and do them adequately."

And what of the argument that having raised a family gives him more real-world insight, in turn making him a better priest? "I don't buy that," he fires back. "I don't think I'm a better priest than anyone else. But I *do* think that each of us brings unique experiences to the priesthood. Every priest does that. Some have the experience of coming from big families. Another priest brings with him the great Irish heritage of a deep Catholicism. Somebody else brings along a great business background. Somebody else brings a marriage. Those are all useful, but I don't think any one of those is more valuable, or better, than any other."

Fuld loves his new life, even when it's hard to love. "There are plenty of those days where you sort of throw your hands up and say, 'Hey, is *this* the navy I joined?' You find yourself sometimes so busy taking care of administrative things that you find at the end of the day you haven't spent any time in prayer. But by and large those are rare. Most of the time I find myself totally excited by being a priest and a pastor."

And the kids? They're happy for him, too, even if thinly veiled family experiences turn up now and again in Dad's homilies. Fuld cites the time his daughter was pregnant going into the holidays. "I of course had told people about my daughter and all the adventures of pregnancy from my point of view," he says. Then on Christmas Eve she brought the newborn to Mass, where Fuld introduced them to the congregation. "She was very embarrassed. Nevertheless, she stood and held up the baby. I tell you, it was like presenting the Christ child. Everyone was touched—including this very proud grandfather."

▣ Father
James Conner

AVA, MISSOURI

The drowsy town of Ava, seat of Douglas County, is in south central Missouri, almost to Arkansas. If you take Highway 5 south about twelve miles, you'll hit Highway N. Go east on N for nine more miles, swinging back and forth through the fickle grades of the Ozark Mountains, and you'll find Highway OO. Go north about a mile on OO, or about the point at which the asphalt gives way to rock, and you're at Assumption Abbey, a Trappist monastery carved out of a thick stand of mountain pines. The small abbey, built of block and stone, is low-slung and contemporary in design. Father James Conner, the genial superior, tells me that of the twelve Trappist abbeys in the United States, Assumption is considered the most remote. I can well believe it.

I make it just in time for the start of Lauds and Mass, the ritual of chant and liturgy held each morning at six-thirty. By this time the monks have been up for more than three hours, already having conducted Vigils (prayers that are recited rather than sung) and having had a bite of fresh-baked wheat bread for breakfast. Their spartan chapel is small and square, with white-painted walls of concrete block that the monks manufactured themselves years ago when block making was their chief means of support. Seventeen monks reside at the abbey, two of whom are hermits and so not at Mass. The other fifteen file in from behind the plain cedar altar, around which they form a kind of broken horseshoe, half to the left and half to the right. Each man wears a simple white alb with a hood, set off by a long black garment that hangs front and back. This cloth, called the scapular, is an adaptation of an apron the monks' forebears wore centuries ago.

Two of the men would seem to be in their late twenties or early thirties; the others all are in their sixties or beyond. Each takes his place behind a freestanding wooden lectern, which stores his missals, hymnals, and psalm books—Assumption's version of traditional monks' choir stalls. They consult red vinyl binders for their chants, a dozen or so of which are intoned before and during the Mass. Anyone expecting the rich, reverberant sound of the monks on the best-selling *Chant* albums might be disappointed, as there aren't enough of them to replicate that kind of sonorous tone, not to mention that this rustic space is better suited to contemplation than music making. Still, their mingled voices produce a lovely effect, as when, after communion, they sing the dozen stanzas of "The Song of Zachary." To a visitor, the (mostly) bearded and robed clerics look like the men they are singing about when they proclaim

> *"As he promised by the lips of holy men,*
> *those who were his prophets from of old."*

The Trappist order traces its beginnings to La Trappe, France, where in the seventeenth century a band of Cistercian monks launched a reform movement so that they might lead lives more rigorously patterned after St. Benedict's monastic "Rule of Life." The Rule essentially calls for strict adherence to prayer, poverty, obedience, daily work, and, by tradition, silence. Unlike other Catholic religious orders, which operate in the lay population to serve as teachers, missionaries, hospital administrators, and caregivers to the poor, the Trappists are a "contemplative" order—which is to say their lives primarily are given over to prayer and devotion, in the relative isolation of this abbey. As the Trappists are a cloistered community, most of the monks will never leave the grounds but for a dire emergency. For the most part, their human contact with the outside world is limited to the occasional visitor.

Assumption itself was founded in 1950. A wealthy Chicago businessman who was impressed with the Trappists contacted their nearest abbey, in New Melleray, Iowa, and offered to donate his Ozark property east of Ava for a new monastery. Thirty of the New Melleray priests and brothers came down to get Assumption started, but it was hard going. Because the property was mostly ledge, it couldn't grow the kind of crops that have traditionally sustained monasteries. The monks tried a dairy, then a vineyard, but those failed, too. Then someone realized that Bryant Creek, which snakes through the property about a mile downhill from the abbey, provided more than enough sand and gravel to manufacture concrete block. That grueling business was profitable enough, and in 1970 the monks built the complex they now inhabit. Ten years ago they gave up the block business, which had become less economical and more exhausting for the aging men. Now they support themselves by producing a popular fruitcake, one that, Abbot Conner confides with a smile, "a lot of people think is one of the best—and I say that without prejudice."

The sixty-four-year-old Conner is a shy, soft-spoken man with an unruly thatch of silver and gray hair. He came to Assumption in 1994 when his predecessor had fallen ill, and he was formally elected to the superior's position a year later. As head of the abbey, Conner has responsibilities that range from making sure the light bill gets paid to counseling the thoughtful young man who, perhaps drawn by the same brew that enticed Conner himself years ago ("a lot of idealism, a lot of romanticism"), thinks he wants to exchange his loose-fit Levi's for the robe. The abbot is his community's point man in dealing with the larger Trappist organization, the Church generally, and the secular world. His primary charge, however, is overseeing the spiritual life and commitment of his brother monks.

Born and raised in Tulsa, Oklahoma, Conner from a young age was interested in becoming a priest. But why a monk? He pauses a moment, reaching back a half century to reconstruct a teenager's thought process. "Diocesan priesthood had sort of the best of the lot," he explains. "You were still in the world, you still had your own life to live, you had your own car. The rectory was not your own in one sense, but in another sense it was. All that. I just felt like I wanted something more radical than that. Then I began to look at the religious orders, and it was, again, a mixed bag, in that you had something of both [worlds]. So that was why I suppose the Trappists appealed to me when I heard of them. It seemed like the radical thing to do. I was drawn to that."

Conner was introduced to the Trappists by a popular book of the time, *The Man Who Got Even with God*, whose author, Father Raymond Flanagan, was a monk at the Trappist abbey of Gethsemani, in Kentucky. After high school Conner joined Gethsemani as a novice, and he was ordained there in 1957. Throughout Conner's seminary years and first decade as a priest, his existence was as ascetic as we still imagine monastic life to be. The men had the tops of their heads shaved in the Friar Tuck tonsure. Strict silence was observed at all times; a monk was allowed to speak only to his confessor and the abbot. There was no contact with the outside. Indeed, a monk never left the abbey, even for a death in the family. As with so much in the Church, the reforms of the sixties loosened things up somewhat, even in the cloisters. Today the tonsures are gone, and occasional family visits are permitted. While the Trappists still observe "the Great Silence," which is roughly between eight in the evening and eight the next morning, they may communicate freely otherwise.

Silence was never a vow per se, Conner tells me, merely a traditional part of their discipline. That particular liberalization was necessitated by the advent of modern machinery and technology in their work. Supervisors had to speak to be understood, and in time the rules were modified to allow anyone to speak during work time. Finally, in 1968, the Trappists authorized general communications among monks without special permission. Which is not to say that today the men of Assumption are what you would call chatty. In fact, Conner told me they still have workshops on effective verbal communication. "We're getting more adept at it," he says.

Even so, to this day some of the men aren't comfortable with free expression; the older monks especially tend to remain reserved. But even they can surprise you, Conner says. Occasionally, for a special event or feast day, the abbey will cap off work with pizza and beer and some entertainment. "And one of the brothers, who's one of the most somber and quiet within the community, he comes out with his guitar and his harmonica and sings these old hillbilly songs he learned as a kid," Conner says. "He can be the life of the party when he gets going."

Of the seventeen men in the Assumption community, six are priests and eleven are brothers. (There are also seven women hermits who occupy a remote corner of the grounds.) In monastic orders there has historically been something of a class distinction between the priests, who are ordained, and the brothers, who are not. Brothers were responsible for more of the manual labor than the more-educated priests, whose duties typically involved the ritual prayers and chants. In yet another modernization, the Trappists have essentially done away with that distinction, so that both priests and brothers are considered monks of full rank, as it were.

Certainly at Assumption they share equally in an austere and highly regulated life, one that centers entirely on prayer and work, as St. Benedict maintained it should. The monks rise each day at a quarter past three. (When I asked Conner if one ever gets used to that, he said with a kind of sigh, "Well, yes and no . . .") At three-thirty are Vigils, at six-thirty Lauds and Mass. Terce (for the third canonical hour), a short prayer, is at eight-thirty, after which everyone heads off to work. Sexth (sixth hour), another short prayer, is at eleven-forty-five, followed by a communal lunch, the main meal of the day. (The meal is accompanied by a reading, which Conner says can be about theology, Trappist business, or most anything. During my visit they were in the middle of a biography of C. S. Lewis.) After lunch the men have an hour or so of private time. At two is None (pronounced with a long "o"), another short prayer, and then it's back to work. Vespers, the main evening prayer, is at five-forty-five, followed by a fifteen-minute period of meditation. The monks pick up supper on their own, and at seven-forty is Compline, the last canonical hour of the day. The monks may retire any time after that. Most are in their spartan cubicles by eight or so.

The abbey has one television, in the reception area. The men don't watch it, although it can be used for instructional or inspirational videos. Conner says a few of the monks have radios in their rooms, mainly for news, but none is for community use. The abbey gets the weekly Ava newspaper, as well as *Time*, *U.S. News and World Report*, and various other periodicals for its library. Conner says the men attempt to stay abreast of what's happening in the world and within the Church. A few also retain a strong interest in sports, but that can be frustrating considering that they're deprived of regular scores. Conner was reminded of a story from his years as chaplain for a community of Benedictine nuns in Oklahoma. "The [mother] superior there was from St. Louis, and she was a very *avid* St. Louis Cardinals fan," he says, the memory prompting a grin. "So whenever the baseball season came along, especially if they got into the World Series, she would be praying for the Cardinals. Well, I sort of objected to her about it; I thought it was out of place. So then she started praying for *all* the cardinals of the world."

The Trappists are one of the better-known monastic orders, in large part because of their most prominent member of recent times, Thomas Merton, the monk and writer who lived at Gethsemani. With his best-selling autobiography, *The Seven Storey Mountain*; his works of poetry; and his books on meditation, prayer, and monasticism, Merton remains influential among Catholics and non-Catholics alike. Gethsemani is about forty miles south of Louisville. When Conner first arrived there, in the late forties, it was already the largest Trappist abbey in America, with about one hundred fifty monks. The population peaked in the fifties at about two hundred seventy-five monks, but today there are only sixty-five. Conner initially became acquainted with Merton in the latter's capacity as master of students, or "Father Master," in which Merton functioned as a kind of mentor to the apprentice monks. The young men were fond of him not only for his aggressive intelligence but because he was friendlier and more empathetic than some of the intimidating principals of the abbey. Merton's conferences gave the young men a strong sense of themselves as people and as monks. "I've always said that one of the great graces of my life" was to come under Merton's sway, says Conner, who after ordination went on to spend several years as the older man's assistant.

In 1968 Merton was permitted to travel to Asia, where he met with the Dalai Lama several times and was able to explore personally the Eastern monastic traditions that had long fascinated him. In Bangkok he gave the featured address at a conference of superiors from Asian Christian contemplative orders, after which he retired to his hotel room. There, in a freak accident, he was killed when a faulty electrical fan fell on him. Conner still recalls hearing the stunning news back at Gethsemani. That day when the monks finished their communal meal, the abbot rose to address them—something that virtually never occurred. "We knew something extraordinary had happened," Conner remembers. "He made this announcement that he'd just received word from the embassy that Merton had died in Bangkok, but at that time he still didn't have any of the details about it. It was certainly a bolt of lightning for the whole community."

For Conner, the most remarkable thing about Merton was "his humanity. He was a very down-to-earth person. At the same time he was a very spiritual man." Where some of his brother monks were personally and intellectually unyielding, "Merton was much more alive, more human, thinking about possibilities." Perhaps most important for the monks, Merton's grasp and explication of monastic tradition made him an unequaled advocate, both inside and outside the abbey walls, for the monks' unique place in the world.

◈   ◈   ◈

For the priests, nuns, and brothers in Catholicism's religious orders, understanding their place—having a fixed sense of purpose—has never been more imperative. There are nearly one thousand orders active in the United States, but since the early sixties their populations have fallen more than forty percent, and many are flirting with extinction. This decline more or less mirrors a simultaneous falloff in the number of Catholic schools, hospitals, and seminaries in operation these days—institutions that in many cases the orders existed to serve. On top of that, the average age of the men and women who remain in religious orders is over sixty, and climbing. In other words, America's religious communities are confronting an identity crisis without parallel in modern times.

Religious orders have sprung up throughout Western history to meet particular needs, not only within the Church but within society at large. The hermits and holy men who took to the desert in biblical times were the forerunners of the monastic orders. (The Cistercians, the parent order of the Trappists, celebrate their nine-hundredth anniversary in 1998.) Mendicant orders, such as the Franciscans, arose in the Middle Ages to help those being left behind by the new mercantilism. Apostolic orders, such as the Jesuits, were formed in part to counter the humanism of the Renaissance and Reformation. Additional orders, including some in emerging areas like the Americas, surfaced to meet pressing needs for schools and hospitals, as well as education of the clergy. By 1962 the number of religious men and women in the United States reached its peak at more than 206,000. Of that number, eighty-four percent were nuns, ten percent priests, and six percent brothers.

But around this same time a variety of factors converged to begin the steady erosion of those ranks. Vatican II came and went without seriously addressing the role of the religious in the new lay-empowered Church, which left the orders confused (a development that seems to have been exacerbated by some symbolic changes, such as when many nuns abandoned their habits for civilian clothes). The feminist movement and the secularization of the culture helped trigger an exodus of women religious and a dearth of new members. Meantime thousands of urban parochial schools were closing in the wake of suburban flight. Catholic-run hospitals were being shuttered or turned over to the private sector. And the dwindling number of vocations meant fewer seminaries and convents were required. The upshot was that by 1995 the number of men and women religious in the United States was down to one hundred twenty thousand. Beyond that, the orders were greatly perplexed about their functions, not to mention their viability.

Against that gloomy backdrop a pair of DePaul University psychologists, David J. Nygren and Miriam D. Ukeritis, in 1990 undertook the most comprehensive survey of American religious ever done. More than academics, the two are themselves Catholic religious—Nygren a Vincentian priest, Ukeritis a sister of St. Joseph of Carondelet—and their aim was not only to assess attitudes within the religious orders but to devise some survival strategies. For their study, Nygren and Ukeritis got back extensive questionnaires from more than sixty-three hundred men and women religious, which they followed up in a variety of workshops and "visioning groups" (sort of ecclesiastical focus groups). They presented their findings to more than a thousand superior generals, or heads of religious orders, at the Vatican and published them in a 1993 book entitled *The Future of Religious Orders in the United States.*

Nygren and Ukeritis found that while most religious remain personally satisfied with their vocations and hardly consider themselves anachronisms, they are acutely aware of their parlous circumstances. The study concluded that if the orders are to remain viable, a variety of things must happen: middling leadership must be replaced; creeping materialism must be checked; "loners" within the communities must be brought back into the group dynamic; the charisms of the orders' founders must be revisited. (Every order has a charism, or guiding purpose, which is considered a gift of the Holy Spirit.) However, far and away the biggest concern Nygren and Ukeritis identified is that "a significant percentage of religious no longer understand their role and function in the Church."

In an interview I asked Nygren, who is an executive vice president at DePaul, to elaborate on this last point. He explained that in the wake of Vatican II many religious simply have experienced the sense of no longer fitting in. While this is true of priests, they at least have had their traditional ministerial and sacramental roles to fall back on. But he said nuns and brothers have felt particularly at sea, which no doubt explains why a much higher percentage of them have left their orders than their priestly counterparts. According to Nygren, the orders that will survive and prosper are those that, like corporate entities, can rally themselves to redefine and then commit to their roles in a changing world. For instance, if an order that was founded to build hospitals has pulled out of the business, it must identify some similar need consistent with its charism and aggressively pursue it—operating hospices, perhaps. Whatever it is, that need must be genuine, Nygren emphasized. "Many [charisms] are irrelevant because they don't respond to a real need that society cares about," he said. "They've got to be responsible to their charism, but are they doing something of recognized value?"

Nygren suggested that current reductions in government services might help some orders refocus, especially if working with the poor was part of their original mission. At the same time he reminded me that that's not what every order was established to do, and he cautioned that Americans shouldn't assume that religious orders (and charities) can step in to fill the void left by shrinking government expenditures. "To suggest that all orders should work with the poor or be involved in the social safety net is not to recognize the hand of God in all this," he said.

The Trappists, for instance, share their surplus with the poor, but as a contemplative order their charism is one of prayer rather than social work. Indeed, as Conner and I discussed the health of his order, I asked him how he would describe the value of an ancient regime like monasticism at the dawn of the twenty-first century. "Personally, I see it as being very, very essential," he answered. "When I first entered the monastery, the abbot at that time always used the image, almost ad nauseam, that the monastery can be a 'powerhouse of prayer,' the dynamo which was giving power to the whole rest of the Church and the rest of the world. I think that can be exaggerated, but fundamentally there's still a great deal of truth in it. Every prayer, whether it be by a monastic community or the prayer of an individual in his room at home, has a universal value and a universal effect." Beyond that broad impact, he went on, the value of monasticism to individual laypeople and nonmonastic clerics "is in just providing a place and an atmosphere and circumstance where they can come and begin to listen to their own heart, to be in touch with the Spirit speaking within their own heart. When people [would ask], 'How do I know what the will of God is for me?' Merton used to say, 'Simply listen to the deepest yearnings of your own heart.' I think if a monastery is able to provide an atmosphere and a place, an example and an incentive for that, then it can have a tremendous power and bearing on what's taking place."

In fact, Conner, who concurs completely with Nygren and Ukeritis about the need for orders to redefine their missions, believes the key to the future of the monastic orders can be found in the broader spirituality he sees moving through society—a movement, he adds, with which the Trappists are "very much connected." As part of this trend, he says, many monasteries, including Assumption, are hosting more retreats and entertaining more guests than ever. And Assumption for one fully intends to do more yet.

Conner believes the resurgence in spirituality is more than a rejection of pop culture or a response to rampant secularism. "I think there's a very general interest in Christianity in society, and specifically Catholicism today, and in the whole area of prayer and spirituality," he says. "You're constantly seeing advertisements for workshops and new books coming out on prayer and spirituality. A number of new lay associations are springing up, wanting to be associated with the monasteries. Personally, I see that as a very positive sign. There's a great deal of hope for the future."

❖   ❖   ❖

The fruitcakes made at Assumption Abbey are not quite as heavy as the concrete blocks the monks used to turn out, and they're infinitely tastier. The abbey sells about twenty-seven thousand cakes a year, including eight thousand through the upscale Williams-Sonoma culinary stores and catalogs. Showing me around the abbey's humble kitchen, Conner explains that the monks acquired the recipe from a St. Louis pastry chef who once worked for the duke and duchess of Windsor. I watch as a trio of monks, dressed in jeans and work shirts, go about their business. One man is hunched over a big tub to mix the batter, which is the color of light caramel and studded with fruit. Two others carefully ladle the mixture into ring forms for baking. As I peek over their shoulders, one monk turns and teases, "Welcome to heaven." I glance about me and say, "Who knew?"

In the next room back, two more monks take the baked cakes, by then a rich brown, paint on a syrup glaze, and decorate the tops with cherries and pecan halves. In another room the cakes are placed in white tins for shipping. Elsewhere in the building other monks in a cramped office are filling orders, arranging for deliveries, and handling all those related tasks familiar to any small business.

Before the monks discovered the joy of fruitcake, Assumption Abbey nearly closed its doors. A decade ago its population, once thirty, had dwindled to twelve. "There was very serious talk about whether it was really viable to continue here, or whether the place should just be closed down," Conner says. "But the community was adamant about staying put. They were very attached and dedicated to the place. So they managed to weather that. And now, hopefully, we're beginning to show new signs of life."

By that he means Assumption, like most of the Trappist abbeys, has finally taken on some new members after years of decline, and inquiries continue to come in. Indeed, Conner is so optimistic that he's trying to raise several million dollars for a major expansion and renovation of Assumption. To some extent the project is being driven by the cake business, which long ago outgrew the existing ramshackle operation. The renovation would create a new kitchen and offices as well as processing and shipping facilities. But the master plan also greatly expands the number of rooms available for guests and monks alike; the latter might even be equipped with plumbing, which the current quarters are not. The leaky roof would be rebuilt. The new facility might even have a garth, or courtyard, enclosed by a proper cloister walk. Ambitious stuff, but the monks hope to see it all in place by 2000, Assumption's golden anniversary.

Quite a turnaround for an abbey that not long ago was a candidate for extreme unction. On that subject, I ask Conner whether he ever thinks he belongs to a dying breed. "I think we've all had the feeling, since the [Vatican] Council in the sixties, that our generation will probably be a transition generation—that things will never be settled, or certainly never the same as they were, in our generation. But I think there's always been a sense that the phenomenon of monastic life, and the reality of monastic life, *will* continue in some form or another. It's just a question of what form it will take."

As the monks confront that future, Conner is aware that he must tread gently. "The whole dynamic of trying to do that can be very ticklish," he admits, because change is always scary, especially for a community that has operated more or less the same way for a millennium. So even though the monks take a vow of obedience, getting them to agree on something as ambitious as a master plan is no mean trick. Conner says he recently spoke with a fellow abbot who has been through several building programs of his own. The colleague advised ("half seriously, half jokingly," Conner says) that if you need to get a consensus within a cloister, "the only way to do it is to make it appear to the community that you're against it, and then they'll all be for it." Conner laughs heartily.

When we finish the tour, I ask Conner what the monastic life means to him personally. He reflects for a moment, then says, "It gives me the opportunity to be more in touch with the depths of my own heart and being, and to be in touch with what the Spirit is doing within me, and through me." In that sense, he says, the isolation is an invaluable gift.

I suggest that the tedium of such an existence surely must be a trial. "Always," he replies, this time without hesitation. "The standard temptation of monks, from the very beginning of monasticism back in the second and third centuries, has always been that of what they called the *taedia*, which is really tedium. Or what St. Bernard called 'the noonday devil.' It's just the idea that for every monk, particularly the ordinary people who are really living the monastic life, there *is* a sense of sameness, a sense of inevitably wondering at times, 'What am I doing? Why am I doing this?' Like the Scripture says, 'Why this waste?' That is a very real and crucial temptation."

So how *does* one deal with it? "Partly sweating it out," he says, "partly asking God for the grace and the help to go through it." And does it ever get easier? By the time a monk is, say, in his sixties, as is Conner, is he still battling the noonday devil? "Always," the abbot repeats, with a smile. "It's just like sexual life and temptation. We always tell the story of St. Alphonsus Liguori. Somebody asked him when he was an old man, 'When do sexual temptations cease?' And he said, 'Fifteen minutes after the undertaker carries you away.'"

▧ Father James Sullivan

NEW HAVEN, MISSOURI

A drive of several hours up Interstate 44 brings me to the fetching country-side of eastern Missouri, just this side of St. Louis. My destination is Holy Family Church, located eight miles outside New Haven amid the round-shouldered farmland that north of here gives way to the Missouri River. Holy Family was built as a rural outpost more than a century ago, and it's pretty much a rural outpost today, with only one hundred ten families on the rolls. On a Saturday afternoon I find Father James Sullivan training a handful of new acolytes, or servers, as they're more commonly called. These are the young people who attend the priest during Mass, and this kind of training drill, equal parts choreography and oral exam, has been going on in Catholic churches for centuries. Yet it's a discrete sign of these times that all four of Sullivan's anxious recruits, who look to be fifth- and sixth-graders, are girls.

Holy Family is not a large church, so by the time you account for the altar, the pulpit, the chairs for the presider and servers, and sundry tables for cruets and other paraphernalia, the sanctuary is rather cramped. Navigation is tricky even if you know your way. At first the girls—two of them identical twins—move about with the tentativeness of boot-camp recruits caught up in their first close-order drill. But as Sullivan walks them through the intricacies of the liturgy, he demonstrates an easy rapport. After an ersatz communion service, the priest, flanked by the twins, has a seat. "There's a reason that we sit right after communion, and it's not because Father can't think of what to do next," he says, prompting a giggle from the girls. "We're supposed to pray, right? To take a moment to thank God for this special gift."

So it goes for nearly an hour as the trainees take turns practicing their paces. When he thinks he's finished, Sullivan asks the girls if they have any questions. Meekly, one holds up her hand. "I've been here all afternoon, and I haven't gotten to ring the bells yet," she says.

"You haven't?" Sullivan replies. "Anyone else have something you didn't get to do?"

"I didn't get to pour the water between your thumbs," says one.

"I didn't get to do the towel," chimes another.

"Well, let's *go*, then," Sullivan says, delighted by their enthusiasm.

He brings them back up to the altar until each girl has rehearsed to her satisfaction. Then, before turning them loose, Sullivan remembers one last point. "If you're out here in church and right before Mass you see Father putting out the things the altar boys and girls usually do, that means he doesn't have anyone to help him yet. In that case you might want to come on up," he tells them. "That happens once in a while, especially at the Saturday night Mass."

This is isolated country. The western fringes of St. Louis are pushing relentlessly to meet it, but this isn't exurbia yet. Even so, most people make the forty-five-minute commute into the city to work; in farm country almost no one can get by on farming alone anymore. Still, the early-to-bed, early-to-rise regimen is in their blood. In fact, soon after Sullivan arrived as pastor he suggested to the parish council that Mass on Thanksgiving Day be pushed back to ten o'clock, as is often done in urban parishes, so that even those who wanted to come to church could sleep in. The council members looked at Sullivan as if he had just flown in from another planet— which in a sense he had. "Why? What would you do *that* for?" they told him. "We're up *way* before that."

A man of fifty-six, with a square build and a broad, open countenance, Sullivan has been pastor here for ten years. Though he lives and works at Holy Family, his pastorate includes a second parish, St. Gerald's, which is ten miles down the road from Holy Family in the town of Gerald. In the Catholic Church these days it's hardly uncommon for pastors to have more than one parish; some priests, with four or five rural parishes, are virtual circuit riders. This so-called clustering of parishes is a product of the priest shortage, as well as an effort by American bishops to keep small or failing parishes open as long as possible. However, St. Gerald's actually began forty years ago as a "mission," or auxiliary, parish, meaning the pastor lives elsewhere. It is not surprising that this situation at times engenders some low-grade parish envy. But of late St. Gerald's has grown a little larger than Holy Family, with a hundred twenty-five families. It also enjoys a more convenient Saturday evening Mass—five o'clock rather than Holy Family's seven-thirty. The lateness of that second Mass is one reason it is often lightly attended.

Nonetheless, the previous Saturday night the place was packed, Sullivan tells me. It was Holy Family's annual "deer hunter Mass," an event that quite by accident has become a local tradition. As Sullivan explains it, the opening day of deer season, on a Saturday, always draws thousands of hunters from St. Louis and around the state to this area. The hunters spend all that day in the woods and are anxious to get an early start on Sunday. Some years ago the more observant among them discovered the conveniently late Mass at Holy Family. Word spread, and soon it was SRO among the camouflage-and-orange-cap crowd. "Oh, yeah. They come right out of the woods," Sullivan says with a laugh. Their guns, and sometimes their fresh kills, adorn the pickup trucks that jam the small parking lot. A few years ago one hunter approached the priest before Mass and asked about buying a plot in the cemetery behind the church. The man explained he wanted it for his mother, who had grown up in the area and wished to be buried there. "He gave me a check," Sullivan says, "and there were bloodstains on it! I was going to ask him, 'How soon do you *need* this plot, anyway?'"

Jim Sullivan was born and raised in St. Louis, one of the midwestern cradles of Catholicism. He was trained in the archdiocese's seminaries, then worked as an associate pastor in various St. Louis County parishes. Holy Family–St. Gerald is his first pastorate; the two also represent the smallest churches he has ever worked at and the farthest he has ever ventured from home. Juggling two parishes, even small ones, can be hectic. Sullivan makes the winding trip down Highway C to Gerald and back at least once a day, and sometimes three times, for meetings, funerals, prenuptial conferences, confirmation classes, and the like. Two parishes means two sets of books to keep, two parish councils to consult, two bulletins to prepare, two congregational agendas to consider, and twice the paperwork ("There's so much of it it just drives me nuts," he laments). He gets part-time help with the accounting, but Sullivan can't afford a secretary. Even when he tries to recruit volunteers, he encounters a nettlesome fact of life that might be called Mayberry Syndrome: everyone around here tends to know everyone else's business. But Sullivan wouldn't trade the Mayberry pace of the place. He loves that when he hears confessions at St. Gerald's, he has to hang out a sign, like Lucy in *Peanuts*, to let people know the "Priest Is In." He particularly relishes the country solitude, a commodity his classmates in the big urban parishes can only imagine.

There's one other thing about being the only priest for two parishes: you say Mass—a lot. It is probably fitting that I catch up with Sullivan as he is going over the rudiments of the liturgy with the fledgling altar girls, because celebrating Mass is perhaps the most important and representative function a priest has, not to mention one of the most time-consuming. In Sullivan's case he says a Mass every morning (except Thursday, his day off), generally alternating it between the two churches. He has the two Saturday evening Masses, then two more Sunday morning. Throw in the occasional wedding, funeral, and holy day of obligation, and he averages ten Masses a week. Ordained thirty years ago, Sullivan has celebrated between fifteen thousand and twenty thousand Masses in his career. A load like that, increasingly typical for many priests, challenges their ability to keep the service fresh; it's hard to put enthusiasm into a liturgy you're conducting for the fourth time in less than twenty-four hours. On the other hand, the people in the pews, for whom the Mass is the centerpiece of their spiritual lives, will hear this particular liturgy only once. If the priest is simply going through the motions up there—and every Catholic has seen that—their experience is diminished.

Sullivan and I discuss this reality at length. "It *is* a challenge," he admits. "You'd like to do more than just *say* Mass—just kind of spin it out, you know." He reminds me that not too long ago priests weren't supposed to say Mass more than once a day; one reason was to keep the experience from sliding into drudgery. He says his private prayer life is important to keeping a fresh outlook on the liturgy but adds that "on my day off I don't say Mass at all. Partially that's because I want to be a little bit renewed when I get back to it again. I really do think that when you celebrate Mass you try to put yourself into it. You try to really make it meaningful. But it does get to be impossible after a while, when you have to repeat that much. It's been all right, but I sure get tired by the time I'm finished on Sunday."

At its most elemental, Mass is the ritual reenactment of Christ's Last Supper. Yet it is also a Catholic's source of connection: more than popes, more than saints, more than shifting doctrines, this ancient act of reverence and remembrance is perhaps the single strongest thread tying Catholics to one another and to generations of forebears. Still, "going to church" becomes such an ingrained part of Catholic life, and at such an early age, that many of us—even those in that forty percent or so who attend with regularity—never stop to contemplate what the Mass actually stands for or why it is constructed the way it is. Formal worship can become something that we do by rote, like memorizing the Hail Mary, and that we continue to do because, well, we're supposed to. Chipping away at that apathy is a priority for every committed pastor. That Saturday evening I have the opportunity to watch Sullivan conduct Mass at both St. Gerald's and Holy Family, and in the process I see how one priest tries to make it the solemn yet intimate experience it is meant to be.

Mass comprises two distinct parts: the Liturgy of the Word and the Liturgy of the Eucharist. The first part centers on sacred Scripture. The second is marked by the consecration of plain bread and wine into Christ's body and blood and culminates in the sacrament of the Eucharist. A liturgy can be short or long, plain or filigreed with rituals, tuneless or full of music (alas, too often unsingable modern compositions that seem to be supplanting the great hymns). But at bottom it is always the same. Each begins with the celebrant's welcoming the congregation and offering introductory prayers. This is followed by what many of us still know as the Confiteor (Latin for "I confess") but what is more blandly called the penitential rite. Herein the congregants admit their transgressions, after which they pray for forgiveness in the Kyrie. Through most of the liturgical year, this is followed by the Gloria, a joyful song of praise.

The people presumably having readied heart and mind for what is to follow, the actual Liturgy of the Word commences. I daresay for most Catholics this is their only regular exposure to Scripture. (The liturgical calendar is set up so that over the course of three years virtually the entire Bible will be covered at Mass.) In a typical Mass, lay readers, or lectors, offer two initial readings. The first is a passage from the Old Testament, the second from the New Testament (more often than not one of St. Paul's first-century letters to the Christian communities then forming across the Mediterranean world). Sandwiched between the readings is the Responsorial Psalm, which, as the name suggests, is a selection from the Book of Psalms that is prayed in a kind of call-and-response between lector and congregation. This sets the stage for the primary reading, the Gospel. Since it conveys the life and teachings of Christ, the Gospel is always read by a priest or deacon, and the congregation stands to hear it.

Next up is the homily, which is usually a parish priest's best shot at reaching his congregation on moral issues, to put across the messages of the readings in the context of contemporary life. Some priests are terrific at this, others dismal. In my experience most sermonizers fall into that great middle ground; they are adequate but uninspired, offering the laity ten- to fifteen-minute recapitulations of that day's theme but no real passion. (I was fascinated to learn there are sermon "services" that crank out boilerplate texts a priest can use if he hasn't the time or inclination to write his own.) Until very recently Catholicism has not embraced homiletics in the way, say, many Protestant traditions have, and it shows. Surveys consistently find that churchgoing Catholics want better preaching.

Sullivan is no Jesse Jackson, as he would be the first to admit, but he has a talent for preaching. It is important to him. Indeed, most priests sermonize only on Sunday, but Sullivan has at least something to say at each weekday Mass as well. Every cleric has his own routine for preparing a sermon, and I inquire about Sullivan's. "To be completely candid with you—" He breaks off, then grins sheepishly. "I use an electric shaver, and while I'm shaving I'm looking at [that day's] readings. And by the time I'm finished with the old buzz job, I'm thinking, 'Ah, I know what I'm going to do with that.' And I go back and make a couple of notes."

He will invest more time than that in a Sunday sermon, of course, but otherwise Sullivan's preparation is the same. By first light (like his flock, this shepherd is decidedly a morning person) he organizes his thoughts and writes out key points in longhand, on five or six sheets of plain white paper. Though this weekend's liturgy marks the feast of Christ the King, Sullivan decides to take his broader theme from Thanksgiving, which is only days away, and from the children's participation in Mass at St. Gerald's that night. When he does finally address the congregation, the priest has rolled the sermon around in his head quite a few times. Notes in hand now, Sullivan half reads, half declaims in a slow, almost stagelike delivery that punches certain words for effect. His style is one you seldom encounter in a day when most Catholic priests prefer a more natural approach. "We really don't have to wait till Thursday to give thanks to God," he tells his parishioners. "Tonight we have gathered here to offer Mass together. We remember that Mass is our most perfect prayer of thanks. We remember the very name 'Eucharist' means thanksgiving. So that's the main thing we do here every time we celebrate a liturgy."

There is one other noteworthy aspect to Sullivan's sermons: they are blessedly succinct. The one he delivers at St. Gerald's (and will reprise at Holy Family) is six or seven minutes, tops, and the audience is attentive. Sullivan feels the brevity works to his advantage. "People have a way of looking at me as I'm talking," he says. "They seem to be trying to listen. They know I'm not going to keep them too long."

After the sermon Sullivan leads everyone in the Profession of Faith, actually a recitation of the Nicene Creed, which since the fourth century has summarized the core tenets of the Catholic faith. ("I believe in one God, the Father, the Almighty, maker of heaven and earth, of all that is seen and unseen. . . .") The Liturgy of the Word then concludes with the Prayers of the Faithful, which are general petitions that the community as a whole, and individual parishioners, put before God.

Mass now shifts to the Liturgy of the Eucharist. The priest-celebrant moves to the altar, bare up to this point, making it the liturgy's focal point. This section begins with the Offertory, now called the Presentation of Gifts. Members of the parish carry forward cruets of water and wine, as well as gilt plates containing the wafers of unleavened bread (an echo of Passover) that later will be distributed at communion. Also at this juncture dozens of children file out of their pews to bring up their own offerings: canned goods and other packaged donations for the poor. Meantime Sullivan has moved on to the preparation of the gifts, which includes pouring some of the wine and a splash of water into his chalice. (Every priest has his own chalice, usually made of silver or gold to his specifications. When I was a boy these tended to be ornate affairs, rather like Hollywood's conception of the Grail itself. In our postmodern era, however, priests generally have opted for simpler, goblet-style chalices, like precious-metal versions of the rustic cups Christ would have used.)

The priest blesses the bread and wine and asks God to accept them. He leads the community in the Sanctus ("Holy, Holy, Holy"), then proceeds to the Eucharistic Prayer. Known until Vatican II as the Canon, it is this long prayer, proclaimed by the priest alone, that explicitly recalls the final Passover meal the night before Christ's death. As Sullivan goes along, his delivery is animated but solemn. Then slowing, he raises a single large host and once again intones the Lord's own admonition to his disciples: "Take this, all of you, and eat it: this is my body which will be given up for you." Genuflecting, he then turns to his chalice. Raising it, he proclaims: "Take this, all of you, and drink from it: this is my blood, the blood of the new and everlasting covenant. It will be shed for you and for all so that sins may be forgiven. Do this in memory of me."

This is the moment where one of the most profound of all Catholicism's faith mysteries occurs. The Church holds that upon consecration this bread and wine become the actual body and blood of Christ, his "real presence" among the faithful. As mentioned previously, a substantial majority of Catholics have come to consider consecration a symbolic act only, albeit a deeply affecting one. Nevertheless, for a priest it represents the fulfillment of his calling, the act he was ordained to perform in a direct line from the apostles. I ask Sullivan about that intimate moment and whether after thousands of repetitions it ever becomes commonplace. "Well, the presence of the Lord—that you're united with God in a very special way—that's all still very much there," he replies. "You know, when we were small kids, you were thinking in terms that God is circumscribed by the size of the host. But at the same time, the whole [Mass] is God giving himself to us in a more dynamic way—first through the Word, then through the Eucharist. In other words, God is there in many different ways, in many different aspects. So even though I do say, 'This is Jesus Christ, our Savior, the Lamb of God who takes away the sins of the world,' I'm well aware of the holiness of God, and the presence of God, at *all* times in what I do."

At the conclusion of the Eucharistic Prayer, the congregation stands to pray the Our Father, followed immediately by the Sign of Peace, during which parishioners turn to their neighbors and, with handshakes or hugs, wish them God's peace. This sentiment of peace is then reinforced in the Lamb of God prayer.

All the foregoing rituals, important in and of themselves, also lead up to what might be considered the liturgy's climax, which is the sacrament of the Holy Eucharist. The priest, today usually accompanied by several lay eucharistic ministers, invites the congregation to come forward to receive communion. With each host he declares, "The body of Christ," to which the communicant responds, "Amen." Prior to Vatican II, Catholics received the host directly onto the tongue; now they have the option of taking it in their hands, as most do. At many Masses they may also partake of the sacramental wine.

Once communion is finished, there is a moment for silent prayer, after which parish announcements are made or special business attended to. At St. Gerald's and Holy Family, for instance, it is time again to cast ballots for parish council members. At last everyone rises to receive the priest's benediction. "The Mass is ended," Sullivan declares. "Go in peace to love and serve the Lord."

▨   ▨   ▨

Every year the St. Louis archdiocese asks its pastors how they're faring, what they might like to do next, and when. Though Sullivan has been very content here, he imagines one of these days he'll move on. "I keep watching for signs that maybe the people would like to see somebody new for a change," he says. "But things have gone real well here in many ways, so I kind of have to keep weighing that, too. I see signs of growth in both parishes—new things happening." As an example he cites a popular Bible study group that was started at St. Gerald's by a new parishioner.

If and when Sullivan leaves, it will likely be to another small parish. It's not that small parishes are immune from the problems of the big ones; the difference is usually only one of scale. He still remembers the trauma at Holy Family when, shortly after his arrival, he had the sad job of closing the school. The parish had operated it for decades, but enrollment had shriveled to eighteen kids in eight grades.

On the whole, however, Sullivan simply has come to value what small-town ministry means. "I think I get to know the people better," he says. "I get to see the people, to know their names. I get to know the kids. I have direct contact with them. If somebody was sick, maybe I got close to them at that point. If somebody was getting ready for one of the sacraments, I got close to them at that point. I give instructions to somebody—all these are opportunities where you get close to the people, and I think that's really a joyful thing. With a bigger parish, these things happen a lot of times in much bigger groups, and there's not that immediacy. Like in preparing the first communion class—I visit the class myself three or four times. And I teach them how to make their first confession by using puppets." He smiles hearing himself say this, then explains: "I've been doing it since I was a young priest. We have all sorts of ridiculous confessions. But this way they learn the new rite of penance, which is conversational anyway, and they don't have to feel uptight about it. That ability to do that with these kids—one on one, and I'm still involved—is what I appreciate about being in a parish like this."

That Saturday night at Holy Family, people begin drifting in about ten minutes ahead of the Mass, filling up the old wooden pews from the back forward, as would seem to be a law of congregational physics. Sure enough, shortly before the service is to begin, Sullivan emerges from the sacristy to put out the cruets of water and wine. Then he lights the candles—not a server in sight. Once again he will be going solo.

Father Gregory Le Strange

FAYETTEVILLE, NEW YORK

Immaculate Conception parish in suburban Syracuse has been around for a century and a half, but its current home is an unabashedly modern creation. From afar, the circular church, adorned with a spidery crown, resembles a spaceship that has nestled into a wooded glade. Inside it has the feel of an elegant theater in the round. Window-walls surround the congregation, and on this crisp fall morning they afford a spectacular vista of the sugar and red maples afire in the distance. The theatrical feeling is enhanced by a mini-orchestra massed near the altar and by the way the pastor, Father Gregory Le Strange, not only welcomes us but, rather like an emcee, introduces himself, the lector, the cantor, and the homilist. I've never seen this protocol before, but Le Strange does it before every Mass at Immaculate Conception. "It's important for people to have a sense of who's who," he explains.

It's also emblematic of Le Strange's liturgical style, which is that of a confident, genial host. With outstretched arms he invites people to participate in the service rather than merely listen to it. The Phil Donahue approach, of course, is not for everyone, which Le Strange says is fine; indeed, he is thankful that, for now, there are still enough priests, with enough different styles, to give Catholics a choice. "People shop for the church they like. They should," he says. "I would never delude myself into thinking that everybody who lives in Fayetteville comes here. They don't; I know they go elsewhere."

Maybe, but most don't. In fact, the five weekend Masses at Immaculate Conception routinely draw well over four thousand churchgoers, or about the same number of people who live in this leafy, well-to-do community just east of Syracuse. The congregation, predominantly white, is more diverse when considered from an ideological standpoint, Le Strange says. There are parishioners who think he is changing the liturgy too fast—being in the forefront to use girl servers, say—whereas others want him to move faster yet. That's one reason the Masses are conducted in various gears: the Saturday five-thirty and Sunday noon services are standard, three-hymn affairs; Sunday's seven-thirty is no-frills; nine is a folk Mass with guitars, trumpets, and drums; and the ten-thirty features the parish choir ("phenomenal," the proud pastor says). At each, however, the celebrant embraces the congregation. "It's really important for me to make sure people feel welcome," Le Strange tells me after we've dropped by a post-Mass gathering for coffee and doughnuts, a monthly occurrence and yet another effort at congregational outreach and icebreaking. "Every parish is different in terms of its style of prayer. And yet you have to be yourself."

Gregg Le Strange is just shy of forty and looks younger. He is a tall, handsome man who reminds you of a trimmer version of the actor Tim Curry. He took over Immaculate Conception, one of the largest parishes in the Syracuse diocese, in 1994. Then just a year later he suddenly lost his full-time associate pastor. Given the shrinking number of active priests, Le Strange knew the associate was something of a luxury, but it was one he expected to have at least a few more years. (He says he knew it was trouble when "I got a call from the [diocesan] personnel director, who's a friend of mine, saying, 'Uh . . . , Gregg, . . . uh . . .'") As such, I saw this energetic young pastor as someone who could speak not only to the nuts and bolts of running a big parish but to how one tries to be creative in a time of shortage; he seems to be the clerical equivalent of private-sector managers who find themselves in "downsizing" environments.

The development has clearly made more work for Le Strange. But he contends that it hasn't been the trial most people assume. "People say to me all the time, 'How are you doing this all by yourself?' My response is pretty standard. I am not doing it all myself. I am doing it with twenty-two hundred other families. In two weeks we're having a liturgical ministers day—kind of a workshop/day of recollection for people who are lectors and eucharistic ministers, ushers, et cetera. There's like three hundred people in that. We have a hundred people who teach in the religious ed program. We've got people involved."

It's true there are fewer priests in the contemporary Church, he goes on, "but I am convinced that we have more ministers available. Far more than we ever had in the past. And while this is not a perfect parish, I just see the number of ways in which people minister the message of the gospel. Some people would no more come into the sanctuary to proclaim the word of God than they would jump off the Empire State Building. Others would find it terribly mundane to be over there setting up coffee and doughnuts for after Mass. But thank God we have enough people who recognize the value in both."

Despite the Gallic cast of his name, Le Strange's roots trace to Ireland, not France ("I'm sure someone swam across the Channel," he says). He grew up in Binghamton, New York, seventy miles south of here. "I came from a real strong Roman Catholic, Irish American family, in the best sense of all those words," he says. "My family took church seriously but were not terribly pious. There was never a question of 'if' we are going to church this weekend. It was just a question of which Mass. There were Sunday mornings when you would groan in your bedroom, 'Oh, I don't feel good, I'm not going to go to church today.' The response would quickly come back, 'Fine, then just plan on staying there all day.' Well, I mean, who would go to Lourdes when you can have a miracle like that of instant recuperation?"

He was a senior in high school when he began contemplating the priesthood, but his plans were by no means sure. As luck had it, that same year the diocese established a program at Le Moyne College, a Jesuit-run school in Syracuse, designed for just such undecideds. It afforded them a typical campus existence, but they lived in a house with like-minded candidates and priest-advisers who could field their questions. It was precisely the environment he needed at that juncture, Le Strange says. Unfortunately, it no longer exists. "I think the program folded because they weren't getting a lot of the guys going on from there," he says. "I still maintain it was one of the best things the diocese did."

Le Strange did go on, to seminary at the University of Toronto. While pursuing his theological studies, he made time for a kind of ministry that remains close to him: care of the sick. Both as a college student and seminarian, he worked in various hospitals and one summer took an intensive course at City Hospital in Boston. "That was a great experience," he says. "I spent half the time in class and half the time on the floors. I saw my first baby being born, my first autopsy. The reason I stayed focused on hospital work was that I have always felt that the Church, which can sometimes seem awfully big and impersonal and not very caring at times, should be none of the above when we're sick or someone we love is sick. That's why I've always thought that the [work] is real important—not only for hospital chaplains but for those involved in parish ministry." In conversations around the country, many priests told me that working with the sick and dying is perhaps the most emotionally grueling aspect of their job, and few are overly fond of it. Le Strange appreciates that, but its difficulty makes the work all the more critical to do well, he says. "You know, you've got to be really responsive. We've got a person now—one month ago this guy was doing construction work, fifty years of age, perfect health. Now they have just diagnosed him with less than three months to live. That was yesterday."

Ordained a priest of the Syracuse diocese in 1982, Le Strange served several stints as an associate pastor, first at a largely Italian American parish in Syracuse, then at a big suburban church. In 1992 he took advantage of the diocese's unusually generous sabbatical policy: after ten years a priest can have six months to travel and further his education. Le Strange spent six weeks in Israel and the remainder of his break taking classes at the University of California at Berkeley. He returned to what he calls a "village" parish in another suburb and was in that job a year and a half when the pastorate of Immaculate Conception opened up.

When a parish becomes available in this diocese, all priests are notified and anyone can apply. Before his ordination Le Strange had been a deacon at the Fayetteville church, and he had worked at a nearby hospital, so he was familiar with the parish. Yet excited as he was by the prospect of running such a big operation, he frankly didn't know whether he was up to it. Aside from the generic administrative challenges, Immaculate Conception has an elementary school with two hundred children and handles another thirteen hundred in its CCD classes, which offer religious instruction for Catholic kids who attend public school. Trying to sort things out as the deadline approached, Le Strange called the departing pastor, whom he knew, and asked whether he might drop by for a chat. As Le Strange remembers it, "George comes in with great gusto, plops himself in the chair next to my desk, and says, 'Well, have you written your letter yet?' I said, 'What do you mean?' He says, 'That's what this is about, isn't it? Well, there's only one [parish] you can apply for, and that's this one.' So I wrote the letter—knowing that I wanted it and knowing that I was qualified for it, but never thinking I would get it."

When he did, the familiar subtle waltz began: Le Strange's new flock began to size him up, and vice versa. "I am not real smart, but I am smart enough to know that you don't make a lot of changes the first year," he says. "You smile a lot." Gradually, however, he began to suggest new ways of addressing old problems. A good illustration is how he went about assembling a parish council. The old council was full of "wonderful" people, he says, "but by their own admission they had served too long"—twelve to fifteen years on average. When Le Strange allowed as how it might be time to introduce some new blood, most of the council members were grateful to step aside. Then he told the congregation, "I want an advisory body of twelve people who are committed to this parish. I don't need twelve new directors of maintenance. We have a director of maintenance, and he does a great job. I don't need twelve new principals for the school. We've got one; she's wonderful. But I do need twelve people who are prayerfully going to tell me what they see as being the direction of the parish."

He also didn't want yet another election, as that tends to favor longtime parishioners over newer and younger ones and sometimes creates hurt feelings. Instead, he invited all interested adults to submit their names, and Immaculate Conception would choose its new council—out of a hat. "People said to me, 'You're just going to draw names out? What if you get twelve women?' I said, 'Well, we could *elect* twelve women.'" More than sixty names were submitted, after which Le Strange met with the candidates to explain his goals and the demands of the job in detail. He said if any of them wished to withdraw, they could; only one did. Not long after, following a Sunday Mass and with a hundred or so people staying to watch, Monsignor Edward Ryan, a retired priest who lives at the parish rectory, pulled twelve slips from a hat. For his part, the pastor listened with relief as the names were called. "Boy, I couldn't have gotten a better deal if I had handpicked them myself," he says. "Four of them have been in the parish twenty years, four have been in the parish fifteen to twenty years, and the other four have been in the parish less than three. It was real diverse—some married, some widowed, some divorced, some single."

Le Strange also changed the way sermons were handled. Aside from introducing the homilist at the opening of Mass ("There has been no audible groaning," Le Strange tells me), he tries to rotate the job enough so that neither the priests nor the audience get complacent. At Immaculate Conception the duties generally are divided among Le Strange; Father Neal Quartier, who works at the diocesan offices but lives at the rectory; Monsignor Ryan; and another retired priest in residence, Monsignor James McCloskey. Once in a while the pastor even invites an outside lay speaker, a real departure from general Catholic practice. Recently, for instance, he had in the director of a Syracuse spiritual renewal program, a married father of four. "It may have been one of the best homilies we've ever had here," Le Strange says. Whoever has the sermon delivers it at all five weekend Masses. Although Le Strange may take two weekends a month, no one else has more than one. "I think it's good to give the people a break and to give the [priest] a break," he explains. "I know there are a lot of guys in parishes who preach every weekend. I can't."

If these were not exactly seismic changes, it must be remembered that in a parish, as in any close community, even small matters can be sensitive. Besides, the principles are the same. Le Strange contends there are three imperatives to successful change in a congregation. First is doing your homework. "Very important," he says. "Find out what is the teaching of the Church, what is the fine print. Oftentimes we get a lot of our information through the secular media, and not all the details of the teachings of the Church are always put forth." Second is educating the congregation: *why* is a certain change happening? "Little things," he says. "I know a couple of parishes that have gone through renovations in their sanctuaries and people say, 'Why didn't he move the altar out further into the congregation?' or 'Why don't the servers sit up next to the priest anymore?' There's nothing worse than coming into a place of worship that you are accustomed to, much like our own homes, and [finding] it rearranged." The last essential, he says, is to "always make these changes with charitable, compassionate hearts. I think it's real important to listen to where people are at and bring them to where you would like them to be. You can't listen enough. [But] that doesn't mean you should ever be afraid of making decisions."

Of course, the biggest change in Le Strange's life at Immaculate Conception, the loss of a full-time assistant priest, was not his doing. However, that triggered other changes, if for no other reason than to keep the pastor's own schedule manageable. Le Strange's day typically begins at five-thirty, and most weekdays he will handle the six-twenty-five Mass. After a full day of routine pastoral duties—Masses, funerals, visitations of the sick, school activities—and at an hour when other people are winding down, Le Strange's schedule heats up with meetings and appointments. Various church and school groups are convening (parish council; liturgy, social justice, and finance committees; school board; Parent-Teacher Association; Bible, confirmation, and baptism classes; etc.), and the evening hours are when he generally does his personal counseling, because that's when people can come. That means his day goes until nine o'clock, and often later.

Since the associate pastor shared many of those duties, Le Strange's first step was to ask his staff and the various parish committees for their help. One step they took, which left some parishioners "a little stressed," was to eliminate the Saturday morning Mass. Another was to chip away at the meeting load. Le Strange says, "One of the things I really pushed was that no meeting should go more than an hour. I said, 'Folks, we're all dizzy.'" He attends as many of the meetings as he can but has made clear to everyone that he can't and won't stay for the entire session (the only exception is the regular parish council meeting). Still, much of the associate's liturgical duties fell to Le Strange, because weddings, funerals, and anointing of the sick require a priest. "Now when somebody calls about a marriage," he says, "there's not a question of 'Whom should I contact?' They don't have any [choice]. That's it."

Spreading the administrative load allows Le Strange to focus more on personal ministry, which is where he, like most priests, would rather spend his time. A favorite example is the realm of marriage counseling. At a parish the size of Immaculate Conception, you can count on a wedding virtually every Saturday. "I mean, I have seen every kind of bridesmaid dress imaginable—the good, the bad, and the ugly," he says. The priest had long been bothered by what he regarded as inadequate marriage preparation on the part of many Catholic couples and a missed opportunity for the Church to reassert itself in people's lives. "I guess over the thirteen years I've seen and married an awful lot of people between the ages of twenty and thirty-five who have been on sabbatical from the Church," he says. "If they are going to come back, it's going to happen either at the time of their marriage or the birth of their first child. It's [been] too easy to get married, and too easy to get divorced."

So he puts a premium on working with engaged couples. Over the course of a year as a wedding approaches, Le Strange will meet with the couple five or six times. During my visit the parish also was about to launch a program for engaged couples to attend daylong workshops, where speakers and young married couples would talk about what married life really means. Le Strange tells engaged couples up front what he expects and the time commitment involved. He also tells them if they'd rather find another priest, he understands. "I've got to say that in thirteen years there were a few couples that did. And no regrets." As for the ceremony itself, "We never talk about [it] until six weeks before." Le Strange likes to do that by inviting the couple over to dinner.

In all this it should be said that it's easier for any minister to concentrate on the spiritual side of things when the material side is not an overriding problem. Immaculate Conception is a relatively affluent parish—the kind, Le Strange admits, that other churches sometimes look at and say, "Oh sure, all they worry about is credit cards and country clubs." He's sensitive to that impression and quick to refute it. "I mean, when my head hits the pillow I am thankful for the fact that I don't have to worry about where the money for the utility bill is going to come from." Indeed, much of what the parish takes in goes to charities, including shelters for battered women and homes for the poor. "Every month we have a food drive, and we get over a hundred brown paper shopping bags. We pass them out one week with a list stapled on it in terms of what [the charity] needs. All the bags go out, and all the bags come back full." And he says a few years ago Habitat for Humanity, which at the time was not really established in Syracuse, announced plans for one of its home-building "blitzes." As usual, the organization approached local churches for sponsorship. "I said, 'Sure, we'll be a part of it,'" Le Strange says. "So I turned it all over to our social justice committee. They just took the ball and ran with it. We were the only Catholic church—which I say with great pride but embarrassment—in the county that got involved with [the blitz]. There have since been a couple of other parishes that have got on board, but it's people from this parish, who are financially stable people, who were down there moving lumber, driving nails, putting shingles on roofs every morning."

Since a congregation can derive as much energy as direction from its leader, I ask Le Strange what he does to keep himself charged up. For starters, he says he makes a real effort to take some time off: at least part of Thursday and all of Friday. Like other people, he enjoys spending some of that downtime at home ("in here on a Friday morning watching *Regis and Kathie Lee* in my sweats"). But when the living quarters are part of the church complex, as is the case at Immaculate Conception, business headaches are always just a door away. "I am learning—it has taken me a long time, and I am *still* learning—that if I am taking a day off, I cannot go into the office part of the building," he says. Lately Le Strange also has resolved to get more sleep: "in bed by ten, lights out by ten-thirty." Before, he was getting only six hours a night, and he says, "I was finding that around two-thirty or three in the afternoon I wasn't worth much." As for the two ten o'clock television programs he enjoys (*ER* and *Chicago Hope*, unsurprisingly), "Well, thank God for VCRs."

In excellent trim, Le Strange also testifies to the value of exercise. Certainly he is the only pastor of my acquaintance who rollerblades, an activity he recently added to his jogging regimen, and he's a regular at the local health club. It was there, he told me, that he and another man fell into conversation one day while running laps. "He said, 'What do you do for a living?' I said, 'Oh, I'm a Catholic priest.' Boy, did *he* drift back all of a sudden! He got real winded and just sort of drifted back. But then he caught up and said, 'Are you really a priest? I didn't know priests ever did stuff like this.' I said, 'Oh, there's *lots* of them here. There must be three dozen priests who are members of this club.'"

◩   ◩   ◩

I first met Gregg Le Strange at the National Federation of Priests' Councils convention in San Diego. We were talking about the priest shortage, and I learned that he had done a lot of vocation work for his diocese and as such had listened to many young men who had at least considered the priesthood. He told me what one teenage boy had confided: it wasn't the idea of being celibate that frightened him but the prospect of growing old alone.

"I remember that conversation," he says now, as we sit in the rectory living room, a mute American League playoff game on TV. "And I remember the conversation with the individual involved." The whole question of relationships—or more specifically, the lack thereof—is one he heard often from such young men. "I guess a lot of times younger guys just don't see any significant relationships in the lives of the priesthood. It's not accurate, but that's the perception," Le Strange tells me.

"Unfortunately, some individuals only experience priests who are tired and growing old," he continues. "Obviously, there is a great fear that all of us have. But I think there are people who *are* growing old alone, because I think that for too many years in the Church, priest friendships weren't encouraged. They were discouraged. I can't imagine not being able to socialize with my family, my friends, with other religious and laity. I can't imagine that."

Why was that? I ask. Was it a question of avoidance of temptation? Partly, he answers. But it was also a matter of image. "I think—now this is just a supposition on my part—there was a quasi-official teaching that just being a priest would be enough to be fulfilled—twenty-four hours a day, seven days a week. I don't think that's realistic. I don't think a marriage can grow and be nurtured if the couple doesn't work at it, if the couple doesn't constantly bring into that relationship other interests and that kind of thing. The same is true with priests."

Aside from his other friends, inside and outside the parish, Le Strange belongs to a support group with six fellow priests that "through God's direction or dumb luck" has been together for more than twelve years. They meet once a month on a Sunday afternoon, first to talk about a predetermined book, movie, or magazine article having to do with some issue of faith or the culture, and then to have dinner. It's a time for debate, shoptalk, and relaxation. Much of their conversation, naturally, turns to the secular crosscurrents and their impact on young men who once might have followed them into the priesthood but no longer do. "We live in an age where sexual encounters are just"—he snaps his fingers—"you know, like going to market. I think a lot of potentially great relationships are really botched" by that sexual pressure, he says. And a lot of vocations: culture-generated expectations increasingly make the prospect of an ascetic lifestyle so alien as to be virtually unthinkable. The dearth of replacements means, among other things, that more and more demands will be made of Le Strange and his peers. At thirty-nine, he can handle them, but what about at fifty-nine? He admits to wondering that himself; indeed, one reason for his fitness regimen is that very prospect.

And what of the laity? Are we in the pews beginning to understand the shortage? Perhaps on an intellectual level, Le Strange replies, but he says it really doesn't sink in until it touches people directly. "This past week a longtime parishioner was in the hospital," he says. "The family called and asked that one of the parish priests come to visit. I don't think they realized . . . that there was *only* one." (He adds dryly, "It makes great committee meetings because now they're over rather quickly.") He then cited the recent experience of a Syracuse colleague, the lone priest at his church. One Saturday, not long before the evening Mass, he suddenly and violently came down with the flu. "There's no way he could possibly have celebrated three weekend liturgies, not to mention infecting other people," Le Strange recounts. "So, with all the strength he could muster, he went over and posted a note on the church doors explaining that he was sick and the times of the liturgies of other parishes." Thus did that particular congregation, he says, come to appreciate the precariousness of their situation.

But if this is a predicament, priests themselves must take some of the blame, he adds. Unlike men who were already ordained when Vatican II played out, those in Le Strange's cohort could see the statistics and read the actuarial tables. Yet for some there was a kind of denial, Le Strange says. "I certainly went to school with individuals who were moving toward ordination with the thought in their mind—mistakenly, I think—that soon into their priesthood the laws of the Church would change in terms of both married clergy and women's ordination." Though Le Strange says he didn't peg his own career or future emotional happiness on the occurrence of either of those things, he believes strongly that both issues must be examined and debated. "If we don't," he says, "some people are going to be denied the sacraments, which I think would be one of the greatest sins the Church could ever make." Even so, "It probably will not happen in our lifetime."

For now, the pastor moves ahead, trying to avoid what he calls the "trap" that snares many of his colleagues: becoming synonymous with his parish. As he explains, "One of the big red flags for me is when someone calls me or stops me on Sunday and [says], 'I would like my baby baptized at *your* parish' or 'have my wedding at *your* parish.' Or, 'Why haven't *you* fixed the air conditioning?' Well, it's not *my* air conditioning. It's not my parish, you know; it's ours." And the advocate of change believes it's good for pastors, too. As cozy a match as he would seem to be with Immaculate Conception, he asserts that no priest is ideal for all parishioners, for all time. "I am smart enough to know that not everyone likes the way Gregg Le Strange moves. Not everyone likes the way he celebrates liturgies, celebrates sacraments; not everyone likes the way he teaches or preaches. Hopefully the next guy will come in and be able to touch the hearts of those people." Then he adds, "I hope in twelve years we'll address that."

▣ Father Alfred Burnham

CULVER CITY, CALIFORNIA

Approaching St. Augustine's Church for the first time in my life, I nonetheless had the distinct sensation of having seen it before. Later I would learn that I probably had, perhaps many times. It seems that the stately church, situated down the street from the huge Sony-Columbia lot and convenient to four other Hollywood studios, has for years put in cameo appearances in television shows and movies. Says St. Augustine's pastor, Father Alfred Burnham, "Everybody wants to use our place. They're always calling up to say, 'Can we film in your parking lot?' And I usually have to say no, because we *use* the parking lot."

Indeed they do. Aside from its heavy Mass schedule (three services daily, six on Sunday) and the activity that attends an elementary school with more than three hundred children, St. Augustine's at any given time is apt to be hosting a meeting of the Knights of Columbus or its charismatic-prayer group or the local chapter of Alcoholics Anonymous. There could be a Filipino breakfast going on or a Cinco de Mayo celebration or a "citizenship day" for those in the neighborhood holding visas or green cards. The local contingent of French immigrants might be getting together, or perhaps this is the day the church is sponsoring a mammography clinic. Like Immaculate Conception in suburban Syracuse, St. Augustine's is one of those places where the Church is robust. But unlike the affluent New York parish, with its predominantly white congregation, the parishioners at St. Augustine's are white, black, tan, and brown. Half the congregation is Spanish-speaking, but the number of Asian parishioners—especially Filipinos—is surging, too. In other words, St. Augustine's looks a lot like the future of America, and certainly the future of the American Church.

Culver City, while incorporated, is surrounded by Los Angeles and is a kind of crossroads, geographically and metaphorically. A short drive in one direction is Hollywood; in another downtown; in another Westwood and

Beverly Hills; in another the international airport; in another South Central. Once a community largely comprising professionals and the middle class, many of whom worked in the film industry, Culver City today is more of a blue-collar area and home to a growing immigrant population. "It is really like a cross-section of Los Angeles," says Burnham, who arrived at St. Augustine's in 1993 and became pastor two years later. "There are Cuban refugees who have been here thirty years; they still hope someday that Castro will be gone. We have people from all parts of South and Latin America. The majority of our Hispanic population is from Mexico. But we have people from El Salvador, Nicaragua, Guatemala. And because the universities"—UCLA, Southern Cal, and various smaller colleges—"are close by, we have a population of students. That's a segment I have tried to address, because they really are an enthusiastic bunch. But I'm going after it kind of late." Many of those young Catholics have gravitated to surrounding parishes, including St. Monica's Church, which has experienced extraordinary growth in recent years in part because it *has* courted that sometimes disaffected constituency. The hip Santa Monica cachet doesn't hurt either, Burnham concedes.

Hip Culver City isn't (despite the presence of some first-rate coffee bars and an emerging high-tech corridor), but things are bustling as I visit St. Augustine's. It is a Sunday, a few weeks after Easter, and by coincidence the third anniversary of the riots that devastated Los Angeles when four of its police officers were acquitted of beating Rodney King. There is heartening irony, then, in seeing so many ethnic groups assembled in amity. The nine-thirty Mass looks as diverse as a United Nations conference. Close to a thousand people are here, filling about three-fourths of the capacious building. There is none of the high-church hush you find at many parishes; throughout the service babies squawk and toddlers carom in the aisles. Returning from communion, many parishioners rush up to various statues of Mary along the side aisles to say devotions. The Mass itself is boisterous and full of ritual. Four servers attend the celebrant, and their entrance processional circles the church twice. Ten huge arches define the large, bright space, graceful ribs that run the length of the nave, each coming to a point like a bishop's mitre. When everyone joins hands to recite the Our Father, the collective prayer rises until it gathers in the old man's hat.

Halfway through the service there is a baptism ceremony. Nine young schoolchildren—Priscilla, Candelaria, Alex, José, and five others—join their parents and godparents at the font near the front of the church to recite their baptismal vows and have their foreheads daubed with the anointing oils and water. Then, turning back toward us in their Easter finery, they hold aloft lighted baptismal candles and receive the assembly's vigorous applause.

At St. Augustine there is nothing stodgy about the Catholic faith or the congregation's manner of expressing it. "I can't take credit for it, because it was here long before I got here," Burnham says of this vitality. "There is a sense among the people that this parish is theirs, and they feel a part of a faith community."

Burnham, forty-six, has been a priest for twenty years. Born in Chicago but relocated to Long Beach when he was small, the priest regards himself as a native Californian. After grade school he moved into the Los Angeles archdiocese's seminary system, where he stayed until his ordination. Though he entered the priest track at the tender age of fourteen and came of age during the turbulent, turnstile sixties, Burnham says he never second-guessed his calling. "The only time I would have wavered was when my stepfather was extremely ill, and it became difficult for my mother to care for him," he says. "I was the only son living at home, so there was a time when I thought maybe I should leave seminary and work for a while and try to help my family out with the bills. But she persuaded me not to do that; she didn't want me to interrupt my studies. And my pastor found some sponsorship for me, so that helped relieve our burden."

Burnham began his pastoral work at a small parish in west Los Angeles ("small" by L.A. standards: fourteen hundred families). After that he was invited to return to his high school seminary to teach. He stayed twelve years, the last three as rector, whose duties essentially mirror those of a pastor. At St. Augustine's he inherited a sprawling parish of more than three thousand families. He has two associate pastors, while a third priest, an African who will return home at the completion of his studies, is in residence. Also on staff are a married deacon, a bookkeeper, a director of religious education, a director of adult education, and the principal and faculty of the elementary school and its after-school care program.

That kind of organization is necessary to oversee a big parish that, like its neighborhood, is in flux. St. Augustine's was founded in 1921, when its congregation was much smaller, certainly much whiter, and, relatively speaking, financially comfortable. A frequent visitor in the fifties was Bishop Fulton J. Sheen, that era's ecclesiastical superstar, who was a friend of St. Augustine's pastor at the time. Recent history, however, has been about change. As longtime parishioners age, some of St. Augustine's traditional fraternal organizations, such as the Legion of Mary, are "graying" out of existence; springing up in their place are such contemporary phenomena as charismatic-prayer groups and lay ministry organizations. The influx of immigrants and the loss (at least as a percentage of the congregation) of professional people have resulted in a drop in the parish's average household income. Burnham says he has also seen a marked increase in the number of families where both parents work.

These changes represent a new incarnation of American Catholicism, and St. Augustine's finds itself in the vanguard. The Church's new look is fueled not only by raw growth—Los Angeles has overtaken New York and Chicago as the largest archdiocese in the United States—but by changing populations and demands. Today about thirty percent of the American Catholic population is Hispanic, a figure that immigration and higher birthrates will continue to accelerate. But there has also been a surge in the number of Asians in the domestic Church, and not only among nationalities with Catholic traditions, such as Filipinos and Vietnamese, but from some non-Catholic communities as well, such as Koreans.

Growth like that poses obvious logistical problems, such as finding enough priests to meet the sacramental and liturgical demands of these new Catholics. But the new face of Catholicism likewise challenges pastors to approach their jobs differently than when homogeneous congregations were the norm. Today they must be sensitive to many constituencies. This means having parish councils that are representative of the entire parish. (Burnham is attempting to resurrect St. Augustine's council, which was disbanded years ago.) It means being sure to know and observe the feast days special to certain cultures. It means altering traditional ideas of social outreach. Hence St. Augustine's sponsorship of such informational programs as those devoted to screening for breast cancer and explaining how to become an American citizen. And the parish has redoubled its efforts on behalf of the less fortunate. For instance, St. Augustine's has operated a food program for poor families for twenty-five years; it has become so efficient that other churches in the area piggyback on it. "This parish has made a major commitment to helping the poor and the homeless," Burnham says, "and I think the people appreciate it."

While L.A.'s still largely Anglo priest population is working hard to meet the demands of an increasingly non-Anglo Church, Burnham says it's imperative that the booming new populations grow their own priests, a trend he is beginning to see. "As it is, people like me have to become bilingual and bicultural—tricultural, in some cases—to effectively deal with our communities."

I ask Burnham to elaborate on what a pastor must do to be effective in a "melting pot" parish. "There are two or three things that are probably key ingredients," he says. "One is having visibility with people and being approachable. Because I speak Spanish and my associate pastors speak Spanish and my deacon speaks Spanish, I consider us very approachable to the fifty percent of our parishioners who are Spanish-speaking. We understand we have cultures we're dealing with here; we try to be sensitive to them. We try also to address the community in our preaching. We have people who are more sophisticated—teaching college at USC, say—and also people who are just arrived from Central America. So we try to preach to our people in a way that is both approachable and authentic in announcing the good news."

Burnham, a stocky man with thinning hair and glasses, is a believer in outreach. After Mass he frequently can be seen working the aisles, making a special effort to chat up the young adults, in either English or Spanish. More broadly, he is networking with other denominations in the neighborhood. In fact, aside from his day job, Burnham serves as the ecumenical and interreligious director for the archdiocese. As such, he works with other faiths and organizations around L.A. and the nation. When we spoke, he had just returned from a meeting in New York between committees of the National Conference of Catholic Bishops and the National Council of Synagogues. Once that would have been a full-time position with the archdiocese, he says, but in this time of shortage, staff priests are moving back into the churches. Every Catholic clergyman is being called on to "wear more hats," he says.

For all the effort that goes into molding his ministry to a changing Church, and notwithstanding the diversity apparent in the pews, Burnham emphasizes that his central message never varies. "For me, the focal point is Christ, and the parish is based on the message of Jesus Christ and the person of Christ," he explains. "So I don't really feel like we're missing the mark. I'm not trying to run a corporation here with an eye toward profit. What I'm looking at is a community made of people who come from all segments: the poor and middle class; blue-collar workers as well as some who are university-educated; some immigrant people, with a wide variety of faith experiences. So the one central unifying experience is the Holy Spirit guiding people to worship. I have to keep Christ the center of the parish."

Of course, that can be particularly daunting when you labor in the epicenter of Western culture. "West L.A. is very materialistic," he says. "I mean, our teenagers could tell you the twenty-five top brands of lipstick, but they wouldn't necessarily be able to articulate the Ten Commandments.

"I believe that we priests have to be teachers and preachers of the truth, and we have to stand in opposition to all forms of deceit and indifference," he continues. "The big temptation for us would be to sail along with our society's ho-hum attitude about genuine spiritual growth and the sacrifices implied by living a holy life, being in the world but not of it."

At such times Burnham takes solace in the knowledge that he isn't fighting alone. He cites an episode from the Acts of the Apostles, when the disciples were arrested and threatened with death for spreading Christ's teachings in Jerusalem. A Pharisee, Gamaliel, admonished the chief priests to leave the Christian proselytizers alone. Burnham paraphrases Gamaliel's argument: "If this movement is man-made, it is doomed to fail. But if it comes from God, then you will be fighting against the Lord himself."

▣ Father
Camillus Ellspermann

ST. HENRY, INDIANA

While it would be incorrect to suggest that a young lady drove Camillus Ellspermann to the priesthood, she may well have pointed the way. His clerical career began in 1939, at the tender age of thirteen, when he turned up at a high school seminary. "I got sore at my girlfriend when she wrote me a snotty note," he tells me, a smile widening across his roseate face. "I said 'I'll fix her; I'll go to St. Meinrad.'" His beloved St. Meinrad, the Benedictine seminary and monastery where he studied for the priesthood and spent so much of his career, is only a few miles down the road from the small St. Henry's parish in southwestern Indiana. A restful and bucolic place, the village of St. Henry is situated two miles off the main road to Jasper, just past the Weaver Popcorn granaries. The tall, classic spire of the church is a focal point for miles in every direction.

When I drop by to see him, Ellspermann is about to celebrate his sixty-ninth birthday, and St. Henry's is the kind of light-duty parish where a priest can ease into retirement. But as it happens, it's also a growing parish. When Ellspermann arrived a few years ago, there were just over a hundred families on the rolls; now there are nearly one hundred fifty. "It's not *my* doing," the pastor is quick to assert, explaining that the situation has more to do with the locals' less transient nature these days. His parishioners are about what you'd expect of country people: conservative, trustworthy, friendly. As we spoke, mothers were dropping off children at a volunteer-run day-care service at the parish center next door. "Oh, they're good people," Ellspermann says, shaking his head, "*good* people."

Unlike the other priests on my itinerary, Father Camillus (as everyone who knows him calls him) is an acquaintance of some years. I can't say I had known him well, but I'd been around him enough to appreciate him as an unusually thoughtful and kindly man. He is a placid presence, with his silvery white hair and spectacles, and almost demonstrably soft-spoken. Perhaps that's why he surprises me with the vigor of his feelings this day.

Turns out he had surprised himself, too. "It's only been since I've been here, at St. Henry, that I realized how angry I was," he says. "People—the religious hierarchy and people in the Catholic communities—do not see how priests today are being chewed up and spit out by multiple demands that are made upon their time, their energy, even upon their spirituality. They're not seeing that [the priesthood] is an impossible situation that is being asked of men in today's Church and today's world." If the words are strong, the tone isn't. His intensity is plain, but Ellspermann's calm voice never rises. It merely bespeaks sadness and concern.

Ellspermann isn't referring to his situation at St. Henry's. Rather, it seems he is still coming to terms with that difficult period in his life that brought him here in the first place, in 1991. For nearly fifteen years prior to that, he was pastor of St. Benedict Church, what was then the biggest parish in Evansville, the diocesan seat for this corner of Indiana. Running St. Benedict's was a pressure-cooker of a job, one that ultimately exacted a toll on him. By chance this tense passage coincided with the height of the pedophile scandals, which torpedoed clerical self-esteem and credibility, and with the sudden decision of several of Ellspermann's young colleagues to leave the priesthood. As a result, the discouraged pastor suddenly found himself navigating the darker side of the contemporary priesthood, where even good, dedicated men flirt with doubt and burnout. With time, I am happy to say, his outlook would be repaired considerably. But his concerns for the priesthood, which he fears is being eroded "to the point where the institution is gone," are no less acute. "I say it because of my love for the Church, and I say it because it needs to be said in all honesty. And I'm not the only one saying it."

In 1939 Camillus Ellspermann could never have imagined invoking such sentiments. He didn't even know if he wanted the priesthood, and the priesthood certainly didn't know if it wanted him. When he stumbled into the seminary as a boy, it was a time in American Catholicism when there were so many vocations that not every candidate was permitted to go on to ordination. And on the face of it, the young Ellspermann didn't seem an auspicious prospect. He grew up in an Evansville family with ten children, two of whom died in their youth. A middle child bent on getting attention, he was a self-described troublemaker with little use for school. Yet he had a strong influence in his oldest brother, Leo, who had also gone to Meinrad and became a priest the same year Camillus arrived. (A younger sister, now married, was a nun for sixteen years.) Somewhat to his surprise, then, the boy found that he loved Meinrad—the people, the regimen of Latin and Greek, the solitude, even the monkish discipline in which talking after dark was, literally, sinful behavior. "The [seminary] high school . . . was my salvation," he says, "because it was either going to be the priesthood or penitentiary for me—and that's no exaggeration." That first Meinrad class was and remains a tight group, Ellspermann says proudly. "Of thirty-one freshmen in high school, fifty percent of us were ordained priests. And of that group, only one has left the priesthood. In our day that's something. That's unbelievable."

Meinrad became the center of his world. In 1945 he entered the monastery there, and after five years of formation he was ordained a Benedictine priest (in May 1950, eleven years to the day after his brother). It was there that he taught sociology and theology off and on for nearly twenty years, and during Vatican II he worked on committees that successfully advocated treating the seminarians less like monks-in-training and more like regular college students. For seven years, he traveled to other dioceses as director of a deacon internship program he helped develop. Finally, after a quarter century spent in the service of the institution, he mentioned to his Meinrad superior that he thought he was ready for some parish work. He figured to land a small, rural parish. Instead, in 1975, he went to St. Benedict's as an associate. The next year he became co-pastor, and the year after that pastor.

"I was almost ecstatic with the privilege of working with so many people, of seeing [them] respond to the vision of Vatican II," he says of those heady first years. Often before, he had pinch-hit for parish priests, but he found being a full-time boss both exhilarating and sobering. "I learned to pray on a personal level in a manner that I never had before, even in the monastery. I learned insights into theology from people's lives that I had never gotten from books. I was forced into examining my own belief in eternity because of helping people prepare to die and burying them. You reach a point quickly in parish work where the rubber hits the road, and you have to say, 'What *do* I believe personally about all this?'"

Ellspermann had inherited a good situation at St. Ben's, as the parish is familiarly known, and for a long time he was energetic enough to enjoy all aspects of it: the children and the school, the various parish committees and fraternal organizations, and the large recreational component (bingo, basketball, baseball). "It was complete fulfillment," he says. For years, the centrally located St. Ben's not only was the largest Catholic church in Evansville but the most well-to-do. By the time Ellspermann arrived, however, many of its more affluent families were moving to newer homes, and parishes, on the edges of town. The school's enrollment began to decline. Some poorer families in the parish couldn't really afford to send their kids there. Other families who could, and who were interested in St. Ben's as an alternative to public schools, didn't belong to the parish.

In retrospect Ellspermann considers the "golden age" of his tenure there the early eighties. He can't really cite a turning point, saying only that things began to change "imperceptibly" so that by the late eighties problems were developing. On the personal front, he was by then into his sixties and losing energy even as the demands of the job were expanding. He grew weary of refereeing the internal disputes (e.g., who gets the gym Tuesday night?); he says some days it felt like he had exchanged his collar for a striped shirt. Life's balance—between work and recreation, peace and anxiety, dialogue and prayer—was something he had always cherished at St. Meinrad and in his early years at St. Benedict's. Now things were out of balance.

Ultimately, though, the major rub was a sharp debate that arose over the elementary school and its place in parish priorities. The fundamental issue, he says, was "whether you were going to use a 'contractual' relationship to the church—you put your money down, you get your education, you get your spiritual service, *that* model—as opposed to the model of: this is a parish, this is a faith community, these are the people of God, our first priority in a parish is the spiritual life of the people." Ellspermann was strongly committed to the latter model, yet with each passing year he saw mounting "divisiveness" between adherents of that view and those with the "let's keep the school open at any price" mindset. Many of the latter were parents who were well intentioned, he says, but myopic about the greater good of the parish. "It isn't school as school," he explains, emphasizing his lifelong commitment to Catholic education. "It's one-third of the parish getting the benefits of efforts of three-thirds of the parish. Many people have their children in Catholic schools—and I'm not the only one who feels this way—simply for the discipline, the education, and then accidentally for religious formation. And that's not right. It is *not right* in terms of distribution of assets in the parish."

Spinning out of this situation were increasingly tough and unpleasant decisions he was forced to make. A case in point: "For two summers, I interviewed families with [school] applicants, sometimes six a week. It was just a meat-grinder. You'd talk to people who didn't belong to the parish or who were single parents, who had children with physical and emotional handicaps, and you had to say to them, 'No, because you're not members of the parish.' This type of clash and tension, and where the money went, value-wise, really began to get to me and to tear away at my personal identity as a pastor. I know this now. I didn't know it then."

In the end, Ellspermann says, things simply reached a point where he realized he couldn't be a pastoral minister for all the administrative demands and the school tensions. He was unhappy and felt ineffective. His stamina was ebbing, and he began to worry about his health. "I just never resolved it," he says of the dilemma. "Well, I resolved it by leaving.

"I don't want to make the parish a scapegoat here," he emphasizes. "I hope you understand. I'm just trying to identify the factors" that prompted his angst. The problem was not people but "the system," he maintains. On the other hand, "where [the experience] touched priestly ministry—the sick, the children, religious education, the dying, baptism, marriages, counseling—I didn't regret one second of it. I loved it, and I miss that."

This is a familiar priestly refrain today, according to Father Philip Murnion, director of the National Pastoral Life Center in New York. The center's primary aim is to help priests in parish work. This it does in a variety of ways, including conferences, workshops, tapes, even personal counseling. But its best-known means of outreach is an award-winning quarterly magazine, *Church*, which goes to almost half the parishes in America and deals with everything from the mystical side of the priesthood to standard songs that should be in any parish hymnal. Murnion is highly regarded in clerical circles as a kind of "pastor to pastors" (my words, not his).

Murnion told me that experiences like Ellspermann described are increasingly common and symptomatic of a post-council priesthood still in transition. Today's pastor has so many agendas to juggle—those of his bishop, the chancery, his ministerial staff, (often) a school, the parish council, and the congregation, to name a few—that his own feelings and priorities can get pushed deep inside. Like Ellspermann, Murnion doesn't point accusatory fingers at any one segment. But he says the modern expectations of the people in the pews have definitely contributed to an anxious climate. "Parishioners are more challenging than once was the case," Murnion says. "[Pastors] might more likely use the word 'demanding.' They have their own notions of what they want and their entitlement to what they want. We have a whole culture of entitlement in our country; if you want something, you are entitled to it. So they direct that at the parishes. It's very tough."

Pastor burnout is real, he agrees, though in his experience "it comes not from the amount of work one has to do but from the *kind* of work one has to do. It's to the extent that they are involved in work that's very management-oriented or that they don't feel trained to do." Time after time Murnion talks to parish priests who say they are exhausted from dealing with Church bureaucracy or finances or parish politics. But challenge these same men with "real ministerial opportunities"—he cited the popular Renew programs, which are work-intensive, three-year efforts at spiritual renewal—and "suddenly they are not so tired. Priests who before [said] they can't take on another thing will take on those things. Suddenly they are dealing with . . . the central questions and feel like they are opening up the power of the people."

As for Ellspermann, well, St. Henry's, with its slow pace and open spaces, leaves a man plenty of time for introspection. He indulged in long walks in the countryside and secluded himself in the prayer room of his rectory. As the sociologist in him gradually worked through what had happened at St. Ben's and why, the minister in him determined to pay more attention to younger colleagues and friends. Many of these are big-church pastors themselves and therefore grappling with some of the same issues Ellspermann was. He worries about these men. The support group he belongs to once had ten members; now there are seven. Two younger men in the group abruptly decided to leave the priesthood altogether. It saddened him terribly; one of the men in particular "was like Christ himself," Ellspermann says. "They [know] the mean age of priests, and they can project themselves into that future, and they don't see the personal dimension of priesthood being possible like it was when we were younger priests." The best thing Ellspermann can do now, he figures, is offer advice when it's asked, and support regardless. "When you get to be my age, you realize that you've pretty well lived your life and you can't be that crusader out there anymore. You just can't affect certain institutions. You do what you can, where you are. That's where I am now—and probably a little more effective."

The worsening shortage of priests makes him shake his head. "We'll be like the dinosaurs," he says. Ellspermann finds the raw numbers—how in ten years there may be only one priest for every three thousand American Catholics—intimidating enough. But not long ago a colleague in the support group, one who likes to crunch numbers, put the problem in truly chilling perspective, because he brought it home to southern Indiana. He charted the priest decline in the Evansville diocese, where we all live and where there are more than seventy parishes. In the past twenty-five years, the number of active parish priests here has fallen from one hundred eighteen to eighty-two. Should this trend continue unchecked, it is projected that by the year 2020 there will be forty priests for nearly one hundred thousand Catholics in this area. By 2045 there will be exactly *two* priests in the entire diocese. By 2050 there will be none.

Some months later I happen to bump into Ellspermann at a party. It is just after Christmas, and I am glad to find him in much improved spirits. He reports that he had recently been back to St. Ben's on several occasions, for weddings and other social affairs, and the feelings had been warm all around. He is at peace with everything, he says. "I finally was able to come to terms with all that anger."

That turn has helped restore his natural optimism. For all the pain of losing friends and associates, for all the shocks the priesthood has sustained, Ellspermann believes it's happening for a reason. "My own personal feeling is that it's the work of the Holy Spirit. That over these years the dross has been burned out in the furnace, that the gold is being purified." He says that's not a commentary on those priests who left, some of whom made "absolutely the right decision." But he says, "Sure, we've lost numbers in priesthood, but the counterpart of that is an accepting of a sense of responsibility on the part of the people of God, the laypeople in the Church."

He says the Church has moved from what he calls the "Bing Crosby model," where Father was respected just because he was Father, to one where he has to earn that respect based on example. "That is a good change, but it's a shocking change for some people. In priesthood—and I have the deepest respect for the young men who go into it as they see it now—you're really walking the Way of the Cross with the Lord. That's the way priesthood has always been. But it's like learning to be the good, sacrificing parent. It ain't easy. And so the priesthood is being purified," he says.

"This is the bottom line: to hang on, to try to give witness in a time of transition, in a time of pain, in a time of purification. Not to be too abrupt. To try to encourage those persons who are faltering for running out of energy, not faith."

◈ Deacon
Daniel Leary

EMMITSBURG, MARYLAND

Each summer during his college career at Villanova University, Daniel Leary, though an English major, worked as an intern at the accounting firm Coopers and Lybrand. When he graduated, in 1990, he was invited to join the company in the field of health care consulting. So here he was: a regular guy, with a great job in downtown Washington, D.C., and room and board at his parents' home in the upscale environs of Bethesda, Maryland. "Yeah, I led a very social, active life," he says. "I dated a lot. College is a very self-ish time; so is the time right after college. If you want to do something or go somewhere, you do it." As is evident in that observation, however, life was not entirely copacetic. Seven or eight months after picking up his diploma, when Leary might have been his most carefree, he was spiritually restless.

"I wasn't away from the Church per se, but I was away from the sacraments—which is the same thing, but not to me at the time," says Leary, who is last of six siblings. During that season of Lent, which his father observes by trying to attend Mass daily, Leary began going with him. As he did, his outlook gradually metamorphosed. "I began to have the feeling that God was calling me," he says. "It was like a path that he was laying in front of me." His father gave him a rosary that Leary's grandmother had brought with her to America from Ireland. "I began to pray that rosary. The inclination got stronger. And little by little, I believe God started to clear my mind. What he said was, 'I've been calling you; will you listen? Will you just come and try this? Come and see.'"

Today Leary is a fourth-year student at Mount St. Mary's in Emmitsburg, a national seminary with more than one hundred fifty candidates for the priesthood. It's actually his fifth year here; the first year is considered pre-theology, followed by four years of theology. A fourth-year student is finishing up his training, with advanced studies in such subjects as the Pauline epistles, homiletics, and sexual morality, as well as practicum

courses in celebrating the liturgy and sacraments. Last June he was ordained a deacon. Next June he will be a priest. On a journey that once
seemed impossibly long, the days now "are moving very quickly."

Dan Leary is twenty-eight, but with his wire-rim glasses and enormous
smile he looks closer to twenty than thirty. While there's no such thing as a
"typical" seminarian, Leary might be viewed as representative of some contemporary trends: he came to the vocation later than his predecessors, after
some outside career experience; his theological outlook is more traditional;
and he has the kind of enthusiasm more often associated with eager young
athletes: he's anxious to get in the game. He has seen and heard plenty of
stories like that related by Camillus Ellspermann. Intellectually, he understands the demands awaiting the relatively few young men coming out of
America's Catholic seminaries today—about five hundred a year, or half the
number there were three decades ago. But he reminds me that the Church
has survived previous periods of weak vocations. And his excitement is palpable.

Then again, enthusiasm is endemic at Mount St. Mary's Seminary. The
picturesque campus, located just south of the Pennsylvania line and only
miles from the Gettysburg battlefield, is built into the foothills of the Blue
Ridge Mountains. It's so serene that it's hard to work up worry. "There's
great hope here," Leary says. "This place is going nuts with vocations."
The seminarian's life revolves around two things: study and prayer. Devotion to the seminary's patroness, Mary, has been especially important since
the school's founding in 1808. Here, unless a seminarian is headed for the
gym, he'll probably be wearing his clerical black. Says Leary, "If you ask
these guys, 'Do you have a rosary on you?' I bet you ninety-five percent of
them will."

Leary was born and raised in Bethesda, part of the Archdiocese of Washington. He attended high school in Rockville, Maryland, at Georgetown
Prep, which is operated by Jesuits, and went on to Villanova, run by Au-
gustines. The men of these orders were strong influences, Leary says, but
not as much as his parish priests, role models he will try to emulate when
he, too, becomes a diocesan priest somewhere in greater Washington. The
influence of these men "was never anything incredible—you know, knock-
you-down breathless. It wasn't television priests at all. It was their simple,
day-to-day caring for the people. When you're in grade school, they come
to the baseball games, the football games. They give you a blessing after
serving Mass. They take you out for pizza." On further reflection, however,
Leary says their service "*was* incredible, because each of these men let me

know the joy of their vocation. Were it not for their joy, following Christ in his footsteps would have been much more difficult."

Still, priesthood was hardly a lifelong goal. "I have to say that I'm not what's called a lifer. You know, the four-year-old kid who as soon as he can stand up can practically say Mass. I never was like that." The calling wasn't some mystical event ("It's like a mosquito in your ear—you can swat it, and it will go away, but it always comes back") and didn't arrive until that post-collegiate epiphany. Even when Leary yielded to it, he didn't know whether it would lead to ordination. "More than anything else, I knew that God would be with me, forever."

The decision thrilled his parents. His brothers and sisters had some initial misgivings but came around. Many of his friends were caught off guard, he admits, the women apparently less so than the men. "They were, well, sur-prised but not surprised, you know? They'd say, 'Dan, we'd seen that side of you.'" No one tried to change his mind, and in fact within weeks of his announcement friends were asking Leary to perform their marriages and baptize yet unborn children. His stock reply: "Let me make it through the first year of seminary, and then we'll talk."

Since Leary's decision came just as the pedophile scandal was surfacing, I wondered whether its ugly implications had given him pause. On the con-trary, he says, the scandal made him more resolved to go on. Why? "Be-cause people didn't understand who went into priesthood. They thought priests were kind of 'hatched.' So I was never intimidated."

After passing a gauntlet of tests and interviews designed to gauge his mo-tivations and determine his emotional and psychosexual stability—screen-ings that have become much more rigorous in recent years—Leary was di-rected by archdiocesan officials to Emmitsburg. Mount St. Mary's is no cloister; in fact, it is run in conjunction with Mount St. Mary's College. But the setting, the prayer, and the slower pace work changes on the men as "the grace of God begins to take effect," he says. The secularism and self-absorption of the outside world subside. Goals can change, too. Leary says he first was driven by a desire to "do good." Now he wants "to bring Christ" to people. The difference? "I mean [Dr. Jack] Kevorkian can say he's doing good, but he has no right to take a life. So that is the key: to start with Christ and the Gospels, and then go out" into the world.

Outsiders can appreciate a spiritual calling in a young man, but it's harder for them to fathom his making a commitment to be celibate for the rest of his life. Leary only formally took the vow of chastity when he be-came a deacon, though as seminarians they live the discipline. Leary considers celibacy an intrinsic part of the priesthood, "but it isn't easy, I should make that clear, if we only see it as a rule." As they learn to live as celibates, Leary says he and his colleagues talk about it, yet they minimize television channel-surfing and try to sidestep other sources of temptation. But "one of the most important things is to develop a serious prayer life and a relationship with a spiritual director," another priest who helps them with the struggle. Prayer, Leary says, is "a great source of peace" that enables one to make sacrifices. By that he means intense prayer, preferably spent before the Blessed Sacrament. "Let God talk to you," he says.

"It's a very spiritual thing, and I don't know if I really grasp it," he continues. "I think it takes a very long time. Instead of seeing it as a negative, we have to see it as a great gift, a gift from God given to man to bring others to God." Does he worry that other young men and women will think that he is, well, weird? No, he insists. Celibacy "makes me available to everybody. And I think people understand when someone is making a sacrifice for them." Indeed, Leary believes his friends have come to understand more about "God's gift of sexuality through this gift" of celibacy. He has his doubts about whether a married clergyman could be as effective, but he doesn't even dwell on the possibility. He says that would be like joining a football team hoping the coach will be fired. "Why waste the time?"

As he surveys the environment he's about to join, the seminarian doesn't seem to fear the demands that will be made of him, except to the extent that they may impinge on prayer time. Much more troubling to him, it seems, is the ideological fighting going on in the Church. "It's a little bit disheartening," he says. "[People] want to change things, and that's not the role of the Church. That's not what we're supposed to do. Before you know it, nobody knows what we believe, what we stand for. A case in point is Catholics for choice. Now, that goes against the basic tenet of the Catholic Church in supporting life as a gift from God. If that's what you really believe, fine. But don't call yourself Catholic, because that is not what Catholicism is all about."

Leary maintains that the shouting in the American Church is more about control than religion. "I think what happens is that those who have their own agenda are the ones who have lost their desire to pray. There's a great desire for power. You know, the pope is the servant of all—especially this one. He will be remembered forever for his work with the families, his dedication to the poor, and his role in supporting women."

A year from now Leary hopes his work will be more about parishioners than politics. It would be easy to focus on the problems before today's seminarians, he says, and sometimes they themselves do. He passes on a story one of his instructors ("a very holy priest") told him. In it, a young seminarian seeks out the advice of a wise abbot to unload his complaints about how things are going with the priesthood. After listening patiently, the abbot replies, "Well, I have an idea. You work on you, and I'll work on me, and then there will be two." In other words, numbers don't matter as much as commitment, Leary says. "And that is the attitude priests have to have. It's not a numbers game. Each soul is vital. Each soul waits to be brought closer to Christ. So what are you doing for that soul today?"

Father Egbert Figaro

CHICAGO

More than fifty years ago, Egbert Figaro had *his* heart set on the seminary. Like a lot of precocious, serious young men of his time, he had been encouraged by his Catholic elders in Atlantic City, New Jersey, to pursue the priesthood. Unlike those contemporaries, Egbert Figaro is black. "Oddly enough, even though the diocese of Camden now has ten or eleven black priests, in 1940-something, when I applied, they said they didn't need them," he tells me. "They didn't want them. I was turned down by many diocesan people. I was turned down by many religious orders. The Holy Ghost Fathers were doing ministry on the weekend and touring the city, and that was almost my last outreach."

The Congregation of the Holy Ghost, better known as the Holy Ghost Fathers, was founded two centuries ago to do missionary work in Africa. Since that time the order essentially has been in the service of black Catholics, including in the American South and at various schools and colleges around the country. Figaro's parents were from Trinidad, where his father was educated by men of the order. After the older Figaro prevailed on two of his former instructors, the Holy Ghost Fathers agreed to accept the son on a trial basis. Not only did he pass his apprenticeship, Egbert Figaro was ordained in 1951 and would become one of the order's most distinguished educators. His has been a life devoted to tipping over barriers and helping prepare other young people of color to do the same.

Now seventy-one, Figaro is assistant pastor at St. Mary Magdalene Church in Chicago. The immediate neighborhood is a pleasant oasis of modest but tidy homes amid the general dishevelment, even squalor, of the greater south side. Until the sixties this neighborhood and its parish were made up almost exclusively of Polish Americans. The closing of the steel mills triggered their exodus, and now the area is mostly Hispanic. There are also African Americans and Haitians at St. Mary Magdalene, as well as some Poles who never left. With the dearth of diocesan priests, the Holy Ghost Fathers took over the multicultural parish about ten years ago.

Figaro's order is affiliated with the nearby Catholic Theological Union, a seminary that trains young men destined for certain religious orders. In the brick rectory behind St. Mary Magdalene, Figaro lives with a handful of other Holy Ghost Fathers and some of the seminary's faculty members and students. He is a short, lean man with close-cropped silver hair. Figaro's deep and resonant voice betrays the slightest hint of his West Indian lineage. As he recounts the events that shaped his life, including the bruises, there is no bitterness in that voice. This was just the way things were, his even, dignified mien seems to suggest—in America and in the Church.

When Figaro's parents immigrated to Atlantic City shortly before he was born, they joined a small group of black Catholics there. "We were not too welcomed in the white church," he says, and in time a mission church, St. Monica's, was established for them away from the white parish. It was "a separate-but-unequal kind of a thing," Figaro remembers. His parents, devout Catholics, saw to his religious education. But when time came for high school, Figaro was one of a handful of black students selected to integrate a previously white-only Catholic institution. While the young man understood the importance of the example he was setting, he admits, "It wasn't a very pleasant experience."

In a country and time where segregation was the law in the South and a fact of life everywhere else, the Church was no haven from the ugly practice. When he was a young man, Figaro says, there were black priests, but they generally went into the Society of the Divine Word, which had its own seminary for black candidates. Black Catholics were steered away from mainline orders. I ask Figaro whether the discrimination caused the young man to reconsider his vocation. No, he replies, merely to refocus his thinking. "I was no longer interested in integrating [certain clerical ranks] or anything like that. But if I could become a priest and come back to my own people, at St. Monica's, or to a black community or a black mission . . ." The bias he encountered in Catholic institutions was like that he felt everywhere else, and he treated it the same way: as something to be beaten, not beaten by. "All my life I *had* to roll with it," he says. "As a teenager, I rolled with it when they sent me down to an all-white high school. I said, 'Well, I'll prove I'm not just as good as you but even better.'"

After ordination Figaro taught at his order's seminary in Ann Arbor, Michigan, where he went on to become principal. Meantime he continued his own studies at the University of Michigan. Eventually he would earn a doctorate in education and English. More important, he settled happily into his life's work. That career culminated with his tenure from 1957 until 1971 as dean and director of St. Emma Military Academy, "the only black military academy in the entire United States," he says proudly, and a touch wistfully. St. Emma's, now closed, was a boarding school operated by the Holy Ghost Fathers outside Richmond, Virginia. It was situated on a bucolic, five-thousand-acre campus; an affiliated academy for girls was run by nuns on the other side of the campus, across the James River.

Imagine the challenge: taking over an all-black, all-male Catholic military school in the South just in time for the civil rights movement, the sexual revolution, Vatican II and its fallout, the education revolution, and the rabid antimilitary sentiment of the Vietnam era. "And here, in a country area, thirty miles outside of Richmond, I had all five of those things to deal with in boys who were fourteen through eighteen," Figaro says with a smile. "Three hundred and fifty of them—and two hundred and fifty girls." Were there occasions when he was left to grope for his sanity? I ask. "Yes. Many times," he says. Then, turning serious: "I enjoyed it tremendously. That was the highlight of my priestly career."

St. Emma's black students were of course aware of the racial turmoil abroad in the land, but given the academy's remoteness, they were to some extent insulated from its repercussions. Insulated but not immune. Segregation was still the norm when Figaro arrived. He determined to help change it, and because St. Emma's was a military academy and affiliated with other like institutions, he had occasional opportunities. For instance, "We played the first integrated basketball game in the state of Virginia," he says. This was in the early sixties, and St. Emma's played against another Catholic academy. "I told the bishop, 'Hey, these are both Catholic institutions, and we're both playing in the Catholic league. If we can't play together, something must be wrong.'"

Figaro says what made the job so gratifying was that "you were formulating young black minds to take their right and proper place in society. Whenever the question came, 'Are you prepared?'—'Yes, we *are* prepared.' Toward the end of my two terms there, we were getting ninety-nine percent placement in college." Figaro remains in touch with some of his graduates and is obviously proud that so many have become successful in business and the professions. Says he, "I see myself in the kids I taught."

And one lesson he always taught was the importance of not standing still. As he puts it, "The whole thing in my life has been change. I've seen change in the civil rights movement. I've seen change in the education movement. I've seen change—I hope I see even *more* change—in the Church. The thing is to be *open* to change. Change means growth and development."

That change invariably has bettered the human condition, he asserts. In the Church, too? "Oh, yes," he replies vigorously. Contemporary Catholicism is much more welcoming of all people, irrespective of race, gender, or station, he believes. Pointing to his own parish, he says that not long ago such a diverse congregation would have been unthinkable. Then he offers some poignant personal testimony. Not long before my visit, the current president of Catholic Theological Union had been installed at a certain Chicago church. "In 1951," Figaro says, "I knocked on the door of that church and asked them if I could say Mass there, and I was told no. Because (a) they didn't believe I was a priest; (b) they didn't believe I lived in that area; and (c) they told me the 'colored' church was over in another area, and I could go to the colored church."

Does this mean Figaro, once an enthusiastic young man rejected repeatedly by his Church because of his skin color, has at last been made to feel at home? "Oh, yes," he says—then qualifies: "Two things. Not only because of my color but because of my faith. Because of my education. I don't want to be accepted because of my color; I want to be accepted because of *what I am*. You want a Ph.D.? I have it."

Figaro predicts more change in store for the Church. For instance, he sees the laity taking on much of the work traditionally handled by priests, such as administrative functions, and in his estimation that's all to the good. "As more and more theologians examine the priesthood, who knows where it will take us? Into the married priesthood? To lady priests?"

He raises the questions but doesn't answer them, and our visit concludes sooner than I might have liked: Figaro must take one of his housemates, an older priest, to the doctor. As he goes, he says only, "We have to be prepared to accept the change, wherever the Spirit leads us."

Father
John Smyth

DES PLAINES, ILLINOIS

In 1994, when Chicago police came across a west side apartment where nineteen unsupervised children were living in filthy, vermin-infested conditions, the appalling discovery made headlines around the country and was dissected on all the morning talk shows. President Clinton likened the abused children's surroundings to Calcutta. Vice President Gore said he hoped the outrage would prompt an "all-out war against crime and drugs." The nation simply was shocked.

Father John Smyth wasn't shocked. Things like that happen all the time in Chicago, he tells me; the only thing unusual about the circumstances in that particular apartment, with its windows broken out and soiled mattresses strewn on the floor, was the large number of children involved. The kids, ranging in age from one to fourteen, belong to six different mothers, five of whom are sisters. The parents were found and charged with child neglect and placed in drug treatment programs. "When people are hooked on that crack cocaine, they are nuts," Smyth says. "They don't care about anything except the next hit, and the kids are starved."

As often happens in such dreadful cases in Cook County, when these children were discovered Smyth was the first person authorities called. He is executive director of Maryville Academy, a nationally acclaimed agency that every year takes in thousands of Chicago's abused children. Sadly, repairing broken lives is a booming business these days: Maryville has grown to encompass seventeen separate organizations, from shelters for runaways to a nursery for crack babies to a witness protection program for kids who testify against pimps and pedophiles. "Any case that's in the paper," Smyth explains, "they always say [the victims] are in a 'safe environment.' They are in one of Maryville's settings. I am proud of that fact. We can reach out in a crisis, when children are in harm's way, and change it."

Maryville, headquartered on a parklike ninety-eight-acre campus here in suburban Des Plaines, was established in 1883 to care for children orphaned or left homeless by the Great Chicago Fire. For most of its life, Maryville was operated by the Archdiocese of Chicago as a Catholic charity. Today it is financially independent and one of the largest residential child-care facilities in the nation, annually treating and sheltering thousands of victims of physical, sexual, and emotional abuse.

Maryville's remarkable track record has received widespread attention in recent years: first in 1995, when Republican leader Newt Gingrich was promoting such latter-day "orphanages" as one solution to rampant child neglect; and later as politicians grappled with welfare reform even as they constricted the social safety net. In the national debate on these issues, privately operated agencies like Maryville are being asked to step into the breach left by government cutbacks—a situation the already taxed agencies contemplate with alarm. As Smyth says, "We've never had an empty bed."

Called by some a child's "home of last resort," Maryville rests on two pillars. One is its guiding principle of treating youngsters with love and respect. Once Maryville takes in a child, it sticks with him, regardless of how much trouble he makes or how long it takes to stabilize his life. The other pillar is John Smyth. Now sixty-two, the priest has been here since the day he left Chicago's Mundelein Seminary in 1962. Back then Maryville was in a shambles and on the verge of collapse. With a steely will, salesmanship, and a lot of help, Smyth has turned Maryville into a model of social outreach.

At six foot six, Smyth towers over most everyone he meets, and when you shake hands with him, his swallows yours. A generous beak of a nose punctuates his handsome face. The priest indulges a taste for Marlboros and an Irishman's sense of humor. (His father came to the United States in 1927; an immigration agent decided the family name should be "Smyth" instead of "Smith.") It's only nine in the morning, but arrayed before him on a half-moon-shaped desk are eight message slips and a long "to do" list with half the items already checked off. The phone rings often. One call is from a well-heeled friend offering him a ticket to that night's Chicago Bulls playoff game. He says he is free and would gladly accept; when he hangs up he confesses that he actually has a conflict. He stares at the offending appointment in his daybook, wondering how to make it disappear. "How could I refuse?" he asks.

On the face of it, John Smyth is about as unlikely a priest as you'll meet. Born and raised on the northwest side of Chicago, he went to college at Notre Dame, where he caught the attention of professional scouts as the star captain of the basketball team. Well, not exactly a star, he says. "I was a journeyman, a hatchet man. I still hold the record for the most personal fouls at Notre Dame. [The St. Louis Hawks] wanted somebody to 'protect' Bob Pettit, who was the superstar in that day. I didn't mind protecting people. Sometimes I would make Dennis Rodman look like an altar boy when I was playing. God gave me two good elbows and I used them." After Smyth's senior season, he jumped at the chance to tour with other Chicago-area stars as opponents for the Harlem Globetrotters. He did this for six weeks—in lieu of classes. "I don't know how I graduated," he says. "Well, I got down on my knees and begged when I came back."

As much as he loved basketball, Smyth wasn't sure about it as a profession (in those days basketball players made little more than priests). He had been contemplating a religious vocation, but he wasn't certain about that either. Then he learned that St. Louis planned to make him its first pick in the National Basketball Association draft. Given his indecision, Smyth suggested that the team look elsewhere. The Hawks drafted him anyway, and that made up Smyth's mind: it would be the seminary.

The NBA might have been easier. Smyth was no scholar: "I had a lot of problems in the seminary," he recalls, the memory prompting a trace of a grimace. "I didn't know a word of Latin. I never learned a word of Latin in my five years there. I had a tough time, but I made it. They ordained me and [said] I had to go back to the seminary and learn Latin. I just kept walking."

This was in 1962. Perhaps because he *didn't* know Latin (use of the vernacular at Mass was still a year or two away) Smyth was assigned to Maryville, a facility he had never seen and knew nothing about. Once there he was smitten. "It was a place that really practiced our faith in a basic way of the virtues that the Lord talks about. I just saw it was very evident here."

First assigned as a teacher, Smyth took to the work with the enthusiasm of the newly ordained, and in 1970 Chicago's Cardinal John Cody appointed him Maryville's executive director. Unfortunately, Cody, a formidable man, also informed Smyth that he was about to close the place. By this time Maryville's nearly century-old physical plant was dilapidated, the agency was losing money, and social service practice was moving away from institutionalizing troubled children in favor of placing them in foster care.

But John Smyth is formidable, too. It doesn't take much time in his company to peg him: if he were in politics, he'd be the ward healer. In a POW camp he'd be the scrounger. But as a social services professional, he was in the business of saving kids, and he would do whatever that required. Cardinal or no, Smyth opted to build. Calling on friends in the private sector, he embarked on a surreptitious program of repairs and new construction. Then six months into his tenure, Smyth learned that Cody was coming out to visit. Since at the time the only road into the campus led right past a gymnasium obviously under construction, Smyth had to think fast. In a scene out of a sitcom, he barricaded the lone access road and then prevailed on the city of Des Plaines for some gravel to improvise a new one. He also got his hands on some horses. (The campus *had* been a farm, once.) When Cody's car arrived, Smyth was there to intercept it. "I put the horses so that he couldn't see the building," he says, lighting another cigarette and shaking his head. "We talked about twenty minutes, and he turned around and left. He didn't find out that I'd put up the building until they were all finished."

The cardinal and the priest would develop a relationship of mutual respect, punctuated by sometimes stormy discussions about Maryville's direction. After several years of Smyth's stewardship, the cardinal was pleased with the turnabout and lifted Maryville's death sentence. Today it gets no money from the archdiocese. A little more than eighty percent of its sixty-million-dollar annual budget comes from contracts with the State of Illinois. The remainder must be raised from private sources.

How? In a variety of ways, including Maryville's annual Chuckwagon Day, which clears three million dollars in one giant party. The bulk of Maryville's donations, however, results from Smyth's networking. Every week he puts another six hundred miles on his car, most by driving into the city for business and social functions (and to drop by various Maryville operations, which are scattered throughout Chicagoland). He's a familiar figure among the city's business and political elite. "I love Chicago," he says. "There are circles in Chicago. If you get in the circle, it's terrific." Some in that circle, like Chicago Blackhawks owner Bill Wirtz, have been especially generous to Maryville through the years. Still, Smyth insists it's not his style to directly put the arm on a potential benefactor. "I try to give them the *opportunity* to give," he explains tactfully. "It's been very, very successful. I think people who are more direct would probably accomplish it faster and probably get more. I am satisfied.

"I think God created worriers in this world to take the place of those who don't worry," he continues. "I never worry about a thing. I really don't. I am concerned, I work hard, but I don't worry about things. That really gives you a lot of freedom."

Freedom, that is, to devote personal attention to the Maryville operation, which is vast in scope and ambition. The main campus alone has numerous residences, two gyms, a pool, skating rinks, a high school, and a vocational school. Maryville has more than a thousand employees and hundreds of volunteers. There are three hundred full-time residents, and at any given time some fifteen hundred kids can be found in one or another of its facilities. On average a child at the main campus will be there four years. Smyth figures that in his tenure Maryville has tended to more than forty thousand children.

And make no mistake: this clientele is society's refuse. Many of the children, especially at the main campus, arrive after having been through a revolving door of foster care and group homes. Nearly half the boys and eighty percent of the girls are victims of sexual abuse. In their brief lives they have known little but torment. "If I had the background of seventy-five percent of these kids, I would be a disaster," the clergyman says bluntly. "Kids come in as fifteen-, sixteen-year-olds, and they haven't been to school in six years."

From a child's first day at Maryville, the staff offers emotional support and a sense of stability. "Permanency to a child can be anywhere as long as you give that child the ability and capability to exercise his potential," Smyth believes. Toward that end, the youngster not only goes right into school but is encouraged to pursue special interests, whether in books, sports, or the arts, thereby promoting self-esteem. (Children come here regardless of denomination, and there is nothing overtly spiritual about the Maryville regimen.) When students finish high school, those who want to go on to college will have their tuition paid. Others avail themselves of the campus's extensive trade school, where they can be trained in carpentry, cosmetology, auto repair, the restaurant business, and countless other occupations.

The education continues in their living quarters. Maryville tries to make its homes as family-like as possible. The older residents live eight or ten to a house, each house supervised by teaching parents. Everyone pitches in with the chores, and they gradually learn the art of getting along. Through it all Maryville reinforces the idea that it stands behind the kids, even if they screw up. "Once we commit to [children], we never kick them out," Smyth says. "That's easy to say, you know. There are times when you want to but you don't do it." Even if a resident breaks the law, Smyth says Maryville's position is, "We're staying with you. We're not proud of what you did, but you are going to face the consequences. Then you're going to come back and put the pieces together, and we'll work with you. And it's amazing: when they know that—that, hey, you're going down the pipe with them—they change."

Maryville's success has been so conspicuous that Smyth was a logical poster boy for those advocates of latter-day "orphanages" (which Maryville isn't, but no matter) as one way out of the welfare mess, especially where unmarried teenage mothers are concerned. He's not averse to the publicity, and the academy was featured in articles in major newspapers and on a segment of

Sixty Minutes. But neither is Smyth comfortable being cast in the cavalry role in the ongoing battle over entitlement spending. So far the nation has not turned to a wholesale system of Boys Towns—or Maryvilles—but it has taken a first controversial step toward limiting welfare. And the great debate over who should be tending to America's destitute and desolate goes on.

As it happens, Smyth, who lives with the flesh-and-blood consequences of the welfare system at its most dysfunctional, agrees with those who consider the status quo a disaster. "Working thirty-five years in this field, I abhor the welfare system. People need help; I am not going to deny that. But when you make it a lifestyle—and the system *makes* it a lifestyle by the conditions: you know, you can't be married, you can't work, you can't save anything, you can't own anything. I mean, that's like slavery." Welfare should exist as a bridge between need and opportunity, he contends, but instead it has become a trap. "Welfare kids, after a while, know that the money comes from the post office box, and that's all you have to do. It gets internalized after so many years. That eats the inner strength away. [Welfare children] are not lazy. They can be taught. [But] that's what the welfare system has done for the last fifty years to people."

Smyth does not proffer a magic bullet, though he says any reform of welfare not only must embrace job training but ensure actual jobs, perhaps by enticing private industry with tax credits. Yet as the debate unfolds, he, like directors of charitable organizations around the country, worries when he sees "welfare reform" equated with windfall savings in federal spending. Private charities cannot be expected to deal with all the people who fall through a shredding safety net, they say. Worse, they fear a double whammy, because charities like Maryville, while "private," still derive much of their funds from government grants and contracts. (For instance, Catholic Charities, which has a hand in almost every type of social service imaginable, from adoption aid to shelters for battered women, gets nearly two-thirds of its two-billion-dollar annual budget from local, state, and federal governments.) If welfare and other entitlements are slashed by billions of dollars, the charities argue, more people than ever will need their services even as their own budgets are under siege. "A place like Maryville will be inundated," Smyth says. "I don't think the private sector, as it stands right now, can survive under that onslaught."

For his part, Smyth is working closely with Illinois officials about their spending priorities, but he says when things are tight the debate always boils down to "Which is more important—the kids or the roads?" As for what's happening in Washington, all he can say is, "I wish we could get a more definite reading."

In all this, one thing Smyth does welcome is the fresh discussion about the rightful role of America's churches in caring for the needy, a conversation prompted by the writer Marvin Olasky and others who lament government's twentieth-century usurpation of that function. Vatican II pointedly reminded Catholics that the Church's mission must involve seeking social justice and peace, and Smyth believes a wonderful place to engage that challenge is in the rotting inner cities. "The faith is being expressed to people, which is beautiful and wonderful, but we don't reach out and really help other people who need it," he maintains. "I think much of the Catholic faith is parochialized, tied into the parish." Smyth understands that those parishes have their own needs and priorities and that everyone seems to be strapped financially. Even so, he says, Catholics must force themselves to keep the bigger picture in view. "The Catholic Church has to stay very, very close to the basic virtues of what Christ said: feed the hungry, clothe the naked, take care of your fellow man. If the Catholic Church pulls away from these areas, a tremendous amount of power disappears."

Smyth is especially concerned about a commitment—or a lack thereof—to educate these needy children. "I really think the Church's voice should be heard within the city. I think education is a strong tool for a strong Church. [But] it seems like Catholic education is going to those who can afford it. I think it is a big, big step backwards." Maryville itself helps sustain a Catholic school for almost three hundred children in the poverty-ridden Altgeld Gardens area on Chicago's southeast side. The school loses money and battles every year to keep its doors open. "Could we do more down there?" he asks. "Probably. But we are doing a tremendous amount: saving kids and giving them an education and direction and giving them the Catholic faith—what it stands for."

After more than three decades at Maryville, John Smyth has been in one continuous assignment longer than any other priest in the archdiocese. He intends to keep adding to that record so long as he is wanted, has his health, and hangs on to enough of that young man's enthusiasm to remain creative ("I've never been a caretaker," he says). He proceeds to tell me about a boy who came to Maryville after having been in nineteen different foster homes and group residences. "He's a junior in high school, and there is a court hearing coming up about his future," Smyth says. "Well, I just had a talk with him, and he's done real well. He's a smart kid, and I hope and pray that when he graduates he goes on to whatever school he wants to. He's learning something, and then he'll put his life together."

Father
Thomas Wenski

MIAMI

Walking busy Sixty-Second Street with his German shepherd, Burek, Father Thomas Wenski, a stocky man of forty-six, could be taken for a nose tackle a few years retired from the Miami Dolphins. For that matter, with his shaggy mustache and round Slavic face—his immigrant father was born in Warsaw—Wenski could be taken for one of his own heroes, Lech Walesa. Back in Wenski's cramped office, in fact, a 1989-vintage photograph of the priest and Poland's president-electrician hangs in a prominent spot on the wall. Wenski's blue eyes are twinkling.

What Tom Wenski definitely does not look like is a Haitian. Yet over the last two decades, by watching over both the souls and political rights of the one hundred thousand Haitians of south Florida, Wenski has become synonymous with his oppressed, exuberant flock. Here in northeast Miami's Little Haiti, one of those corners of America where the Third World is local news, Wenski exercises his own flinty brand of social justice. His efforts have endeared the Creole-speaking priest to the once skeptical community.

"Probably a lot of [the respect] is just because I have survived," he says. "I have outlived most everybody else in this community. I am still around—since 1978. It's amazing in a lot of ways because here I am, a white guy. I have Haitians who might not necessarily want to acknowledge a white guy as a Haitian leader, but then they do. I always tell people, only a priest could get away with it."

Wenski not only has survived, but as director of the Pierre Toussaint Haitian Catholic Center and pastor of adjoining Notre-Dame d'Haiti Church he is arguably the most visible Haitian advocate in the nation. When his friend Jean-Bertrand Aristide was reinstalled as president of Haiti in 1994, Wenski rode along as a member of the official U.S. delegation. "Thank God we have someone like Father Wenski," one of his parishioners told a Catholic newspaper a few years ago. "He's Haitian. No, he's *more* than Haitian."

Whatever, he's surely the only Haitian Polish American around. Born in 1950 up the road in Lake Worth, Florida, Wenski believes his own humble pedigree is another reason for his acceptance by the Haitian immigrants, so much of whose lives and attitudes has been shaped by class distinctions back on the island. "My father left school when he was in the sixth grade, and he was a house painter. He worked with his hands. Maybe socially, from my background, I resemble these people more than a couple of these Haitian [professionals] in their community."

Tom Wenski hit the priest track early, at thirteen, when he entered a high school seminary in Miami. It was not an easy passage. A self-described "wiseass," Wenski indulged a rebellious streak and barbed sense of humor—he still does, albeit more discreetly—that kept him in trouble. (He told me he's often wondered how much the Archdiocese of Miami spent to educate the sixty-five members of his original seminary class, of which he's the only surviving collar: "Which is why, they tell me, they only pay us eleven hundred dollars a month.") Because of his heritage, the young Wenski attempted to learn Polish, which was a struggle. But when he tried Spanish, he surprised himself by taking to it like a native, and as a seminarian he would relish the opportunities he got to work in Miami's Cuban community. If the conservative Cubans curbed his then liberal bent ("They weren't interested in liberation theology," he notes), they did reinforce his belief that the Church must monitor and safeguard human rights. "So much of the American [Catholics'] preoccupation seems to be about rearranging furniture," Wenski says, "where in the Third World it's more like a life-and-death issue."

Wenski has always moved easily among the impoverished and dispossessed. After his ordination in 1976, he was assigned to a poor parish, Corpus Christi, in Miami's Allapattah neighborhood. The congregation was predominantly Cuban and Puerto Rican, but the young priest immediately was impressed by its small community of Haitians and their joyful, almost outsized, faith. He picked up a little Creole to better minister to them, then decided to pursue the language seriously. By the mid-seventies the number of Haitians fleeing the Duvalier regime was growing rapidly, and the archdiocese, desperate to find priests to serve this burgeoning community, encouraged Wenski's interest. In 1979 he was sent to Haiti for three months to immerse himself in the language and culture, and the following year he helped establish the Haitian Catholic Center.

Wenski hoped to go further and create south Florida's first Haitian church. There was resistance from diocesan leaders who felt such a move, while well intended, would further segregate the Haitian community. Wenski, the immigrant's son, argued the converse—namely, that people integrate from a position of strength, which their own parish would give them. He believed these newcomers would never become true Americans until they felt at home here, and that feeling could only be incubated in a warm, familiar environment. "Life in a new country with its strange ways can be very frightening, very alienating," he would write at the time. "How, then, to describe the joy an immigrant feels to hear the gospel proclaimed in his own language? This is the joy of knowing that one belongs, that one is no longer a foreigner in a strange land but within the fellowship of believers, that one is a brother, a fellow pilgrim." That logic carried the day: when a former convent school became available on northeast Sixty-Second Street, one of the main thoroughfares in a run-down part of Miami that was quickly becoming known as Little Haiti, Wenski moved the Haitian Center's operations there and converted the old cafeteria into Notre-Dame d'Haiti Church. In no time the complex was a bustling, one-stop agency for the Haitians' legal, material, social, and spiritual needs. Today a thousand people a day utilize some service of the center for day-care or Head Start programs, for English classes, for legal services or job placement or small-business advice. And the Notre-Dame parish is just as vibrant. Every weekend its five Masses—and these can run two luxuriant, music-and-dance-packed hours—are crowded. Although last year Wenski buried a hundred older parishioners (the funerals always on Saturday so everyone can attend), he baptized eight hundred new ones.

In ministering to a parishioner's corporal needs as well as his spiritual ones, Wenski says he is simply following a well-trod path. "This is an ethnic parish," he explains, "but an immigrant ethnic parish. I think it's not unlike what it was for a Polish parish of the 1890s in Detroit or Chicago, because I am dealing with some of the same problems. Some of my people are illiterate. This has happened more than once: people come here bringing me letters with Ed McMahon's picture on it. They think they've won a million dollars; they come dressed up. They will come with a letter from [the Immigration and Naturalization Service] and say, 'Father, should I run or should I answer it?' Or when they are getting legalized, they will need a letter from me to give them a reference. So we do the whole gamut—teaching them English, helping them find a job, providing day care and religious education for their kids."

From its Miami base Wenski's operation expanded rapidly to try to keep up with the Haitian diaspora across south Florida. New missions were opened in Homestead, Belle Glade, Pompano Beach, Delray Beach, Immokalee, Fort Pierce, and elsewhere. Soon Wenski and a handful of associates were church-hopping each Sunday to conduct a dozen or more Creole Masses. Wenski even learned to fly to better traverse his growing domain, but eventually the expense, and a mild case of jitters, grounded him. Some of the most outlying churches now have their own pastors, but even so, when Wenski is not at the Haitian Catholic Center, chances are he's somewhere on Interstate 95. "Yeah, and that's *worse* than flying," he grouses.

All this might suggest it was an easy marriage between the Haitians and their Polish American priest, but that was hardly the case. Early on many Haitians, while grateful to Wenski, were nonetheless leery of his motives. Why? Because be it in Port-au-Prince or Little Haiti, Haitian life has been circumscribed by politics and tragedy. Fleeing repression and grinding privation, Haitians for two decades have tried to navigate the six hundred miles to Florida on everything from pitiful rafts to overcrowded trawlers, susceptible to the elements, pirates, murderous captains, and the United States Coast Guard. Many wouldn't survive the effort; the same year Notre-Dame Church opened, in a particularly grisly tableau the bodies of thirty drowned Haitians washed ashore just north of here. Meantime, as the United States debated how to categorize the Haitian émigrés, those who beat nature and the odds were variously intercepted and detained in Florida, held at Guantanamo Bay in Cuba, or escorted back to Haiti. Against this sobering backdrop, then, the Haitian community—as has been the case with so many of Florida's immigrant communities—reckons that who you are depends to a great extent on who you support. The pastor was a good man, yes, but was he *really* on their side? Some factions weren't sure. Others demanded the archdiocese find a Haitian to run its mission. Wenski never knew where he might encounter politics. He remembers one particular Good Friday service, back when the popular Aristide, a former priest, was still sparring with the Vatican. "There was a special prayer you offer for the pope," Wenski says, "and I had people ready to boo in church. It takes a little bit of tact to survive that." (He adds impishly, "Especially since I know that the pope is infallible because he is Polish.")

But in 1983 Wenski went a long way toward cementing his credibility with many Haitians here. He and a colleague traveled to Haiti and found a Catholic lay worker who had been kidnapped and tortured by the country's brutal secret police, the Tontons Macoute. Wenski interviewed the worker and photographed his injuries, publishing both in his Creole newsletter, *The Catholic Voice*. Haiti lodged complaints, but the prisoner later was released. The fact is that Wenski, a stubborn and passionate man, not only doesn't duck controversy but has been known to court it. If he vigorously denounced the Duvaliers and the coup leaders who turned out Aristide, he was equally quick to criticize American detention of Haitians at the Krome Avenue facility outside Miami, and to slam Presidents Reagan and Bush (whose administrations were quite popular in south Florida generally) for immigration policies that he bluntly labeled racist ("the unavoidable perception is that Haitians are being denied entry because they are poor, and because they are black," he wrote in 1989).

The political angst in Little Haiti has subsided since U.S. troops returned Aristide, Wenski says, but the problem of race continues to occupy the priest. Indeed, sometimes it seems everything reduces to race in tropical Miami, where the melting pot has more ingredients and boils hotter than anywhere else. This fact complicates Haitian efforts to assimilate. Already "outsiders" because of their immigrant status, Haitians aren't considered Latin, like so many other south Florida constituencies, yet neither do they feel connected to the indigenous black community. "There is some tension between the American blacks and the Haitians," Wenski concedes, "just as there are between the Cubans and the American blacks. It's a divide-and-conquer type of thing. You get the poor people fighting each other rather than looking to join each other and make a coalition. What's interesting, though, is when American blacks perceive that the Haitians are being treated in a certain way because of their color, then they rally to the Haitian cause. So when the Haitians were being detained at Krome and it was pretty obvious that the reason they were getting that treatment was because their skin was black, then black Miami championed the Haitian cause. But that's on one level. On the other level there's not a whole lot of interaction."

There are other sources of friction, such as lingering fears that Haitians are transmitters of AIDS and animosity over how the Haitians, in classic immigrant fashion, have occupied thousands of low-paying, servile jobs to get established. But if the Haitians are working hard on the American dream, they don't love everything that comes with it. "In my parish one of the big problems that parents have with their teenage boys is when they come home with an earring on," Wenski tells me. "You know, it's World War II. The parents can't accept that. The mothers cry; they want to send the kid back to Haiti. It's more than a fashion statement. For them, it means the kid is giving himself to a dissolute life."

Wenski observes these cultural differences in their religious life, too. For instance, he couldn't figure out why attendance at Mass jumped some twenty percent on the first Sunday of each month. Then he remembered that back in Haiti "some of these people were coming from rural areas, where they only had church once a month because the priest couldn't get out [there]." Most of the children he baptizes are born to couples who have not married in the Church because in Haiti common-law marriage is customary. Haitians also tend to eschew taking communion at Mass until they feel they have proven themselves "worthy," such as by getting a job, and then by maintaining a certain rectitude. Wenski says it can cause a bit of a scandal if someone the congregation knows has made some recent transgression comes up to take a host.

Then, of course, there's *vaudou*—voodoo. Catholicism in south Florida has always had a tinge of the exotic, courtesy of the diverse nationalities that have settled here. As Wenski himself once wrote, "The Church in Miami, like the early Church of the Acts of the Apostles, is challenged to become truly catholic." Which is another way of saying it must accommodate a lot of traditions—if not approve of them, exactly, then at least recognize they exist. In the Cuban community, for instance, there remains a widespread practice of Santeria, a shotgun marriage of Catholicism and rituals brought by slaves from Africa that include animal sacrifice. And among the Haitians there is voodoo, the West Indian belief in sorcery, magic charms, and the like. Voodoo customs continue to be widely practiced, Wenski says. He doesn't condemn them and he doesn't worry about them. Instead, he adjusts.

"I would say besides being a religion, [voodoo] is a worldview," he says. "An analogy would be, say, American secularism—a consumer society. You might be a practicing Christian, but that doesn't mean the secular worldview doesn't influence you. You get sick, you don't think of going to Lourdes first. You think of going to your doctor. Same thing in the Haitian world. You might have people who are practicing Catholics, [but] in a lot of ways the Haitian worldview is that things happen because of evil spirits, evil plotting, the evil eye—stuff like that. So sometimes people who have the faith, they hedge their bets." Secularism and voodoo are both a kind of paganism, Wenski says. "What you have to do is witness the Gospel in both contexts."

To do so the pastor "finesses" the situation. On the one hand he simply looks the other way at some practices, like the Haitians' habit of rubbing church statues for luck. But on the other he has borrowed island customs and symbols for his own use. "For example, the basic instrument of our [liturgical] music is the drum, which is also the basic instrument of Haitian culture and religion. The drum is used in voodoo, but we use it in the Mass. We baptize the drum. . . . That, I would say, is a type of enculturation in the same sense that . . . the Church in the third century decided to celebrate Christmas around the feasts of the [winter solstice] and built their churches on top of pagan temples, that type of thing."

It amounts to a liturgical balancing act as extraordinary as the one Wenski has managed in his own career. One payoff is that he and the archdiocese are meeting some success in one of their primary goals, that of cultivating new priests from the Haitians themselves. (Four Haitian priests have been ordained here in recent years, and three other men are in the seminary.) Ironically, that success sometimes causes Wenski to wonder how long he will continue in the service of his adopted community; all he knows for sure, he says, is that "the bishop owns my soul." But one thing he doesn't have to wonder about anymore is his place in that community. A few years ago, when Wenski's mother died, the small family home in Lake Worth was festooned in flowers, an impromptu, heartfelt tribute from thousands of appreciative new Americans.

Monsignor
Ralph Beiting

LOUISA, KENTUCKY

As much as I am trying to enjoy this trip through the heart of Appalachia, the devilishly twisty ride gives my stomach palpitations. Kentucky 292 hugs the Big Sandy River, which at this point forms the border with West Virginia, and as the asphalt caroms back and forth through dense timber stands, I look out on other of the region's trademarks: unsteady frame houses, trailers on blocks, the curious "swinging bridges" that span roadside ravines (these rope-and-plank affairs are the only access some residents have to their homes when the creeks run high). It is Ash Wednesday, and Monsignor Ralph Beiting and I are headed to one of his three parishes, St. John Neumann Church in Hode, for a late afternoon service. Hode, thirty-five miles southeast of Louisa, is little more than a bend in the road, so tiny it doesn't even appear on state maps that happily pinpoint the likes of Mattie, Charley, Add, and Milo. Nonetheless, our driver, Marilyn Stefanski, well knows the way, as she and Beiting make this trip three times a week. Now Beiting's assistant, she is originally from Connecticut but came to Appalachia as a volunteer and never left. That was twenty-four years ago.

Beiting's bosses put a stop to his own highway driving after a couple of near-disastrous brushes with the coal trucks that whip down these mountain roads like eighteen-wheel avalanches. (A blood clot behind his left eye has impaired his vision.) As far as I can tell, this is the only concession Beiting makes to his seventy-two years. This man may have snow-white hair, but he has the build of a dray horse and, it would seem, the stamina to match. Waiting for us in Hode are maybe twenty people, which I learn is about two-thirds of the congregation. St. John Neumann is one of nine churches Beiting has carved out in the hills of eastern Kentucky. This one began life as a double-wide trailer; later a proper chapel was cobbled onto one end. Beiting makes a quick round of hellos even as he is slipping the purple vestment over his head, then launches into Mass. He extemporizes a brief sermon encouraging the people to take advantage of the Lenten season for their own penance and introspection ("Let it be the best forty days of your existence," he urges). Then these men and women, most of them old, come forward, single file. With his thumb Beiting marks a sooty cross on the forehead of each, intoning, "Remember that thou art dust, and unto dust thou shalt return."

You cannot talk about social justice and the American Church without talking to Ralph Beiting, whose Christian Appalachian Project, known everywhere in these parts as CAP, embodies the very idea. Beiting came to Appalachia fifty years ago, when most hill people had never seen a Catholic—and didn't feel especially deprived because of it. Over time he has created something akin to a United Way–Job Corps–summer camp for residents of the forty-nine Kentucky counties that are considered part of Appalachia. CAP is the largest charitable organization in the state and among the largest in the nation. Though much of its work involves traditional forms of charity—CAP annually gives away millions of dollars' worth of food, furniture, clothing, and building materials—the agency goes well beyond that in its stated mission of helping Appalachians help themselves. This it has done by spinning off small businesses, employing hundreds of people and training thousands more, building homes, operating thrift stores, offering adult education classes, sponsoring recreation and development opportunities for children, and issuing grants to countless other organizations. Each year CAP entices thousands of volunteers from all over the world, who give their time in a spirit of community and ecumenism. Which is to say that while the Christian Appalachian Project may have been founded by a Catholic priest, it is a nondenominational enterprise that is independent of the Church. Indeed, for the past ten years its president has been a Methodist, and people from every faith and hollow hereabouts have been known to pitch in.

Beiting is CAP's chairman of the board, but in recent years he has pulled away from its day-to-day operation. Now most of his work is given over to being the agency's chief ambassador and fund-raiser. (CAP has grown into a forty-million-dollar operation, in terms of money and goods distributed annually.) Besides, he also has three parishes to watch over. The largest, and his home base, is St. Jude's in Louisa. Then there's St. John Neumann and St. Stephen's Church in Inez, twenty-five miles south of Louisa. He celebrates Mass six days a week at St. Jude and three times a week each at the other two. What with those commutes, visiting the sick, and his CAP duties, Beiting runs up more than sixty thousand miles a year on his car. He fuels this schedule with equal parts enthusiasm and Diet Coke.

From his teens Beiting wanted to be a priest. Back then he scarcely knew a place called Appalachia existed, despite growing up only a hundred miles away on a small farm in northern Kentucky. He was the oldest of eleven children, then not an unusually large number for a German Catholic family. It was also not unusual for such a family to yield one or two of those siblings to the clergy, and after high school Beiting entered the seminary in Cincinnati, just across the Ohio River. Years later Cincinnati, Detroit, Indianapolis, and other urban points north would bear the brunt of a great postwar migration of mountain residents, but when Beiting was a seminarian Appalachia remained mostly a forbidding concept, "kind of an ecclesiastical Siberia. You know: if you screwed up in northern Kentucky then you would get sent to the mountains." As it happened, Beiting's bishop at the time wanted to change that perception and began a program of sending seminarians into the hills during their summers for missionary work. So it was that in 1946 Beiting got his introduction to the region, assigned to do street preaching, lead Bible classes, and see about starting a Catholic school. He found that Appalachia lived up to its stereotype as a world of heartbreaking beauty and desolation. "I was seeing poverty that I hadn't seen in my growing-up years," he says. "And remember, I grew up in the depression."

When Beiting was ordained in 1949, he returned to his old high school in Newport, Kentucky, to teach algebra and geometry and kick off what he assumed would be a conventional career track. Then one day the bishop paid him a surprise visit. That usually meant trouble, of course, and Beiting was filled with trepidation, especially because he had no idea what he might have done wrong. Instead, the bishop stunned the freshman priest by announcing that he was going to make him a pastor. "I am ordained one year; nobody in our diocese at that time is getting made pastor before fifteen years," he recalls, eyes crinkling. "So I thought to myself, my God, what they teach us in the seminary is true—the Holy Ghost *does* run the Church." Then Beiting asked where the parish was. The bishop replied, "Well, there isn't a church there yet." That, Beiting says, is when he began to suspect that "the Holy Ghost wasn't involved here at all."

What happened was that through the good graces of the writer and diplomat Clare Boothe Luce, a fresh Catholic convert, a chapel was to be established in Berea, a mountain community south of Lexington, Kentucky. The chapel primarily was meant to accommodate Berea College's Catholic students, but it also was to be a base for the diocese's continued efforts at Appalachian outreach (and just maybe in the process dispel some unflattering impressions there about the Catholic Church). Beiting found out that several previous arrangements for staffing this new church had fallen through, and so the bishop, somewhat in desperation, had turned to him as one of the only priests available with even minimal mountain experience. "I turned out to be Secondhand Rose," he says.

In this roundabout way did Father Ralph Beiting find himself back in Appalachia, not quite sure what he was doing there and never imagining, at least at the time, that the assignment would be permanent. It's fair to say the locals were even less enthusiastic. Among those churched at all—and the great majority weren't and still aren't—they were mostly Baptist, and Beiting remembers too well that "the anti-Catholic feeling was profound." Not long after his arrival in Berea, a woman pulled the priest aside and told him, "Do you know what people are saying? They're saying, 'Last year a pool hall and this year a Catholic church; what in the name of God is coming next?'"

In those first years when Beiting and his seminarians took to the streets, they were sometimes shouted down, pelted with tomatoes, and threatened with chains. Nuisance lawsuits were lodged against the parish. Then there was the time a hostile native trained his shotgun on Beiting. The pastor, Bible in hand, gathered himself enough to ask the source of the man's irritation. He replied that Beiting was the first Catholic he'd ever seen and that as a patriot he was duty-bound to shoot the priest. "He said, 'There's three things wrong with this country: there's those Communists, there's those niggers, and there's those Catholics. And if it takes shooting you to keep you from ruining my town, I reckon I'll do it.' " Beiting would talk his way out of that scrape, but when he returned a few weeks later the man was waiting for him, this time with an unpleasant German shepherd. Turned loose, the animal chomped Beiting's helper on the leg. "I said to him, 'Ed, good news. You're bleeding; you could be a martyr for our cause.'"

Such contretemps only spurred the stubborn pastor's missionary zeal. Certainly he didn't lack for opportunities to put Christ's teachings into practice. Mining, the only real industry in the mountains, gave the region a momentary lift during World War II, but afterward demand fell off and the poverty was more crushing than ever. This triggered an extraordinary exodus; between 1950 and 1972, a quarter of a million people left eastern Kentucky in search of work. Of those who stayed, more and more turned up at Beiting's rectory door seeking help. When Beiting drove home to northern Kentucky and described the despair to his family and friends, they would load up his car with food and clothes to give away when he got back. After several years of dealing with the poverty in this heartfelt but ad hoc way, Beiting had a painful revelation one evening on the highway back to Berea: "I was thinking to myself, 'My God, all you are is a truck driver. They eat the food. They wear out the clothes. You're not changing a thing.'"

In that insight was the genesis of CAP, for Beiting decided that what Appalachians needed more than his handouts was opportunity. Jobs and education were the only way out of poverty's trap. Yet in working with adults, Beiting found that their attitude was, understandably, "pretty defeatist." So he chose to concentrate first on the children. By jawboning a real estate agent, he obtained some property along Herrington Lake, northwest of Lancaster, and with family help he built a camp there. It opened in 1957. Beiting's idea was to transport these kids from their dispiriting environment, if only for a few days, and show them a world beyond. Though there were just six children in that first group of campers—none of them Catholic—the camp quickly caught on. In fact, before long Beiting found that when he took the campers home their parents said, "The kids sure love what you are doing for them. But what are you going to do for us?"

What they wanted, of course, was work—jobs in the mountains. Slowly, Beiting began to sponsor modest enterprises that might make sense for the inhospitable region. He employed one man to try greenhouse horticulture. Another cleared timber. A third began a woodworking shop, a fourth a dairy farm. As small as this initial effort was, Beiting still didn't have the money to pay for it. Then came an inspiration. He sat down one day with half a dozen big-city telephone books and marked all the ethnic-sounding names. Then he pulled together a primitive newsletter that he called *The Mountain News* and mailed it out with appeals to these strangers, over his own Teutonic name. "And amazingly, people answered them," he says. (Needless to say, CAP's fund-raising now is considerably more high-tech: this year the agency will mail out twenty-five million appeals.)

Soon the operation needed a name. To avoid alienating anyone wary of Catholics—and to demonstrate the agency's independence—Beiting called it the Christian Appalachian Project. And from that inauspicious beginning in the late fifties CAP has never stopped growing. It added new programs and industries. It built more camps. It began soliciting volunteers. And it became so successful in luring donated goods that they now come in by the semi-load to distribution centers all over eastern Kentucky (CAP recently bought a seventy-thousand-square-foot warehouse in Corbin to help keep up). But if today's CAP bears little resemblance to its humble origins, Beiting's goals were always big. "I think what we were doing in those early days was trying to decide how to end poverty," he explains. "We weren't satisfied with temporary things, just giving things away. That never answers poverty; all it does is perpetuate it and make it worse. We had to find ways in which we could get people working and involved in changing their attitudes and lifestyles, and hoping out of that would come the excitement that once had been the Appalachia of Daniel Boone and all those pioneers, that made this a wondrous place."

As CAP has grown, it has been inevitable that Beiting would become synonymous with it. He constantly travels on its behalf—countless people have been introduced to him, and CAP, by his flatboat preaching excursions down the Ohio River—and every year he writes another book for CAP to distribute, by the hundreds of thousands, as donor premiums. Like most entrepreneurs, Beiting is not without ego. Over the years he has enjoyed plenty of attention for his achievements. But he calls the recognition simply a means to a greater end. "Presidents have given me awards. I have walls stacked full of that junk. That wasn't me; that was God. That was spirituality. That's the beauty of what the Church is. It's saying to us that there is more than bread that man has to live by. There's the word of God, the spirit of God. Let him have the reins, let him have a chance."

❖ ❖ ❖

We drive on, and my stomach returns to spin cycle. From Hode we take a roundabout way back to Louisa so that Beiting can confer the ashes to a homebound woman, then stop in to give communion to an elderly man who had just returned to his nursing home after a few days in the hospital. We get back to Louisa a few minutes late for Beiting's seven o'clock service at St. Jude's. When Mass is done, we retire to a cozy room off the vestibule, where five men and women who are taking RCIA catechism classes are meeting to discuss the Ten Commandments in modern life. So it is almost ten by the time we return to Beiting's modest home and sit down to a dinner of tuna casserole and macaroni and cheese that Marilyn Stefanski has left for us.

At the end of the long day, Beiting is tired but still talkative, albeit in a more reflective mode. I ask what, if anything, discourages him. He takes his time. "You get discouraged at times because people don't respond to God," he says finally. "You work with people. You do all this for them, and boy oh boy, as soon as they get something they forget about God. They don't do prayer. They start doing their own thing and hurting God. That bothers me because I hate to see him hurt. We know theologically God isn't 'hurt,' but nevertheless his son died because of all this.

"And yet, you know, you just have to say that maybe this is not the time. I have to look at the whole realm of life. Maybe ten years from now they are going to do something that now, today, they're incapable of. But they will remember what you said or what you did."

Then Beiting turns at length to a subject that other priests, especially those who consider themselves in the ideological mainstream, also have told me bothers them a lot—more than the priest shortage, more than fallout from the pedophile scandal. And that is the increasingly acrimonious political division within the Church. These men aren't bothered by the simple existence of political differences: after all, given such emotional issues of the age as abortion and feminism and overpopulation and such contentious Church matters as the question of authority, priestly celibacy, and the use of inclusive (others would say politically correct) language in liturgical texts, how could there not be divisions? But these differences have grown more acute in the last fifteen years, as individual Catholics have tried to decide whether Church reforms have gone too far or not far enough. What's relatively new in all this, and what concerns the priests, is the rancorous soundtrack. Increasingly, it seems, Catholics consider their differences as not so much fodder for debate as shouting points. The trend is not unlike and is doubtless related to the eroding civility in society at large, and many priests despair as they watch whole segments of the faith move into opposing camps. Matters have become so contentious that in 1995 Bishop Fabian Bruskewitz of Lincoln, Nebraska, threatened to excommunicate Catholics in his jurisdiction who belonged to any of a dozen organizations, such as Catholics for a Free Choice or the Hemlock Society, whose views he deemed incompatible with Church teachings. One of the taboo groups was Call to Action, which challenges Vatican positions on women priests, celibacy, and birth control—and whose membership numbers at least three Catholic bishops.

Perhaps tension is inescapable, given that this fight basically shapes up between equally passionate people: those who think the Catholic Church is big enough to accommodate innumerable views and those who maintain that if Catholicism stands for everything then it stands for nothing. Still, Chicago's Cardinal Bernardin was so alarmed by the acrimony that in 1996, shortly before he died, he unveiled an initiative aimed at conciliation. In announcing the Catholic Common Ground Project, Bernardin said he was "troubled that an increasing polarization within the Church and, at times, mean-spiritedness have hindered the kind of dialogue that helps us address our missions and concerns." He hoped that his committee of high-

powered Catholic clergy and laity could function as a bridge between factions and supplant rancor with dialogue. Although the initiative has outlived its sponsor, it is telling that the mere announcement of it prompted
criticism from organizations on both ends of the Catholic spectrum.

"I worry about the division in the Church," Beiting begins. "I've got ul-
traconservative friends, I've got ultraliberal friends, and I've got friends in
between. I was in Lourdes in May and went into the baths there. What I
asked for was one thing: to be a peacemaker. To try some way to reconcile. I
am working on that very hard. Sometimes you get so discouraged. You say,
dang, I can't get this one side to give an inch. They think it's got to be [their]
way alone. Then you have the other side, [the people] who want everything
to change. And you think, where in the world is it ever going to end?"

He tells me about a friend, a fellow priest, who always seems to be at
war with their bishop. He is a wonderful and kind man, Beiting says, but
an adamant opponent of change. For instance, he was pastor of a small
mountain church when the liturgical changes prompted by Vatican II began
filtering down. The bishop kept after the priest to turn his altar around to
face the congregation, but he refused. At length the bishop prevailed on
Beiting, as the man's friend, to see what he could do. Eventually the priest
told Beiting he *would* pivot the altar but it was permanently fastened. This,
finally, was something Beiting could fix. "I came all the way from Lancaster
to his place and brought him an altar, and that's how he got it facing the
people. I could have sat back and yelled and screamed at him forever. But,
you know, it was what needed to be done.

"I've got a dear priest friend that denies purgatory," he goes on. "I have
another who denies angels. What the heck? [These] have all been defined by
the Church. Why in the world should they be doing that?" Beiting attributes their attitudes to a culture that says you're not valuable unless you decide things for yourself. "I mean, pride is at the basis of all faults. If you always have to be the leader, if you always have to be the initiator, if you
always have to be this or that, then there is something wrong with you. We
now think that we have to be the leaders. We have denied the leadership to
Christ; we have forgotten that we are the followers. Christ said to those
apostles, 'Come follow me.' And he didn't tell them where he was going.
Now everybody wants to make his own decision."

This is especially important for the clergy to bear in mind, he goes on.
"What we are is servants. The essential quality of leadership is a recognition that you are truly a servant, a servant of the people of God. That's the
last of all the pope's titles. They give him 'Patriarch of the West' and

'Bishop of Rome' and all of this, and the last one is 'Servant of the Servants of God.' I think that's part of our problem today.

"We are living in a cynical world where authority seems to be bad. Look what our country is going through. We have to be against government. Nobody is in favor of marriage: we'll have no-fault divorce and swap people off. We don't like the Church. We don't like the school system. The industrialists are all crooks. The labor unions are corrupt. What we need is that kindness back, that gentleness back. Give people a break, a chance. If we had a little of that in our society I think the Church wouldn't be so torn apart.

"They asked Mother Teresa once, did she think that she was really successful? They said, 'You take care of those old people, they die, and you don't change that.' She said, 'Well, I didn't know I was supposed to be successful. I thought that I was supposed to be faithful.' And there's the answer."

By now it is past eleven, time to turn in because Beiting has some packing to do. After tomorrow's seven o'clock Mass, he will be rushing off to Lexington, there to catch a plane for San Francisco. Beiting had been to California a few weeks earlier, where he cultivated some leads for charitable activities. Except for hills, the Bay Area is about as far from eastern Kentucky as the mind can imagine. But now Beiting will be back and spreading the word—about God, about amity, and about his beloved Appalachia.

▧ Father
William Jenkins

When it comes to frequent flying, Beiting has nothing on Father William Jenkins, pastor of Immaculate Conception Church in Norwood, Ohio, a working-class island enveloped by sprawling Cincinnati. For him, weekends mean airports. One day Jenkins might be bound for Cleveland, then Baltimore, then Saginaw, Michigan. Another day the itinerary might be Oyster Bay, New York, to Rochester, to Albany. "We travel all day Sunday, from one place to the other, with just enough time to offer Mass, go to the airport, fly to the next city, go to the chapel, offer Mass, hear confessions, try to talk to the people, go back to the airport, and fly home," the priest says. He is usually back in Cincinnati by midday Monday. "I do most of my sleeping on airplanes," he says.

Jenkins and his associate at Immaculate Conception, Father Joseph Greenwell, log that kind of travel in order to serve dozens of affiliated churches that don't have priests of their own. The two men belong to the Society of St. Pius V, a small order of priests who reject the changes in the Church since the Second Vatican Council, and who eschew the contemporary liturgy in favor of its "traditional," or Tridentine (for the sixteenth-century Council of Trent), form. Indeed, attending Mass at Immaculate Conception amounts to Catholic time travel. The service is conducted in Latin. The altar is at the rear of the church, and the priest faces it rather than the people. Communicants kneel at a marble rail to take the host on their tongues. Women's heads are covered with lace shawls or prim hats, and some of the female students from the Immaculate Conception school bobby-pin hankies to their hair in the same manner girls did when I was young. The Tridentine Masses pull so-called traditionalist Catholics from all over greater Cincinnati, which is a conservative area anyway, and from as far as Dayton and Louisville.

Immaculate Conception and these various mission churches (there are forty or so, most in the East and Midwest) exist in a kind of ecclesiastical gray area. Jenkins's church is not sanctioned by the Archdiocese of Cincinnati, and the Society of St. Pius V is not recognized by Rome. Jenkins doesn't acknowledge the authority of Pope John Paul II. Yet he hasn't been excommunicated, nor have his colleagues or their congregations. He admits the society's churches "walk a fine line" in terms of their identity, but he insists they are not schismatics. Rather, these Catholics contend that *they* are the orthodox ones, observers of the "traditional Roman Rite," holders of the true faith. The rest of the Church has moved away from them, they say, not vice versa.

"What we're doing here is basically carrying on the parish life that Catholics had before all the changes came in: the traditional Mass, the traditional sacraments, the traditional catechetics, and so on," explains Jenkins. "We're not setting up a separate church or a separate religion. We're just trying to hold on to the old faith, pass it on to the children."

When I visit Immaculate Conception, things are still in a bit of disarray. The congregation had taken over the Norwood complex only months before. This afternoon a workman is repairing the church roof, and in the rectory carpenters and plumbers are making a din. Several times Jenkins is called away to inspect the progress on a new ceiling. Later he shows me around the school, which has one hundred and twenty-five students in grades kindergarten through twelve. The children wear crisp blue uniforms. Their nun teachers—more time travel—are in black habits and white wimples.

The congregation actually originated across town, in 1980, at St. Gertrude the Great Church. For several years, growing pains there had Jenkins quietly on the lookout for roomier digs. Then, ironically, the archdiocese closed two Norwood parishes and put them up for sale. Jenkins acquired one, the old St. Matthew's, through a third party, because "from past experience" he felt sure the archdiocese would not have dealt with him directly. Then the pastor rechristened his new home, because "I promised our Blessed Mother if we did obtain the church through her good services that I would dedicate it to her Immaculate Conception."

Jenkins is a handsome man of forty-five who has Steve Martin's prematurely gray shock of hair and a Kirk Douglas dimpled chin. He wears the floor-length black cassock. He speaks firmly but softly, which is to say there is nothing alarming in his manner even as he utters views many Catholics find alarming, even heretical. Jenkins was born upstate, in Cleveland, but because of his father's career the family moved often. By the mid-sixties he was in high school in Fort Lauderdale, a thoughtful and conservative young man already troubled by much of what was happening in society and in the

Church. "By my junior year, things were beginning to become . . . *bizarre*," he says. "During the Vietnam War, one day we were all ushered into the school cafeteria—not the church—for a liturgy. It was a guitar-driven liturgy, celebrated on a table. The propers of the so-called Mass were taken from a book called *Good Old Plastic Jesus*. It was a 'Vietnam Moratorium Day' Mass. This to me was something totally alien. It had no place whatsoever parading as divine worship." He was disaffected by matters both inside the classroom (teachers advocating concepts like "Christian socialism," he says) and outside. He tells me about the day the school's principal, a priest, ran off with his own brother's wife. The priest's brother was a teacher at the same school, and Jenkins sarcastically sums up the man's Aquarian reaction to being cuckolded: "he was somewhat distressed by this, but in the spirit of peace, love, and joy we can overlook anything."

After high school Jenkins joined a California seminary of the Norbertines, a conservative order he knew was doing its best to resist alterations in the liturgy. He went on to study theology at Innsbruck, Austria, and in Rome, but he would leave the order in 1974. It had become clear, he says, that even the Norbertines would be unable to hold back the tide of change.

Back in the States he did some teaching at Catholic schools, but that only exacerbated his frustration. "I got into hot water at one point because I didn't use the religion text they gave me," he says. "I was just teaching the old Baltimore catechism. And I found out the children didn't know anything about the traditional faith. You ask them about the Ten Commandments, they knew nothing. They didn't know the Apostles' Creed. Very basic things; they had no concept." Jenkins says at one school, when he did try to instruct students in the commandments and basic prayers, he was chastised by his superiors for "confusing" them.

In 1976, unready to abandon his priestly aspirations, Jenkins simply turned up one day at the Swiss seminary of dissident Archbishop Marcel Lefebvre and was persuasive enough that he was invited to stay. The French cleric was a foremost critic of Vatican II and its modernizations, and he formed the Fraternity of St. Pius X to uphold the traditional Mass, theology, and sacramental rituals. After two years of additional study in Lefebvre's system, Jenkins was ordained by the archbishop, after which he returned home to teach in Lefebvre's small seminary in Michigan. (The seminary later was moved to Connecticut.) Their affiliation would prove a short one, however. In 1983 most of the fraternity's American priests, including Jenkins, parted company with their mentor. The problem, Jenkins says, was that he and his colleagues came to differ with Lefebvre on both philosophical grounds (with the fraternity's willingness to accept modern annulments, for instance) and logistical ones (such as the lack of a uniform standard for ordinations). In short, these priests felt the fabled archconservative was becoming too liberal for them. (After years of disputation and failed efforts at compromise, John Paul II excommunicated Lefebvre in 1988. The archbishop died in 1991.)

After the split Jenkins and his colleagues re-formed as the Society of St. Pius the V, in honor of the pope who declared, in 1570, that the Tridentine Mass was to be used "in perpetuity." Jenkins himself came to Cincinnati shortly thereafter, in 1984, to join the staff of St. Gertrude's, the forerunner of Immaculate Conception.

Traditionalist Catholics reject what they call the *novus ordo,* the new order, that was promulgated by Vatican II and has been transforming the Church ever since. They feel that in the name of reform Church leaders disregarded clear prior instructions from the Holy See against deviating from traditional practices, the upshot being that modern Catholicism is "a different religion," unrecognizable as the faith they grew up with. Says Jenkins, "You can walk into one of these modern churches now and find two people sitting side by side in the pew, at the same liturgy, and ask them afterwards, 'What do you believe about the Blessed Sacrament?' One will say, 'I believe the Blessed Sacrament is truly the body and blood of Jesus Christ, really present and offered on the altar.' Talk to the person next to him, and he'll say, 'Oh, I believe Jesus is there, like he's in the birds and the flowers and the trees and the grass.' They don't have the same *faith.* But they can both worship at the same liturgy, because that liturgy essentially isn't saying anything concrete. It is whatever you interpret it to be."

Vatican II was "a contradiction from beginning to end," he continues. "They talk about the importance of maintaining the Latin, and then the very next paragraph they start talking about the virtues of using the vernacular. It's an absolute gold mine of ambiguity." In his view leftist elements in the Church capitalized on that ambiguity to implement an agenda of change. Yet it's the bishops Jenkins blames for allowing it to happen, and he says one must assume they knew what they were doing. "I don't think it is really accurate to say there is a distinction between the 'spirit' of Vatican II and the fact of Vatican II. Those men were implementing what they understood Vatican II to be all about; they *were* Vatican II. The fact is that for years and years after Vatican II those who did outrageous things were applauded, promoted. And those who tried to resist by refusing to give way, by resisting the parish councils, by writing the dioceses—by writing Rome—they were the ones who were always slapped down."

The most visible manifestation of the traditionalist practice is, of course, the Latin Mass. Even many progressive Catholics who wholeheartedly support use of the vernacular will admit that they miss the beauty and majesty of the Latin service. Major religions have always employed sacred language, Jenkins maintains, "and there's a reason for that. Not only is there an air of mystery involved, but it's a matter of creating a sense of timelessness, too, something solid and lasting and permanent. Pope Pius XI, I believe it was, actually compared the use of Latin in the traditional Mass to the very marks of the Church itself: he said that like the Church itself, Latin is one, holy, Catholic, and apostolic." Pointing out that revered Church texts, such as the writings of Sts. Augustine and Jerome, are in Latin, Jenkins says, "If we cut ourselves off from the fathers of the Church, we've lost our roots. That's how we know we're still Catholic today, because we believe what they believed."

Beyond that, he says, through the years Latin has been an integrating force, tying together Catholics around the world who otherwise have little in common. Use different languages and you shatter the unity of Church culture. He says the practice also invites a kind of freelancing with the liturgy, with no one policing these iterations for suitability or conformity. "We're sort of living through the Tower of Babel all over again," Jenkins believes.

Then there's the touchy matter of papal authority. Where supporters and detractors alike generally see a conservative in John Paul II, Jenkins and his followers see the upholder of "revolutionary" changes begun by John XXIII and Paul VI. Therefore this pope lacks legitimacy, Jenkins says matter-of-factly. "I question whether or not he really is the pope. It sounds goofy at first to even question that, I know, because hundreds of millions of people have no doubt in their minds. But of course to be pope you have to have the faith, and John Paul has done a number of things throughout his papacy which I believe really would give someone honest cause to question whether or not he has the faith. I mean, sure, one day he will show up with the rosary and talk about the Blessed Mother in glowing terms. But the next day he'll praise Buddhism or Shinto. His 1979 address before the General Assembly of the United Nations was shocking, absolutely shocking. It could have been given by Gorbachev—talking about spiritual values. But there's nothing really Catholic about it."

Jenkins specifically criticizes John Paul's aggressive outreach to other religions as dangerous activities that "loosen up" and "denigrate" Catholicism, "as though Christ were just one of many gods," he says. "This is the kind of thing that has been going on for thirty years now. It's no wonder Catholic people are confused, to say the least."

Out of this confusion, then, a movement seems to be growing, though how big or how fast no one really knows. For his part, Jenkins contends that the backlash against modern Catholicism is genuine—and not relegated to nostalgic older Catholics. He says Immaculate Conception is drawing younger ones, too, those born after Vatican II but feeling a void in their faith lives. Families have moved to Cincinnati from other states because of the Immaculate Conception school, and some French families have boarded children here for the same reason. The school, cramped in its old location, can now accommodate as many as four hundred students, and Jenkins believes one day it will.

That kind of commitment on the part of the laity makes his own grueling travel seem trifling, Jenkins says. "There are people who really want to have the old faith. They believed it then, and they still believe it. And they're willing to make sacrifices. There are two families living here now, they used to live in Pittsburgh. Every single Sunday they would load the families—and they're two large families—into their vans and drive from Pittsburgh to Cleveland for Mass. Every Sunday! And then back to Pittsburgh. Just amazing. That went on for two or three years, and they never complained. When I see people doing things like that, I realize I'm an amateur."

▣ Father
Robert Kearns

BALTIMORE

Home of the nation's first English-speaking Catholics, its first bishop (John Carroll), and its first catechism, Baltimore is widely acknowledged as the cradle of the American Church. Less well known is that it also is the birthplace of African American Catholicism: St. Francis Xavier Church, established here in 1863, was the first domestic parish devoted to the black community. The Society of St. Joseph of the Sacred Heart, a small order of priests known more familiarly as the Josephites, began working here in 1871. The order actually originated in England; the Vatican steered its missionaries to the States to work among blacks in the confused aftermath of the Civil War. Today most Josephite parishes are in the urban East and rural South.

The order's headquarters is a stately brick building on the edge of downtown Baltimore, only blocks from St. Francis Xavier, which remains in operation. The American Josephites split off from their English founders in 1893 in order to cultivate their own priests, but with its specialized apostolate of ministering to the black community the order has never been large. Throughout its entire history fewer than five hundred men—most white but some black—have belonged to the society. The population peaked at about two hundred fifty in the sixties; now it's one hundred forty. Still, the Josephites have had an outsized influence in the clerical hierarchy. Three of their number, all African Americans, have become bishops, among them John Ricard, who was a Baltimore auxiliary before taking over Florida's Pensacola-Tallahassee diocese.

Low-key and genial, Father Robert Kearns is superior general of the Josephites. His colleagues elected him to a four-year term not long before I came to see him. (He may be reelected but, like the president of the United States, only for one additional term.) Around here Kearns is better known for the ten years he served as pastor of St. Peter Claver Church in the

Sandtown-Winchester area of west Baltimore. His pastorate was high-lighted by the pivotal role he played in the Nehemiah Project, an ambitious partnership of churches, government, and community organizations that brings attractive, affordable new homes to the blighted neighborhood around St. Peter Claver. The development is named for the Old Testament figure who rebuilt the walls of Jerusalem.

Unlike many so-called black urban churches, which actually were white until their congregations abandoned them for the suburbs, Josephite parishes have always had African American constituencies. Kearns says that's why these institutions enjoy vitality and loyalty even when, as has happened in too many cases, the surrounding neighborhoods have been devastated by riots, poverty, and crime. "There's a sense of identity, owner-ship, pride—it's *their* church, and you are their priest," Kearns says. "The people at St. Peter Claver, when they think of the Catholic Church, they don't think of Pope John Paul II, they don't think of Cardinal [William Henry] Keeler. They think of St. Peter Claver: that's the Church."

Kearns's soft voice informs you right away that he's not from Baltimore but Boston—south Boston, to be exact, where he was born sixty years ago as the seventh of eight children in a working-class home. Since he always wanted to be a missionary priest, and since his March 19 birthday is the feast of St. Joseph, he figured the Josephites were made for him. He went to the order's seminary in Newburgh, New York, and was ordained in 1963.

In the seminary he originally specialized in Latin and Greek, thinking he would teach. But given the socioeconomic changes already rocking the cities where they operated, the Josephites asked Kearns to focus instead on sociology. For graduate work, he was sent to Loyola University in Chicago, where he got the chance to apprentice, under Monsignor John Egan, in the city's groundbreaking Office of Urban Affairs. Looking back, he says, "It was the best thing that ever happened to me." Chicago in the sixties was a cauldron of Catholic liberalism and social activism, and there Kearns fell under the sway of legendary community organizer Saul Alinsky. A Chicago native, Alinsky motivated poor and minority neighborhoods to acquire power through organization and agitation. Kearns, while personally about as different from the abrasive Alinsky as one can be, nonetheless was trans-fixed by his themes.

Though he was there only four years, Chicago was for Kearns a defining experience. Aside from his inner-city work, he also served as an associate pastor at a mostly Polish American parish on the south side. The parish-ioners were not exactly keen to have their priest furthering the cause of the black community; they were especially vexed when word got back that he had gone to Selma, Alabama, to participate in Martin Luther King Jr.'s protest march. Kearns found the home-front reaction unpleasant but instructive. "It kept me grounded, because, you know, you have to relate to certain people and their fears," he says. "And even though you may think they're so-called bigots, they're still human beings."

Chicago whetted Kearns's appetite for community organization just as Vatican II was calling Catholics to a new kind of social justice. He went on to train other religious in how to approach their ministry in this alarming yet exhilarating atmosphere of urban upheaval. "How do you adapt the Church to the new reality?" he asks. "How do you create the conditions that lead to evangelization, openness, in terms of breaking down racial barriers? That was the issue in the sixties."

And how do you do it without the arrogant condescension Kearns often saw in white activists working in minority communities? He was determined to avoid that trap when he began to get his own parishes. His role, he felt, was not so much to lead as to empower the leaders already there. "You flower where you're planted," he says. "I have always followed the lead of the people. What I find in our parishes, wherever I've gone, is that there are always people who know what they're doing, who understand the problems better than anyone [else]. I always pick up my cues from them. [In] meetings, I've always been conscious that they must increase and I must decrease, in the sense of roles—not only as a priest to the people but also as a white and a black."

After running a parish in Washington for four years, Kearns came to Baltimore in 1983 as pastor of St. Pius V, a struggling inner-city church. Soon the Josephites gave him nearby St. Peter Claver, too, and he would handle both for five years. Named for a Jesuit who dedicated his life to ministering to slaves in Colombia, St. Peter Claver was established in 1888 and was intended as a kind of living "laboratory" for Josephite seminarians. Part of that experiment was its school, opened in 1890. The school has been in constant operation for more than a century, an achievement all the more remarkable because three decades ago the once bustling black commercial district along Pennsylvania Avenue began to devolve into something more like a war zone.

On a sunny Saturday afternoon, Kearns and I hop into his beat-up 1987 Plymouth Reliant for a neighborhood tour. We skirt a housing complex that logged nineteen homicides the year before Kearns got to Baltimore. When I ask whether he's ever been in danger himself, Kearns tells how, at

St. Peter Claver, he once had to break a chair over a man who was high on angel dust and had cut three parish employees with a knife. More harrowing yet was the occasion when a thief broke into the St. Pius rectory and held a gun to the priest's head. Kearns cowered there, thinking—incorrectly, he is delighted to say—that he would be shot to death. "The funny thing was, the only thing I could think to do was to cover my ears," he remembers. "I didn't want to hear the gun blast."

Across Pennsylvania from St. Peter Claver is a small wedge-shaped park. At one end some young adults mill aimlessly. Kearns says nonchalantly, "These are all drug addicts, waiting for the man to come, probably around two o'clock. I mean, you can't believe this, but you see it." Yet at the opposite end of the park dozens of children are cavorting, and costumed drummers from a marching band are thumping their instruments. They've just come from a neighborhood parade, and you can readily see that these people are still fighting to be a community. That effort, Kearns says, is what the Nehemiah Project is all about.

As we turn onto a side street, more contrasts: to our left are abandoned row houses, riddled with graffiti, windows broken out. But to our right are bright, neatly maintained single-family homes. These are some of the three hundred residences built during Nehemiah's phase one, completed in 1993. (A second phase will add three hundred more.) These homes have three bedrooms, basements, and central heating and air. The typical monthly mortgage—the homes are purchased, not leased—is a mere two hundred sixty-nine dollars. "Oh, this street was the pits! You can't imagine what this looked like," Kearns says as we turn another corner. Then, coming upon one particularly attractive house, he adds, "This lady is disabled. We wanted to be sure this was open to all types, so we were able to put in a ramp for her and make some adjustments. And look at what she did. She was the first one to put shutters up. She really did a job on it."

Kearns played a primary role in BUILD (Baltimoreans United in Leadership Development), the church-centered group that conceived Nehemiah and then raised a quarter of a million dollars in seed money to attract government grants. The actual construction involved a partnership of the local churches, city and state agencies, and the Enterprise Foundation, a charitable offshoot of the Rouse Company, developer of Baltimore's Inner Harbor, Boston's Faneuil Hall, and other high-profile urban renovations.

There were three thousand applicants for those three hundred homes. Kearns was vindicated—and thrilled, because home ownership is essential to stabilizing this neighborhood, and stability in turn is the first step on its road to rebirth. But he admits to more selfish motives, too. "I was hoping we'd get parishioners out of all this, and of course we have!" he enthuses. "We even get people who may not necessarily be Catholics, but they send their kids to the school, and they're all part of the community now. And the long-term goal, about what the pope is pushing as far as Christian unity— this is how you build it, at the street level.

"The churches, we're not going to move. We have a credibility among the people, and we can be a force," he goes on. "That's what [Nehemiah] demonstrated. I mean, it has worked. And the test is, people have changed. I can tell you, at St. Peter's I'd get calls every day. 'Father, has anything opened up? When can I get in there?' I mean, it was something."

For most of his priestly career, Kearns has worked to ensure that African American Catholics consider themselves, and that others consider them, full partners in the Church. But as superior general of the Josephites, he says, more of his time will involve trying to transfuse the energy of the order's black parishes into the Church as a whole. "What I think African Americans offer to the larger Church is a kind of enriching Catholicism that calls people to involvement," he says. "My nephews and nieces will come sometimes to parishes where I've been the pastor. My nephew J. C. is sixteen. He said, 'If I lived in Baltimore, I would join St. Peter Claver and I'd come to Mass every Sunday, because it's really good. My parish in the suburbs in Atlanta, they've got to drag me to go there. It's an obligation.' There's an energy here. And I think Catholicism needs that." Church leaders apparently agree. "I hear that more and more from bishops as I talk to them. They tell me they like to go to the black churches for confirmations, because they get some energy."

If Kearns will never lack for enthusiasm, manpower is another story. The Josephite churches are apt to outlast their patrons. Back at Kearns's office I look through a copy of the order's quarterly magazine, the *Josephite Harvest*. Aside from a story about Kearns's recent elevation, the magazine features Josephites celebrating milestone anniversaries. Seven men are marking fifty years in the order; nine are celebrating forty. Then in the back of the magazine there are three obituaries. The deceased Josephite priests were ages seventy-four, seventy-five, and ninety-four.

⊞ Father
Peter Gallagher

INDIANAPOLIS

Father Kearns's recounting of the violent side of ministry reminded me of a tale I'd heard from a young pastor working in similar conditions in Indianapolis. Not long after Father Peter Gallagher took up his post at Holy Cross Church on the city's near east side, he learned firsthand just how rough were his new surroundings. Heading back to the church one evening, he rounded a corner just in time to see one of the volunteers from Holy Cross's own food pantry, highly drunk and wielding a pistol, chase down another man and shoot him. The victim died; the assailant, as Gallagher called out to him, simply staggered off, to be apprehended soon after by police. I asked Gallagher whether he had ever seen anything like that before. "No," he replied, "that's one of the things they don't cover at the seminary."

Holy Cross celebrated its centennial in 1996, and "we're trying to hold her together," says Gallagher, a quick, droll man not five years removed from the seminary. The parish is an island in a ragged residential area, where seventies-vintage station wagons sit like rusting lawn ornaments in front of once gracious homes. In a historic district just three blocks away, similar properties have been restored and go for one hundred thousand dollars. The unkempt houses ringing Holy Cross can be had for a tenth of that.

The city's first Catholic church east of downtown, Holy Cross originally was built for those Irish families who'd made enough money to leave central Indianapolis behind. Though many elderly Irish Americans continue to attend the parish, the neighborhood itself has become a transient mix of blacks, poor whites (largely from Appalachia), and Hispanics (many of whom, Gallagher says, are undocumented aliens). The shooting Gallagher witnessed notwithstanding, the church grounds generally escape the neighborhood's worst mayhem. Eighty percent of the children I watched scooting around the parish school blacktop are non-Catholic. Their parents say Holy Cross is the only place in the neighborhood where the kids are safe.

Gallagher actually runs three parishes, the other two being Holy Rosary and St. Patrick's. Considered a pastoral "cluster" for about eight years, the three are situated in the choked area where Interstates 65 and 70 converge. When they were erected thirty years ago, the elevated highways cut swaths through some of the city's most established neighborhoods. As we negotiate their menacing shadows, Gallagher says, "This is what killed all these parishes down here. It just ripped [them] apart. Neighborhoods are gone."

Now all three parishes fight to survive. Running them is a tricky business, and not only because of the time demands and hopeless balance sheets. Gallagher also must contend with entrenched rivalries, particularly that between Holy Rosary and St. Patrick's. These two churches are in fact only three blocks apart. The proximity dates to Holy Rosary's creation: in 1909 St. Pat's, with its proud Irish congregation, was made to yield the nearby property so that a new church could be built to handle the city's poor but growing Italian population. Over the years the relationship between the two churches was at best competitive, at worst contentious. The irony is that unlike the Irish, who continued to push to the suburbs, many of the Italians stayed in the neighborhood even when they achieved affluence. Over a plate of fettuccine at Iaria, a neighborhood institution and a favorite of the city establishment, Gallagher gestures about and tells me, "These people could buy and sell the city. But they live here." When I ask whether someone with his shamrock surname had a credibility problem in an Italian parish, he tells me about his first week on the job there. An elderly woman came up before Mass, and he introduced himself. "Hmmm, Gallagher—that doesn't sound very Italian. It's a shame they don't send us Italian priests," she said. "Well, it's a shame you didn't do a better job with vocations," Gallagher replied. He laughs in retelling it. "It's taken her a while to warm up to me."

In the eighties, when Holy Rosary lost its own pastor, the congregation took it hard. "They interpreted not having a resident priest as closing," Gallagher says, as well they might. Their old grade school already had been closed and turned into the diocesan seminary high school. Then *that* closed. Even so, of his three parishes Gallagher considers Holy Rosary the "most survivable." That's because it is the smallest of the three (due, ironically, to its modest beginnings) and therefore easiest to keep up; it has the most stable congregation (Holy Rosary alone covers expenses with its Sunday collections); and it has the pharmaceutical giant Eli Lilly for a neighbor. Lilly has helped maintain the church, put in a park across the street, and generally taken pains to stabilize the neighborhood. And again, the area retains its strong Italian identity. Every summer Holy Rosary's two-day street festival draws more than a hundred thousand people from all over greater Indianapolis.

Conversely, St. Pat's, the oldest (one hundred thirty-five years) and grandest of the parishes, is most vulnerable. The church has a spectacular marble sanctuary, but fewer and fewer people are there to see it. The beautiful tile roof hides structural rot that will take nearly half a million dollars to repair. One corner betrays major water damage. Last winter the boiler blew up, and the parish had to borrow seventy-five thousand dollars from the archdiocese to buy a new one. The deterioration has caused the parish council to begin a painful but necessary assessment of St. Pat's viability. As it happens, once shuttered facilities there now pay their own way: the former convent is a home for unwed mothers, and classrooms in the old school have been converted into apartments for poor families trying to get back on their feet. But "other than as a basketball court," Gallagher asks sardonically, what use has an empty church?

At thirty-four, Peter Gallagher is a relatively young man to be dealing with such sober concerns. A native of Shelbyville, a town southeast of Indianapolis, he attended college at St. Meinrad in southern Indiana. He stayed four more years as a seminarian in its Benedictine monastery. Then in 1987, closing in on ordination but "not quite ready to make a commitment to anything," Gallagher quit Meinrad and moved to Los Angeles, where one of his brothers was living. Gallagher hadn't ruled out the priesthood, but neither was he sure about it. He took a job teaching religion at a Catholic high school near the South Central district of the city. But he went to church in Santa Monica, an affluent area where he says he witnessed a kind of Catholicism he thought had disappeared in the fifties: huge parishes, plenty of money, authoritarian pastors. When he volunteered to be a eucharistic minister at his new parish, the pastor looked at him as if he were addled. "We have enough priests to take care of that," the cleric told him. "We don't need eucharistic ministers. We don't do that."

In time Gallagher resolved his commitment to the priesthood and finished his studies at the archdiocesan seminary, St. John's, in Camarillo, California. But he also determined that if he was going to be a priest, it should be back in Indiana, where religious were in decidedly shorter supply. "So I asked for permission—well, the Church being the Church, I asked for permission to ask for permission to come back here," he says mischievously. "The cardinal said, 'OK, you can ask for permission.' And then the archbishop back here [in Indianapolis] said, 'OK, you can come back.' And then the cardinal said, 'OK, I'll let you go.'" Ordained in 1992, Gallagher today is the only St. John alumnus working east of the Mississippi.

In retrospect Gallagher calls the hiatus a blessing. It afforded him the chance to recognize and think through all the difficulties ahead—to truly appreciate "the reality that it's a time of chaos in so many ways. I mean, I just look at the fact that I'm [already] a pastor, and my classmates in Los Angeles will be waiting—even with the way things are—fifteen years. In fifteen years' time, hell, I could have knocked off three or four pastorates by then. Am I ready for it? I don't think I was really ready for it. I think of the fact that I may never have an associate [pastor]. I may in all likelihood do this by myself from here on out. It has made me look at what do I do, where do I get my support, so that reality doesn't become a cloud." It also has persuaded him to channel most of his energy where he thinks it will do the most good, which is in nourishing the spiritual life of his parishioners. As for the temporal concerns, he has learned to ask for help. "I'm more than happy to say to people in all three of these parishes, 'If you want to worry about a capital campaign, then I'm all for it, and I'll go and do some of the begging. But if you want that, and it's a need of this parish, then *you* do it. Because it's not what I can do.'"

❖   ❖   ❖

And how have Gallagher's congregations taken to their brash young pastor? It depends, he says. Given their three distinct histories and identities, "it really does sometime revolve around the mood, and what's the latest thing that I've said or done. Holy Rosary and St. Patrick's are pretty traditional parishes. When you see the church at St. Patrick's, everything is intact. You walk in there and it's 1942. Marble communion rail and gates, everything. The altar we use is obviously temporary, just waiting for the move [back].

"Holy Cross has been much more 'church nouveau,'" he continues. "It's at times had a colorful history. It's had a pastor who left—after the homily, [he] walked out the door. That was his exit. It's got a strong social justice thrust to it, I think because of the neighborhood and the poor. Sometimes it's gotten adventurous in terms of how it interprets itself in relation to the Church. I don't say liberal because, well, it's just kind of gotten far afield, and it was kind of ignored for a while. In some ways it's more alive than the others because it is in such turmoil at times."

Just now the turmoil at Holy Cross revolves around Gallagher's liturgies, and especially the question of so-called inclusive language—the controversial effort on the part of some Catholics to make biblical and liturgical texts "gender neutral" and inoffensive to any particular group. (At its simplest this involves substituting "people" for "mankind" or "brothers and sisters" for "brethren"; at its most inventive it might eliminate the masculine pronoun for Jesus or translate "prince" as "leader.") Many in the parish want the modern translations, but Gallagher is cautious. He says the dispute is consistent with Holy Cross's self-image—owing to some extent to the neglect he mentioned—as a congregation of eccentrics. For his part, Gallagher says there's nothing wrong with eccentricity, except when it translates into a kind of reflexive contrariness. "And I've come back at them saying, 'Well, you're unique, but that doesn't therefore give you permission to do some of the things you'd like to do.' They feel really tested right now."

In truth, Peter Gallagher is being pulled in separate directions. He presides over two very traditional churches and a third intent on burying tradition. "Some days," he says, "I think I meet myself coming and going."

Many other pastors experience the same schizophrenic sense from a single congregation. In recent years American Catholics have developed an unprecedented independent streak where Church policies and procedures are concerned. As I write this, dissident Catholics have spent the previous weekend demonstrating outside parishes around the country, demanding that the Church revisit its positions on female priests, homosexuality, and a married clergy. At St. Patrick's Cathedral in New York, a nun declared, "Jesus was open to dialogue with anyone, including people with whom he vehemently disagreed." Added a laywoman from Los Angeles, "The majority of American Catholics are moving ahead regardless of what the pope says. There's a silent majority within the Church that is doing this anyway."

Their comments neatly encapsulate what has become yet another modern dilemma for priests. Some surveys find that as many as ninety percent of the American faithful believe they can disagree with the pope and still be good Catholics. And disagree they do, on the aforementioned topics and a host of others, including episcopal authority, the rights of divorced Catholics, birth control, and abortion. (Indeed, these latter two issues have so thoroughly become matters of personal conscience that priests are seldom consulted about them anymore.)

This buffet-style picking and choosing of what to accept from Rome is often derided as "cafeteria Catholicism." Whatever its merits or failings, the phenomenon puts the priest in a tricky spot. He is criticized by traditional elements if he doesn't aggressively advocate official Church positions, yet if he does he risks alienating those Catholics—and there are tens of millions of them—who feel that arguing with the Vatican shouldn't make them pariahs. My interviews and research suggest that most pastors try to respond with a delicate finesse. While they articulate the "company line" (most assuredly to greater or lesser degrees), they also respect, and allow for, a parishioner's personal judgment and conscience. Except on the question of abortion, which every priest of my acquaintance condemns categorically, I met few priests who genuinely object to informed dissent (though most put a heavy emphasis on "informed").

This approach makes sense, according to Father Philip Murnion of the National Pastoral Life Center. He says Catholics by and large respect priests who respect them, who give them credit for being responsible for their own decisions. "There is some reason to believe that even though the expression 'cafeteria Catholicism' is used, that people pick and choose, it's not quite as capricious as that. The people are trying to pick out what they think makes sense. Actually, they are looking for some guidance—but guidance, not dictation. . . . They are looking for a preaching and teaching that is inviting people into the way of life of the Gospel and the way of life of discipleship. When they hear that, they will come."

Catholics who practice traditional fealty to Rome consider this independent strain another unwelcome offspring of Vatican II. But while the council undoubtedly was a trigger, the modern autonomy of the faithful has broad sociological roots. Many scholars complain that the Church has failed to recognize and therefore respond to the seismic changes that have transformed the American nation, and with it American Catholicism. "No one escapes the impact of this society—not the Church, not its people, not its priests," says John Linnan, a professor at the Catholic Theological Union in Chicago who has analyzed the changing dynamics of the contemporary parish. "We are as powerless as King Canute standing at the edge of the sea, trying to command the ebb and flow of the tide." Linnan says the ancient European-village model of the parish—people of like minds and backgrounds—is nearly extinct. It has been eroded by insistent winds of change: the move from an agrarian to an industrial to a technological society; the education of the population; the migration of people to cities and then to suburbs; economic and immigration factors; the sexual revolution. The upshot is that Catholics in today's pluralistic, urban parishes have little in common but location—and more independent views about everything, including the Church, authority, and right and wrong.

Another of those prevailing cultural trends, of course, is the women's movement. As it happens, in the past decade Holy Cross has attracted strongly feminist Catholics from all around Indianapolis, Gallagher says. His mere appointment provoked some resentment; he summarizes the feminist quarter's reaction this way: "We didn't want you as pastor. The bishop, who represents the male patriarchal, hierarchical imposition of Rome locally, put you here." Gallagher smiles. "I call myself their 'local token.' But they've begun to be able to laugh about that, and that's an important virtue that was lost, and I think we're beginning to get back."

Which is not to suggest he doesn't take their concerns seriously; he does. He knows that Catholics on all sides get emotional about such matters as liturgical experimentation (this can include everything from which prayers are said to what music is played) and inclusive language, because the faith's symbols and rituals are powerful and speak directly to a Catholic's identity. In his search for common ground, Gallagher does a good deal of listening, even to the point of holding focus groups with "a lot of disenfranchised" at Holy Cross. But he also has to worry about longtime Holy Cross parishioners who feel alienated when contemporary and untraditional songs like "A Summer Flower" turn up at Mass. The tensions are real and divisive, he says. "I don't by any means want to drive people away, but . . . I'm trying to draw some boundaries—say, you know, this we can do and this we can't do. Only I can say the Eucharistic Prayer. Those are boundaries that are acceptable in ninety percent . . . of parishes. But then there's places like Holy Cross where everything was pretty much of a free-for-all."

In the beginning, Gallagher admits, he tried to tailor his style somewhat to his different parishes, but he finally concluded the only sane thing to do was to be himself. And just where is he on the ideological spectrum? He shakes his head. When he went to Los Angeles, he tells me, he was "highly suspect"—because St. Meinrad was viewed as a liberal seminary and because he was altogether comfortable with the "vision" of Vatican II. On the other hand, upon his return to Indiana, "I've said nothing differently, and I come to this parish [Holy Cross] and seem to be very conservative." Reluctantly—"I guess it's a fudge"—Gallagher describes himself as a moderate. He finds some of the prevailing conservatism in the Church "very narrow-minded." Then again, "The problem I find with some of the liberal thought I experience in some of these parishes is it's so unreflective.

"There are issues that I know we need to talk about, but their outcome, either way, is not going to affect my life," he continues. "If the Church changes tomorrow and [allows] a married clergy or a noncelibate clergy, then that's the thought in the mind of the Church, that's what the Spirit has moved us to. But is it going to change my lived experience? In all likelihood no, because I made [my] decision when I lay on the floor of the cathedral in '92. This is the choice I've made."

❖   ❖   ❖

In the Holy Cross gymnasium, the church operates a food pantry that provides groceries to one hundred seventy families during a normal week. During my visit, just before Thanksgiving, the parish is putting together special food baskets that will go to almost eight hundred families. The parish will do it again at Christmas. On this afternoon, just before the pantry's closing time, several dozen people are on the gym stage going through a screening and registration process.

Gallagher surveys the scene, then sidles up to a maintenance man who is sweeping the floor. "Are we closed yet? How are the bathrooms?" The pastor has learned that the restrooms can come in for some rough treatment when the pantry is open.

"Holding up pretty good," the man replies, "'cept for your normal problems." He chuckles softly.

"Kids stuff toilet paper in them?"

"Just got one problem toilet everybody tends to mess with. Last one in."

"All right, Sister's gonna hear about it," Gallagher teases as he heads off.

Life here is not easy, for the people or the pastor. A few weeks earlier, Gallagher threw out his back while buffing this same gym floor. Without a priest, that Saturday's Masses had to be turned into a Liturgy of the Word–communion service.

But Gallagher offers no regrets; indeed, he says he wanted to come to Holy Cross because of its respect for the poor. "I also [accepted] because I thought, at thirty-four, I could do it and I have the energy. And I mean this nicely, but if I need to learn how to become a pastor somewhere, I'm not going to do a lot of harm, you know? These places are always struggling, so I don't think anything that I might do can cause things to crash down—unless it's to forget to turn off the gas. But if I was forty-five there wouldn't be enough money to get me to come to these kinds of assignments [without] good structure. There's not a lot of the things that really feed me, like active adult education programs and Scripture study. [Here] if you get three or four people together, you've got a crowd. I'm learning to accept that better. But sometimes it's a disappointment."

Still, he is more upbeat when he returns to his bottom line. "I have a cousin who's now in the seminary. We've talked a lot, and I told him he needed to come and be with me for the summer at Holy Cross and witness the poor. I think that's what really has reinforced my vocation more than anything, being with the poor. All these other things are great to talk about. It's nice to talk about how do we get to the point of good, solid, clean, liturgical inclusivity. It's great to talk about what's good liturgical music and what's a great vision for the Church. Those are great academic pursuits. But our fundamental requirement is to feed the hungry, clothe the naked, visit those in prison." Gallagher says he didn't know until he arrived here that one of the oldest women's prisons in the state is in Holy Cross parish and has been more or less ignored for years. "I've taken to going there once a month, because it's just transformational," he says. "There's a religious experience that sits over there, of these women—especially these women who are in for long-term sentences that, were they men, they would not [have]. There are women in there whose sentences for robbery are twenty years, and I know, for God's sakes, if they were men it might be a year or two. That's really powerful. That's where the Gospels live."

❖ Fathers John Sullivan and Robert Fisher

PLYMOUTH, MICHIGAN

Any other day if Father John Sullivan took to the altar at Our Lady of Good Counsel Church and saw several hundred of his school's students in the pews, he'd be delighted. Today he is upset. Giving them a long look, he speaks soberly but with an edge in his voice: "We've been through a lot this week. I'm not prepared to teach you today. We will all pray, *together*. You will help *me* pray."

Afterward Sullivan explains his irritation, which was not directed at the schoolchildren but their superiors. I had heard that Sullivan is considered one of the best preachers in these parts, that rare homilist who can effortlessly weave the day's readings into a contemporary context—even for seventh- and eighth-graders, who as a rule do not look for relevance from fifty-six-year-old priests. Of course, like all craftsmen Sullivan puts a lot of forethought into these "effortless" presentations, and so he has implored Good Counsel's teachers to give him adequate notice when their students will be at Mass. Unfortunately today, of all times, he'd been sandbagged. It turned out the pastor and his staff were still in mourning. A few days earlier the father of associate pastor James Livingston had died, suddenly and unexpectedly; yesterday, on a cold, rainy morning, he had been buried. Sullivan was in no mood for surprises, especially since some of the kids had been brought to church because their regular teachers were out and substitutes hadn't yet arrived. "See, that's why I was so upset this morning," he says over a steaming cup of coffee back in the rectory, a lovely historic home known around Plymouth as the White House. "They didn't give me the opportunity to do what I do best. And don't use me as a functionary just to fill the time. Eucharist is not 'fill-in.' It's really important to us. So I have righteous indignation today, I think. I mean, I could have spent a little moment taking that 'bread of life' Gospel and applying it to teenagers. But I couldn't do it on the spot because I was drained."

As he talks his ire abates, and Sullivan's usual jovial demeanor returns. He has been a priest since 1966, and Good Counsel is his fourth pastorate in the Detroit archdiocese. It sits smack in the middle of Plymouth, a picturesque, affluent community just west of Detroit where many automotive executives make their home. The parish's location is both a blessing and a headache. This is one of the fastest-growing areas in greater Detroit, and Good Counsel is booming along with it. The church grounds, on the other hand, are cramped and landlocked. With three thousand families on the rolls, with nearly six hundred children in the elementary school (and another hundred on the waiting list), and with parking a nightmare, Good Counsel has long since run out of room. So the parish will soon erect a new church building a few miles away, on a spacious, neighborless parcel off Michigan 14. Ironically, this new construction will occur while venerable churches are still being closed in Detroit proper—for Catholics, a frustrating but familiar demographic reality. As Sullivan admits, "We would love to pick up some of those churches and facilities and bring them here, but unfortunately that doesn't work."

Joining us in the elegant sitting room (the house has been carefully restored to its 1865 vintage) is Father Robert Fisher, who lives in the rectory but works in downtown Detroit. At thirty-four, Fisher has the energy and enthusiasm to tackle one of the most demanding jobs in the chancery: he is director of vocations for the archdiocese. The priest shortage is not as acute here as in other parts of the country, but it's still worrisome. "We are covering everything we have," Fisher says, "but we do need more blankets, you know?"

It has been an emotional few days for everyone at Good Counsel, with this death in their extended family. I ask Sullivan if it's difficult being a consoler when you are so close to the bereaved. "I say to myself, 'What would Jesus do in this moment?' I never worry about what I am going to say because I know those words will come if you really listen," he says. "Just go and sit with them and hold them and listen to their hearts, that's pretty much what you do. Sure it pains. My mother just died three years ago, so, yeah, it brings back all these memories. A priest is not just a functionary. You are very human and very real to them. Sometimes you cry right with them, because I think that is part of what Jesus did, too."

The opportunity for such personal ministry is what attracted Detroit native Sullivan to the priesthood in the first place. Certainly he's busy managing his parish's growing pains—all in all, a nice problem to have. "It's the first time in my priesthood, in thirty years, that I am in the black," Sullivan says, crediting the fiscal expertise of his lay finance committee. But you get the sense that he is mostly grateful for this prosperous state because it frees him, more so than most of his counterparts, to teach and preach. Sullivan spends his days largely in such interaction: with students in their class-rooms; with the church and school staffs; with parishioners who need counseling; with civic groups; with other area ministries. In this outreach, as with his sermons, Sullivan tries to key spiritual awareness to the every-day world. For instance, Plymouth is not far from where Dr. Jack Kevorkian has conducted most of his assisted suicides. So during last year's Lenten season, Sullivan led a seminar every Wednesday that examined the emotional, moral, and theological implications of that issue.

I ask Sullivan what is most important to him as a minister. He replies that he has come to operate from the idea of priest as pontifex, not in the word's contemporary meaning as a bishop or high priest, but in the sense of its Latin etymology: bridge builder. He says that attitude no doubt derives from his coming into the profession during the divisive sixties. "I was newly ordained and thrown right into this whole Vietnam mess," he recalls. "I didn't believe we were doing the right thing, and I knew a lot of other people believed that. I saw a lot of people running off to Canada. Then every other day or so, it seems, I was having a military officer come to the door asking me to go to the home of a family to tell them that their son had died. I had many military funerals. I kept saying, 'Where is the justice? Where's the real honesty?'" About that same time he attended church meet-ings in Detroit on the subject of public housing, and he remembers how people stalked off in anger. He was reminded that a priest is not a politi-cian. That's not to say tact and persuasion aren't useful in the job, he says; they are. But at bottom, "you can't mince the truth. Sometimes you have to say things you don't want to, but you have to say them. But that's also building a bridge."

What's less important to Sullivan—or he contends *should* be—is the po-litical infighting that keeps Catholics agitated with one another. He knows procedures and customs are important; Good Counsel is a traditionally conservative parish, and Sullivan says he talked with the congregation for a full year before moving the altar from the end of the sanctuary to the cen-ter. But he has little patience for those policy and procedural issues (e.g., al-tar girls and liturgical language) that, to him, obscure the true aims of the faith. "A lot of times people get so lost in all the picayune things that can change, and have changed, over the centuries. My job, I really feel, is to help them keep their eyes fixed on Jesus. . . . It's not the things of religion or government [that matter], but what is Jesus really calling you to do? Do you really love?" Whatever a given day's sermon or task might involve, that is the underlying message Sullivan wants to drive home. And should a parishioner feel he is not doing that, Sullivan says that person not only has the right but the obligation to find a priest who can. "I can't be all things to all people, you know. I am a product of my time, too. The majority of people give me the impression that, yes, they are growing and I am feeding them. [But] if you are looking for something else, then God bless you. You have to go where you grow, you really do. That's my principle."

Father Fisher listens to the older man and nods approvingly. It's clear that in the short time Fisher has been here—less than a year—the two have become close friends. Indeed, despite their disparate schedules Fathers Sullivan, Fisher, and Livingston make a point of having dinner together most every night, often inviting parishioners or family members to join them. Though Fisher lives at Good Counsel, he actually spends little time here. His job as vocations director keeps him on the road all week, for presentations, consultations, and counseling sessions. Then on weekends he usually fills in for sick or vacationing priests around the archdiocese. Beyond a professional courtesy, this gives Fisher additional opportunities to proselytize about vocations.

He's been handed a job that few of his colleagues covet, and he admits it would be easy to become discouraged by the gloomy numbers. He chooses not to be. "I have to focus, for my own sanity, on the good news," he says. "The good news for me is that we have forty-seven fine men who are studying for the Archdiocese of Detroit to be priests. They are excited about what they are doing, and I know that is doing more vocational work than I could ever possibly hope to do." In fact, Fisher often uses new seminarians to interact with those young men who might be considering vocations. Close in age and attitude to potential candidates, the seminarians demonstrate that they are "ordinary, everyday guys," Fisher says. "They have the same kinds of interests these kids do."

Yet it's also true that fewer and fewer candidates are coming to the seminary in the traditional manner, which is to say after high school or a year or two of college. Today's typical seminarians are second-career men, as was Fisher himself. Also a native of Detroit, he went to college here and majored in computer science and business, then was in the workforce nearly four years before deciding on the seminary. Ordained in 1992, Fisher was serving as an associate pastor when, last summer, he was summoned out of the blue by Detroit's archbishop, Cardinal Adam Maida, and asked to take over the job of cultivating new priests and religious.

Many contemporary seminarians are in their thirties and forties, and as it happens a good percentage come from the legal profession—so many, Fisher says, that his colleagues joke that the archdiocesan seminary should add "attorneys at law" to its stationery. I ask about the attraction for these older men. "In their experience something has kept tugging at them about checking out the priesthood," Fisher replies. "They are finding fulfillment in this call to priesthood. I think part of it, too, is they are realizing that the promises the culture has made to them have fallen flat. You know, the promises of material things, like nonstop sex. What about that? Who needs the lie?"

These older men not only bring a new worldliness to their vocations but the kinds of friendships that help them get past the isolation and loneliness that can become a major occupational hazard for a priest. The Church once discouraged such outside friendships as openings to temptation, but today most priests consider them essential to their mental health.

Though these men represent a new resource to tap, how much easier would recruiting be if the Church permitted priests to marry? Immensely, Fisher concedes, and he says he can envision a day when that might happen. But he quickly adds that he would welcome the policy reversal only on two conditions: if Church officials truly felt it was the right thing to do and not merely an expedient way of "filling gaps"; and if they continued to underline the value of the celibate lifestyle for priests who choose it—if they still emphasized that it is, in Fisher's words, "a good way of life, too."

Besides, Fisher is wary of ever returning to what Catholics of a certain age remember as the good old days. He says the large number of priests in service at the dawn of the Second Vatican Council not only was a historical anomaly but a factor behind some of the problems John XXIII was taking aim at, such as clericalism and underappreciation of the laity. "I remember one of our auxiliary bishops saying we would never want to have the number of priests that we had twenty or thirty years ago," he says. "We never want it to be that way again because our Church has been so vastly enriched" by the priesthood of the people.

Sullivan concurs. "Even if we had a ton of priests, we couldn't do what some of these people are doing," he says. "Women who have gone through breast surgery deal so much better with women going through breast surgery than we could. Talk about women in ministry—we've got women doing good ministry. It doesn't need to be Roman-collared.

"So yeah, I see some things happening that I never thought I would," the pastor continues. He then tells me that the previous weekend he had done something of a "job swap" with a Presbyterian minister in a nearby town. Each participated in the other's service and gave the homily. Afterward, the minister's wife asked Sullivan if he knew what the Protestant cleric had done before taking up his current ministry. When Sullivan said no, she told him that he had been a priest for twenty-one years. "This man still has a great love for church," Sullivan tells me, praising his counterpart for his ecumenism, his efforts to bring people together in Christ. "His roots are truly planted. I thought to myself maybe that's the work of the Holy Spirit. He's still a priest as far as, you know—" Sullivan broke off, then repeated the biblical injunction that ordained men have been hearing since the laying on of hands began: "You are a priest forever, according to the order of Melchizadek."

▦ Fathers Michael and John Foley

WORCESTER, MASSACHUSETTS

Every Thursday, as often as they can swing it, Mike and John Foley get together at the hilltop frame house in south Worcester where they grew up in the fifties and sixties. John, forty-eight, is pastor of a large parish here, Christ the King. Big brother Mike, fifty, runs the huge (over four thousand families) St. Mary of Assumption parish in Milford, twenty miles down the road. Smart and experienced, the Foleys are among the most accomplished clerics in the Worcester diocese. Yet on their day off back in the old roomy triple-decker, where their parents still live, they are just "the boys" again. "Dad never stood on ceremony," John remarks dryly. "I remember when [Mike] was first ordained, Dad said, 'Look, in my house you do what *I* say.'"

They both remember the scene as if it had played out yesterday, not a quarter century ago. As they settle into familiar chairs in the living room, putting a dent in a plate of pastries their mother offers us, it's clear this is a place where the Foleys are grounded. Since most diocesan priests work close to where they grew up, their families almost always are crucial to their emotional support. Michael and John Foley, however, are those rare priests who also have a sibling who knows precisely what the other is experiencing. They value and use that unique relationship. Over the years, independently and together, they have worked out philosophies of modern priesthood as cogent and practical as any I came across.

The Foleys are close enough that they can anticipate one another's thoughts and finish one another's sentences. But they are very different people, and they arrived at this similar place in their lives after traveling divergent paths. In a sense they're prototypical brothers. In a family of six children, Mike is the family's firstborn—the overachiever, the type A personality, the brain. He turned down an appointment to West Point to attend hometown Holy Cross College. He came to the vocation late, but when he did he studied theology in Rome and did missionary work in

Africa. He had to see the world to temper his outlook and learn about himself. John, secondborn, is more gregarious, the good-time guy, the natural athlete with little boyhood interest in schoolwork. He simultaneously looked up to and competed with Mike. After an unpleasant turn at his first seminary, he stubbornly tried again and came to embrace the academic life.

Both are products of an extraordinary neighborhood tradition that has turned out priests like an abundant apple tree. Their hometown parish, Ascension, has ordained over fifty priests since 1930. The Foleys' block alone accounted for six of these. So even though there was no clerical heritage in the family per se, it was scarcely surprising when Mike and John demonstrated this inclination. And it was the younger brother who committed first. In 1965 John was sent off to St. Charles Seminary in Baltimore. Though Vatican II's changes already were loose in the world, they had yet to penetrate St. Charles, a place as strict and regimented as it had been for decades. It was culture shock for the easygoing John. You couldn't talk to your roommates. Ready knowledge of Latin and Greek was essential. John had no experience with the latter language, and his grasp of the former was unsure. It was suggested he might bone up on his Greek in summer school. ("Now, I don't know where you take summer school in Greek," he allows. "I don't even know where you take winter school in Greek.") Eventually, he was invited—"nicely"—to leave.

Listening to his brother's seminary war stories, Mike nods in sympathy. He interjects that a friend of his was trained in a Montreal seminary where the disciplinary code was notorious. In fact, the story went that back in France, where the seminary's order originated, the candidates were forbidden from skating on the campus pond. When the order branched out to Canada, it brought along its rules intact. And since there was no pond at the Montreal seminary, "they built a pond so there could be no skating," Mike says, grinning. "I don't know if that's actually true, but he swears to it."

Mike didn't commit to the priesthood until after his four years at Holy Cross, the Jesuit-run men's college within a walk of the Foley household. But as it turned out, he says the experience "was a much better formation than I ever would have gotten in the seminary," what with the school's civility, the freer academic climate, and its involvement in the community. Mike went on to Gregorian University in Rome for theology, where he got not only a world-class education but the chance to travel. One summer he participated in an archeological dig in Jerusalem; another found him in India studying comparative religion. Five months of his deaconate were spent in the Kenyan bush. These experiences shaped his perspective in crucial ways, he says. "You begin to see. You could think about what poverty is. Living in these [environments] was the most wonderful thing that happened in terms of making me more gentle and patient, of appreciating what's really good, in recognizing that everyone has their problems to deal with and everyone has things to be afraid of."

Back in Worcester, meanwhile, the bishop asked John if he was still interested in the priesthood. This time he was directed to a Connecticut seminary geared to men with "delayed" vocations. The place was much more to John's liking—tolerant of nonconformists and philosophical debate—and he decided to really hunker down. John calls himself the kind of person that "if somebody says you can't do that, that's all I need to hear. I worked hard there. It was a place to grow—as crazy as it was at times. Here were these guys who were career officers in the [military] services. We had men who had graduated from Juilliard. One guy, John Sanders, played for Duke Ellington for eleven years. Another guy was in the Middle East in the CIA. We had a real array."

As newly minted priests—Mike was ordained in 1970, John in 1974—the Foleys were presented with various career options, from missionary work to teaching to Church diplomacy. But both were intent on doing parish work back in Worcester, an industrial city of about a hundred seventy thousand an hour's drive west of Boston. Mike's journey would begin at an inner-city parish where he also functioned as the chaplain for two nearby hospitals. As for John, his first assignment was at another inner-city parish, this one run by a pastor who had been lobbying for years to get an associate. No young priests wanted to join him because he had a dog so mean it was the scourge of the diocese. Finally the chancery told the older prelate that if he got rid of the animal he could have his priest. Says John, "I replaced the dog."

Setting aside for a moment what that might do to a man's self-esteem, John at the time was wrestling with a bigger issue: whether he had gone into the right line of work. As he says, "I think every priest goes through that time when he really looks at his life and says, 'Why am I here?' And he answers that question one way or another." For John, that moment arrived only two years after ordination. There was no precipitating event, just a nagging doubt as to his place in the world. Then he made a retreat and found his doubts evaporated. "There was a real spiritual renewal," he says. "I turned a corner in my life that day." Later he would confide to a veteran priest how close he had come to leaving the vocation before arriving at that reconciliation. The senior man told him he was lucky. When John asked why, the priest replied, "It took me sixteen years to get to that point."

As for Mike, perhaps his toughest moment came later, when he was asked to leave a small Worcester parish for an exponentially larger challenge at the Milford church. St. John's was close to his heart to begin with, because of its long ties to the Foley family. Mike and John's father had been baptized there, their grandparents married there. Besides, Mike cherished the parish's venerable tradition of welcoming immigrants, the most recent being Vietnamese, of whom some five hundred were enthusiastic parishioners. There was no longer much neighborhood to speak of around St. John's, yet it managed to be a dynamic parish. Foley says they were developing housing in the area and otherwise making some real gains. Then suddenly he was asked to take on St. Mary's in Milford, which is not only a daunting operation in terms of sheer size but one complicated by diverse constituencies. Sunday services are available in English, Spanish, and Portuguese. Whereas St. John's might have one baptism a week, after which Foley enjoyed dropping by the family home to celebrate with them, at St. Mary's he might have fifteen christenings at a time, with six or seven hundred people in attendance. "How do you celebrate things like that in a personal way?" he asks. He's happy now, he emphasizes, but the change forced him to adopt "a whole other way" of approaching his ministry.

The Foleys talk over such experiences a lot. They regard them as necessary if not always expected bumps on the road to ministerial understanding. Some bumps are large, others small, but each is put to use. John recalls the six years he lived with an older priest who had churned through ten previous associates and countless other colleagues because of his alcoholism. "There were hard times, yes," John says, but by offering the older man kindness and respect he evoked a positive response. "He drank less. He was a happier man, a healthier man. We forget to minister to the very people that we profess to be in fraternity with," he says. Then Mike relates how he once lived in a poor parish with a much older, extremely conservative priest. One day the older prelate became quite agitated with Foley: it seems that instead of ordering pricey beeswax candles, Mike had acquired an inferior grade that were still approved for liturgical use but at one-fourth the expense. "We spent two and a half hours one evening talking about candles," Mike says. "What he wanted to express was, you put the best before God. What I was trying to express was I felt that Jesus would rather buy food for some of the people in the parish than have [these candles]. I was trying to find a compromise between this expensive thing and something that was still loving and respectful. We disagreed with each other, but he finished very happy. He says, 'You know, you are the first one to ever really listen to me about this stuff.' That was the best two and a half hours I ever spent."

Another thing experience has taught the Foleys is that in an important sense all religion, like all politics, is local. John says he has found that parishioners "can pick up the Catholic newspapers or the [secular] press and read about the Church going to hell in a handbasket. But if their parish isn't, then there is a sense of well-being. If they like what is going on, I think people are very tolerant, very forgiving. If you minister to the people's needs—you take care of them when they're sick or when somebody dies, or [perform] their weddings or baptisms—they don't care what your politics are unless you are way off the spectrum." He fondly remembers his first pastorate, a small parish that he says had been "devastated" by the time he arrived. The church had such a long French tradition that Foley was its first non-French pastor, which in the beginning was a sore point within the congregation. But John neutralized that stigma with activity. The parish facilities were renovated. The energy level was cranked up. People began to come back. And presto: "you walk on water."

The brothers readily acknowledge that in their large, diverse congregations people come with all sorts of political views and attitudes, which can be a headache if the priest lets it. Mike says St. John's had factions so liberal (as to social matters) and conservative (as to theology) that "there were certain things you couldn't bring them together to talk about, because they just couldn't." He says in such circumstances the smart pastor gets back to basics. At St. John's "there was a triptych up on the ceiling that had the birth of Jesus, the crucifixion, and the resurrection. You would work off that."

Of course, another primary tool for dissipating tension is a priest's style. The Foleys describe theirs as treating the parish as a family. In their view congregations, like families, are made up of people who have different personalities and opinions but an underlying respect and concern for one another. Says John, "When I went into this present parish, Christ the King—which is a very affluent parish [with] an awful lot of very well-educated people, professors, doctors—I said, 'I treat my parish like my family. I demand the same respect, the same love, and you will get that from me.'" And as with a family, both men stressed the importance of listening. The Foleys express moderate concern over seeing some young priests come out of the seminaries wanting to make changes right away. The brothers feel this is a misguided approach and bespeaks a kind of neoclericalism. "In the Scripture, Jesus has three years of public life," Mike says. "He has about thirty years—ten times that—of paying attention, of learning. You have to listen."

And you have to parry some peculiar notions of Catholicism, or spirituality generally. Not long after he was ordained, John got a call from a woman who wanted to know if her marriage could be performed on the church lawn. He told her that wouldn't be possible. What about beside the church? she asked. Can't do that either, John answered. When she asked about behind the church, John said, "Let me ask you a question: why don't you want to be married *in* the church?" The woman replied, "Well, I don't believe in all that stuff."

Perhaps the hardest thing about being a pastor in an age of fewer priests but rising expectations is the triage they must engage in simply to stay on top of things. As Mike put it, "You have to decide what you will *not* do." A good example, he says, was confronting St. Mary's "communion call," where the priest typically brings the Eucharist to the sick and other shut-ins. It can be a lovely experience, he says, but at a place as large as St. Mary's the list can be huge, the names becoming so many items on a computer printout. At the same time, Mike says he usually has eight to twelve parishioners who are in hospices, on the verge of death. So he made the decision to handle the hospice visits himself, while other staff and volunteers do the regular communion calls, where they actually can spend an hour or so in a genuine visit. "I took a lot of grief when I made that move. But this is where you need to be tough. This is the right decision for these people."

Still, when I ask whether such exigencies give them pause about the thinning priestly ranks, both say no. Indeed, the Foleys believe the word "shortage" is a relative and maybe misleading term. Mike recounts how in Kenya he was one of only two clerics serving twenty thousand people. But they had the benefit of an active community of native nuns who handled much of the ministry. "This community functioned wonderfully," Mike says. "The thing is that you just have to use different models." John agrees. "If you have a clericalized model, then we are terribly shorthanded. If you are using a good, healthy parish model, then we aren't necessarily terribly shorthanded."

If they have a concern about the state of the priesthood, it is perhaps that too many of their colleagues are hurting beneath the strain. Besides his day job, John administers the diocese's health insurance program, so he is intimately familiar with the effects of age and overwork. Many of these older men are debilitated but soldier on, he says, because they feel they must. On the other hand, he points out how that same sense of urgency has pulled priests closer together, which both men consider a healthy development. Says John, "I see much more collegiality; I see men working together. I see them starting to offer joint services where before everybody ran their own little fiefdom."

At bottom the Foleys believe that as long as priests properly tend to their spiritual lives, the rest will fall into place. "If this is true—I mean, if God really has come into this world and become one with us, and has risen from the dead, and there is eternal life—if all of this is true, then this energy is there," Mike says. "We are not in this alone."

"God gives you what you need, I really believe that," adds John. "I think he loves his priests. I think he loves his people."

◉ The Life Everlasting

NASHVILLE

No sooner had I embarked on this project when, as I might have expected, "well-meaning" friends began to pass along every priest joke they stumbled across. Equally unsurprising, one was more vulgar than the next. Then, about a year into things, I got a joke via E-mail one day that not only was clean but suggested that perhaps the societal equilibrium was returning to plumb. To wit: there was a truck driver who, whenever he saw a lawyer on the sidewalk, would run him over. Nothing gave him more satisfaction than the thump of an attorney beneath his chassis. Anyway, one day the truck driver gave a lift to a priest who'd had car trouble. As they rode along, the driver spotted a lawyer ahead. Instinctively he took aim, but at the last minute, remembering his passenger, he swerved away. But then he heard that familiar thump and felt sick. "Oh, I'm so sorry, Father," the driver said. "I thought I'd missed that guy." "It's OK," the priest replied. "I got him with the door."

As it happened, a few days later I was having dinner with half a dozen priests at a microbrewery and restaurant in Nashville. As we sampled our pale ales and nut-brown lagers, I was emboldened to repeat the joke. My tablemates laughed heartily, and I detected maybe a whiff of relief, too. Perhaps as I had, they read it as a good portent, however subtle, to find lawyers back as the butt of jokes and priests mere accomplices.

We were in Nashville for another convocation of the National Federation of Priests' Councils. For some months leading up to it, my intuition was that priests in general were feeling better about themselves and certainly more upbeat than just a year before in San Diego. There had been a noticeable decline in exposés and licentious headlines; the pope had made a splash in New York's Central Park; and life just seemed sunnier. Nashville validated that impression, from the livelier bounce in everyone's step to the convention agenda itself, which featured less hand-wringing and was decidedly more forward-looking than its predecessor. While the official theme was "Unity Amid Diversity" (much of the meeting being de-

voted to the growing multiculturalism in the American Church), the real
theme seemed to be "There's Much to Do, but the Worst Is Over." Nick
Rice, a priest from Louisville, Kentucky, and president of the NFPC, said
as much in his opening address. He revisited the "earthquake" that was
Vatican II and recapped three decades of aftershocks. But he said the
Church and its priests are recovering: "As in any earthquake, the recon-
struction often brings something newer, stronger, with more confidence in
survival abilities, an appreciation of the goodness of the human family,
and a deeper sense of what is really important in life." Rice said priests
who had become "worn out" dealing with relentless change are finally
taking comfort in some of its more positive results—among them the
growth of the Catholic population, the emergence of the lay ministries, enhanced Church roles for women, and more bishops devoted to pastoral
rather than bureaucratic concerns. As for me, I was glad to see everyone in
a happier frame of mind, my sincere hope being that the priesthood truly is
outdistancing its torments.

The pleasure of any journey is the doing, of course, yet one still requires
a destination—if not an actual place, then at least some enhanced understanding. Traveling about the country talking to priests, I was constantly
asked, by them and others, what I was learning. My replies usually were
generic and tentative: that "catholic" really must mean universal because
these priests were ideologically all over the chart; that they also represent
an extraordinary diversity of jobs and styles; that many demonstrate remarkable courage and commitment; that they were certainly not the priests
of my youth. I also found that, by and large, I really liked and appreciated
these men. Eventually I think I figured out why.

Most Catholics (most people, I suspect) believe that when a man is
"called" to the priesthood, he is led through some mystical spiritual reck-
oning, or he experiences a Saul-like thunderbolt, or maybe both. The underlying assumption is that these are men who have been singled out, set
apart, to be launched by some divine ignition. And perhaps at some un-
knowable level this *is* how it works. Yet as I pressed each of these men
about why and how they came to be priests, that's not the picture that
emerged. A few seemed to comprehend their destiny from childhood, and
who can say why? Most, however, didn't consider a vocation until years
later and then weren't certain about it. Some were unsure even as they took
the vows, and I suppose it's possible one or two harbor doubts even now.
As for thunderbolts, they would seem rare. As seminarian Dan Leary put it,
the "calling" is more often like the insistent buzz of a mosquito. The point

is, it would be infinitely easier to commit to such a difficult life in response to a clear divine instruction. But when you are not sure, it amounts to the ultimate leap of faith.

To me these priests are special precisely because they are ordinary people who have made this extraordinary commitment. They have the same limitations and vulnerabilities as the rest of us, yet they carry on in faith and hope, trying to do the best they can, refusing to be crushed by the culture or the odds. They don't spend a lot of time talking about spirituality, but they are spiritual men because they live their faith. We are the beneficiaries of their work, yes, but also of their example.

I suppose I learned one other important thing, having to do with priorities. Not long ago, on television, I saw Daniel Boorstin addressing fellow historians, and he made the point that much of what we call history actually deals with historical anomalies—battles, crimes, cults, scandals. Our workaday existence, devoid of all this excitement, is generally ignored. Therefore history and its impatient cousin, journalism, sometimes offer a distorted view of the world, inadvertently conveying the impression that all life is about scandal and strife. And certainly most of what the public sees and hears about the Catholic Church and its priests revolves around controversy, about abortion, sex scandals, papal authority, the role of women.

These are compelling and divisive issues, true enough—so much so that they divide priests, too. As I found, these men hold a diversity of opinions and practices so broad that sometimes it's hard to believe they all belong to the same denomination. But then one is reminded that important as they are, many of these volatile matters reside at the periphery of the faith. I've never much liked the Nicene Creed, which strikes me as verbose, even legalistic. I much prefer the Apostles' Creed, the poetic assertion of faith that every Catholic child commits to memory:

> *I believe in God, the Father almighty, creator of heaven and earth.*
> *I believe in Jesus Christ, His only Son, our Lord.*
> *He was conceived by the power of the Holy Spirit and born of the*
>   *Virgin Mary.*
> *He suffered under Pontius Pilate, was crucified, died, and was buried.*
> *He descended into hell.*
> *On the third day he rose again.*
> *He ascended into heaven and is seated at the right hand of the Father.*
> *He will come again to judge the living and the dead.*

*I believe in the Holy Spirit, the holy catholic Church, the communion
of saints, the forgiveness of sins, the resurrection of the body, and
the life everlasting. Amen.*

Whatever his station or age or politics, not one man I met on my journey
would disagree with any part of the foregoing creed. Nor, for that matter,
would most any Catholic I know, because these are the beliefs that *make* us
Catholic. If issues change from generation to generation, if controversies
come and go, the core principles never do.